PENGUIN BOOKS

New Marketing Practice

...d Mercer is Senior Lecturer at the Open University Business
...ol, Europe's largest business school, where he chairs the team
...cademics responsible for the marketing elements of the MBA
...gramme. He was the first Head of its Centre for Strategy and
...olicy. His previous career includes brand and marketing management
for a range of multinationals, in the consumer goods sector, and general
management in the manufacturing and retail sectors; as well as fifteen
...with IBM. Most recently he has also advised organizations and
...national bodies overseas, as well as governments. He was Director
... School's prestigious programme teaching the MBA at Presiden-
...evel. He is the author of one of the bestselling MBA marketing
...books, selling in both the United States and the United Kingdom,
...well as around the world.

New Marketing Practice
Rules for Success in a Changing World

David Mercer

PENGUIN BOOKS

PENGUIN BOOKS

Published by the Penguin Group
Penguin Books Ltd, 27 Wrights Lane, London W8 5TZ, England
Penguin Books USA Inc., 375 Hudson Street, New York, New York 10014, USA
Penguin Books Australia Ltd, Ringwood, Victoria, Australia
Penguin Books Canada Ltd, 10 Alcorn Avenue, Toronto, Ontario, Canada M4V 3B2
Penguin Books (NZ) Ltd, 182–190 Wairau Road, Auckland 10, New Zealand

Penguin Books Ltd, Registered Offices: Harmondsworth, Middlesex, England

First published 1997
10 9 8 7 6 5 4 3 2 1

Copyright © David Mercer, 1997
All rights reserved

The moral right of the author has been asserted

Set in 10/12 pt Postscript Monotype Bembo by
Typeset by Rowland Phototypesetting Ltd, Bury St Edmunds, Suffolk
Printed in England by Clays Ltd, St Ives plc

Contents

Preface

This is an intensely practical rule-book designed to support and empower the individual manager – you – by offering a range of easy-to-implement rules which have already led to demonstrable success. These simple rules encapsulate the practical experience of some of the most expert marketers in the world. They are intended to help managers who have a less comprehensive knowledge of marketing than these experts, but the unique in-depth knowledge of the specific problems facing their own organization. This help may be in terms of gaining and retaining marketing leadership in the fiercely competitive markets outside their organization or in meeting the needs of the internal markets most effectively.

Since the degree of marketing success or failure can literally make or break organizations this is a book with a very serious purpose. As the levels of competition and uncertainty in the market-place grow over the next decade, this is a threat which will become ever more important to all organizations. Their future is in the hands of their customers and clients, whose choices are becoming ever more sophisticated. In practical terms, that future will be determined by the effectiveness with which managers throughout the organization can deploy the basic marketing skills which lie at the heart of this book – increasing their own marketing sophistication to match that of their customers. It is for this reason that the book does not just give you the practical rules, but teaches you (in easily understandable terms) the very powerful marketing theories behind them. In the process, it painlessly delivers the marketing ideas which dominate the core of the best MBA courses.

Despite this solemn purpose you should find it an interesting read: marketing is a very human subject. It is not easily defined in the mathematical terms that many theoreticians like to use and for this reason is best encapsulated in 'soft' rules of thumb rather than the 'hard' equations academic theorists would prefer.

A separate, but no less important, aspect of the book is its focus on investment in longer-term strategies. The short-termism, which, it is now recognized, has sapped the competitive edge of Western organizations, is especially evident in their marketing strategies. Yet Japanese managers' bookshelves are full of Western marketing books – the difference is that they invest in marketing over longer timespans needed in order to succeed.

Unlike some other authors, I will not pretend that there are grand theories which will magically unlock the inner secrets of the subject and can be applied equally to any marketing situation. Indeed, as already stated, the most important of my contributions are practical rules of thumb derived from observation of what really works – these usually turn out to be the most useful guides of all, perhaps precisely because they are honest about their limited ambitions!

While the book gladly acknowledges the work of those exceptional teachers who have provided significant insights into the processes involved, it aims to rescue their ideas by stripping away some of the less valuable additions which later scholars have made. More often it takes the ideas which drove the original theory and presents them in new forms so that they are easily accessible by individual managers searching for solutions to their specific practical problems. Where no suitable existing theory existed, new ideas have been developed.

This concept, not just of 'rules' but of 'rules of thumb', has been chosen deliberately for a number of important reasons:

• *Practical help* – 'rules of thumb' are derived directly from practical experience, and aim only to help the reader benefit from that experience. They also have a history of working in practice, which reduces the risk involved in implementing them.

• *Immediate (ease of) use* – 'rules of thumb' are, and need to be, inherently simple. In general, they should be no more than one or two sentences long (or a single diagram), so that the reader can immediately understand them and put them into practice.

• *Existing skills and knowledge* – they build upon the practical skills and knowledge that the manager already possesses and typically develop a commonsense perspective, while at the same time stimulating the development of real insight and good judgement.

• *Specific solution(s)* – 'rules of thumb' directly relate to the unique situation facing managers, which only they can solve. Our task is to empower them to handle the related decision-making confidently.

• *Recognized limitations* – even more important, users recognize that 'rules of thumb' are not perfect (as traditional marketing theories often claim to be). They are, justifiably, seen as approximations which will probably help in most (but not all) situations. A realistic awareness of the limitations on what you may do is as important in marketing as being able to recognize the potential development.

Such rules offer a realistic approach to most marketing problems; but no one should expect to apply each and every one of the rules to every situation facing them. The rules provide, in effect, an extended menu from which the user selects just those few rules which apply to a specific situation. The book offers many such rules, to match the many situations which face marketers at different points. Despite the hype generated by those selling simplistic panaceas, there are no universal rules in marketing. That is not to say that some of the rules may not be more generally applicable, and some are more important in terms of their effect on strategy and tactics. In summary, these rules can typically be separated into four different categories:

O **Rule O1 –** *The Hierarchy of Rules*

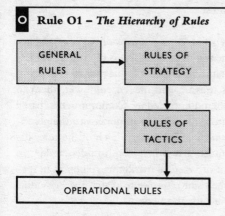

Throughout this book I have identified these different types of rules by a prefix:

G = General rules apply to most management situations; not just to marketing. Although there are fewer of these (only ten in total), they are typically the most powerful in application; precisely because of their generality.

S = Rules of strategy – there are also relatively few of these (just twenty-four in this book), and again they are very powerful, because they generate strategic impact across the whole organization.

T = Rules of tactics expand on the strategic rules, applying them in rather more detail or to more specific areas. There are, accordingly, more of them (forty-nine in total) and they are correspondingly less important in general, but just as important in the specific situations to which they apply.

O = Operational rules – as with the rule above, the bulk of these rules are highly specific, for marketing practice is about detailed activities as much as (and, in many respects, more than) high strategy. Although they are numerous (107 in total), only a few apply in any given situation, and most managers will usually only face one situation at a time (and, depending upon their functional role, be involved in only a few areas of decision-making overall). Their great value is in clarifying individual situations – where application of seemingly 'general' solutions to specific problems tends not just to mislead but also to confuse.

Where I have presented new rules (or new forms of old ones), I have insisted on only one test – the test of practicality. Is the rule genuinely helpful to (and easily understandable by) individual managers in terms of marketing practice? Does it assist, and indeed empower, them to apply their own existing skills and knowledge? Common sense, based on sound practical insight into what is really important to the organization, is the key skill demanded of the reader. Each of the rules has been rigorously tested, to ensure that it helps both understanding in general, and the development of practical marketing responses in specific situations. Specificity, the right response to match the individual situation in hand, is a keyword for the book.

G **Rule G1 – *Rules of Thumb*** are valuable because they offer practical help which is immediately of use in building upon managers' existing skills and knowledge to develop specific solutions to unique problems whilst clearly highlighting the limitations of the 'theory' involved.

To enable me to construct the most logical overall framework of rules, and to ensure that it met the test described above, it was necessary to recognize the underlying philosophies guiding the managers whose expertise is built into the rules. The most important of these philosophies, which have general applicability but are especially valuable in marketing, are best summarized as the **three 'I's of marketing success**. You will meet them again – individually – later in the book, but here they are best illustrated in the form of the Triple 'I' Triangle (the second of the General Rules). They are intended to show that, as basic drivers for management success, they are not just possible but practical and indeed essential, even if they require some mind-bending changes for most managers.

G   **Rule G2 –** *Three 'I's of Marketing Success*

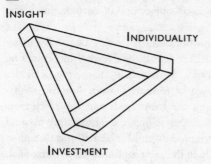

INSIGHT

INDIVIDUALITY

INVESTMENT

•   *Insight* – the basic requirement for success is not a knowledge of academic theory but the ability to use common sense. With a small amount of inspiration and a large amount of perspiration, this will allow you to see what is important in each situation. The rules are designed to take you further, beyond the most obvious common-sense views, to achieve the best possible insight into what is really involved.

•   *Individuality* – and then you must have the ability to deal with each marketing situation individually, directly addressing the specific issues involved, rather than relying on generalized solutions. To this end, the majority of the rules are deliberately designed to address specific types of marketing situation.

•   *Investment* – and, reintroducing the idea floated earlier, you must recognize that the essence of marketing is investment in the longer term, to build the brand value which is normally the organization's most valuable asset, rather than milking short-term profit. The rules have been carefully selected to avoid promoting such short-termism.

Each of these rules is set in the context of a full explanation of the related theory, techniques and practice. Together this adds up to a comprehensive coverage of the whole of marketing. If any of the older, rejuvenated theories – or any of the newer rules I have formulated – help you to understand marketing better, I will have achieved my first objective – and you will certainly have recouped the cost of this book! If they go beyond that point to give you the confidence to act on the basis of your own commonsense judgement (helped by, but not replaced by, the rules which apply in the specific situation) then I will have succeeded in my second objective – of encouraging better market practices.

In terms of my personal contribution, the testing period for many of these concepts lasted something like three decades, incorporating practical experience of successfully managing marketing activities across an unusually wide range of industries, from running multi-million-dollar media campaigns for baby foods and carpet cleaners to managing high-level sales forces selling computers and medical equipment, from advising governments in the Third World on industrial policy to strategic planning in the most sophisticated transnational, from the daily battle for survival in small retail outlets to the calm and tranquillity of the largest university. Over this time I assiduously collected and absorbed the ideas and experiences of literally hundreds of managers with whom I worked. These ranged from senior ministers in government down to the users at the sharp end in implementing customer service.

Over the four years that it has taken to prepare this book I have held more than a hundred in-depth interviews with leaders of industry, across the widest possible range of industries and around the globe. Thus, the book incorporates the best practice of Japan just as much as that of the US – which has traditionally led the field in marketing theory.

Finally, the book incorporates the impeccable quantitative research results from an extensive survey of more than 500 organizations.

It is on their comments, in particular, that I have based the very practical rules which offer the most productive lessons in this book.

1 / *Theory and Reality*

Marketing is the one fundamental activity undertaken by *all* organizations. For most of them it is also the most important contributor to their success or failure. No organization can totally isolate itself from the outside world. Even the most remote monasteries still need to acquire some goods and thus involve themselves, albeit reluctantly, in basic marketing activities. Indeed, marketing, in its practical sense, has existed since before the days of the Pharaohs. It is this *practice* of marketing, now much more complex but still very practical, which is the focus of this book.

In its most general sense, marketing is brought into play as soon as any group, or any individual, needs to exchange goods or services with any other group or individual. To this extent it can be just as important within organizations as outside them. In this wider context it is, therefore, directly relevant to every manager and professional; and may be just as important to those individuals within an organization, in the successful performance of their roles, as it is to the organization itself. However, despite its importance, effective marketing practice is not widely enough implemented, or even recognized as a necessity.

What Then is Marketing?

This is a question which has preoccupied marketing academics for decades. To give a flavour of the wide range of viewpoints that are held by such academics, even about the starting point for marketing theory, some of the most useful of their ideas are summarized below. Throughout the book I will give you brief overviews of more traditional marketing theory which is not directly applicable in practice.

Marketing is human activity directed at satisfying needs and wants through exchange processes.

This is the classical definition of marketing, given by a leading marketing academic,

Philip Kotler, in the earlier editions of his influential book, *Marketing Management*. It perhaps betrays something of the economist's view ('exchange processes' is very much in this camp!). It is, however, very direct – and has worked well for many organizations. But what complications might you let yourself in for when you start to introduce the wider aspects of marketing theory?

Marketing is a social and managerial process by which individuals and groups obtain what they need and want through creating, offering, and exchanging products of value with others.
This is Kotler's later offering, in his 1991 edition. It still has a flavour of economics, but starts to generalize the concept to include, for instance, non-profit organizations.

But what other viewpoints might be adopted?

. . . competitive advantage; without competitors there would be no need for strategy . . .
This is a very Japanese viewpoint, offered by the leading Japanese strategist Kenichi Ohmae – who, though, worked for McKinsey at the time. It is very alien to Western views of marketing, though it has become increasingly accepted as a strategic viewpoint.

The Japanese came to the United States to study marketing and went home understanding its principles better than most US companies did.
On the other hand, Philip Kotler (again, but this time in conjunction with Liam Fahey) retorts that the Japanese learn their lessons well and really are excellent marketers. Perhaps the truth lies somewhere in between.

Marketing is both a philosophy of business and a business function . . .
This quote, from Michael Baker (of Strathclyde University), illustrates one potential area of confusion. On the one hand, marketing is a philosophy, equally applicable to all parts of the organization. One of the key tasks is to get all parts of the organization to recognize the importance of marketing (and to commit to a customer focus). But it is also, much more specifically, a department within the organization which handles, often in splendid isolation, the marketing activities.

Marketing is to establish, maintain and enhance long-term customer relationships at a profit, so that the objectives of the parties involved are met. This is done by mutual exchange and fulfilment of promises.
This more recent European view is from Christian Grönroos. It encapsulates many of the recent developments in terms of partnership, especially those which

emphasize the long-term nature of marketing relationships. This is an important contribution since it looks to a new form of marketing – where organizations collaborate rather than compete (the traditional 'zero-sum' model of the buyer–seller relationship).

It would be much easier for practitioners if marketing could be neatly defined in a few precise words, but the very wide range of ideas illustrated above (not one of which is wholly inaccurate and yet none of which is comprehensively right) indicates just how complex is the situation facing the marketing theorist. In practice, which is what this book is about, marketing cannot be confined to a few neat, generally applicable theorems. It is, instead, a collection of many individual ideas; there are nearly 200 detailed rules listed in this book precisely because there are at least that many approaches to particular situations across the range of marketing practice. On the other hand, the philosophies behind marketing are much easier to describe and it is useful to distinguish two separate levels of marketing approach:

 Rule T1
Marketing is both a RELATIONSHIP with the customer, based upon a series of transactions which, over time, should result in mutual benefit, and a parallel DIALOGUE between you and the customer(s), which communicates the information necessary to define the 'relationship'.

These general processes may become clearer if I describe a particular situation of a salesperson (in a shoe shop, say) making a sale of one product as a result of one-to-one contact – the supposedly classical sales situation. Here the 'relationship' is abbreviated to a single transaction, where the product (a pair of shoes) is exchanged for a sum of money, and there are no more elements to that relationship. Accompanying this is the *dialogue*, which in this special case is the conversation between salesperson and customer that builds up to that transaction (the sale/purchase of the pair of shoes). Typically, much of this dialogue is devoted to finding out what the customer needs and wants (what size, what colour, what style, etc.) rather than being devoted to persuasion, as might traditionally be expected.

In a more general description, this *dialogue* is more complex. Other individuals, especially those who may influence the decision to purchase, may enter the process and other media (letters and proposals, or the mass media, such as advertising) may be used. Still, the principle of the two-way dialogue (exploring what the customer wants, even if this is by marketing research rather than face to face) is much the same.

Similarly, the single transaction, evolving into the more general *relationship*, becomes more complex in two directions. In the first, the elements within it become more diverse. There will be a number of separate transactions involved, not just one. Some of these may be obviously 'physical' in nature: the archetypal product sale. Others, though, may revolve around intangible exchanges, including – most intangibly of all – the corporate/brand image which is needed to reassure the customer. One way in which the description presented in this book departs from most others is that it expects some of these other transactions to flow from the customer, who will not just pay money for the goods (which is traditionally all that is expected of him or her) but will also expend time and effort in buying the product and using it (and perhaps learning to use it), and possibly even purchase related items to enable the product to be used (or to be used more effectively), and will demonstrate a commitment to the supplier (loyalty).

The second aspect is that of time. The traditional single transaction takes no more than the few minutes that the brief dialogue lasts. In the more general model, the more complex relationship, extending over multiple transactions, similarly extends and also develops over time. At the most basic level it is recognized that in most markets the customers make repeat purchases with the same supplier; customer loyalty is hence a major factor. The essence of this on-going relationship is then the investment made by both sides, so that the 'natural state' of the relationship is continuity. It is only in exceptional circumstances, when the relationship breaks down, that it briefly returns to the traditional single-transaction mode.

T **Rule T2 – *Continuity Over Time***
The investment in stronger links between supplier and customer which it implies, is a fundamental aspect of marketing practice.

Surprisingly, in view of its importance to both sides, this relationship over time – and the mutual 'investments' associated with maintaining and developing it – is little debated in conventional marketing theory!

These two elements, *dialogue* and *relationship*, are external elements. While they may be defined in an unconventional way, they will be quite recognizable to the most traditionally minded marketer, since they clearly represent marketing links with the outside world, especially with customers. There is, however, a third leg to marketing practice which is the antithesis of traditional marketing, since it is totally internally oriented. This is the cross-functional **co-ordination** of the organization's operations. This third element is not considered by, and is by most definitions excluded from, conventional marketing theory. Yet it is seen by most practising managers as the most important aspect of marketing. It should be noted, though, that some members of marketing departments take a much more isolationist view! But for most managers, I repeat, it is the element which is seen as ensuring that the organization delivers what it has promised.

These three legs combine to make up what in this book is defined as marketing practice. This compares with the more traditional approach, which has concentrated more mechanistically on a narrower set of discrete topics. Recently these have been most popularly defined as the four Ps (see below) which generally fall within the *dialogue* and *relationship* sections of my own definition above, but only cover parts of these.

There are a number of ways that the separate elements of marketing are traditionally described, but over the past decade many business schools have used the framework of the four Ps (as originally proposed by E. Jerome McCarthy):[1]

* *Product*
* *Price*
* *Place*
* *Promotion.*

The first two are, in effect, the product-related elements. Perhaps influenced by economics, price is split off as an element worthy of separate consideration – though this may, in many cases, overemphasize its importance.

1. E. J. McCarthy, *Basic Marketing: a Managerial Approach* (Richard D. Irwin, 1981).

The other two are parts of the delivery system: *Place* is about delivering the physical product or service, and *Promotion* is about delivering the 'sales message'.

I do not recommend this framework, no matter how popular it is – and indeed suggest that you positively avoid it! As you can see, in its rather desperate attempt to find four categories which began with 'P' it ignores services; it places undue emphasis on *Price* and comes up with a catch-all category for leftovers, called *Place*, which tends to be meaningless, no matter how much time is devoted to trying to explain what it covers. Not least of the problems posed, though, is that the four Ps make no reference to the customer or client – who should be at the centre of the whole process!

I have called the more general, three-legged model used in this book the **marketing triad** (or triad for short – not to be confused with Kenichi Ohmae's 'triad' of international markets).

S **Rule S1 – *The Marketing Triad***

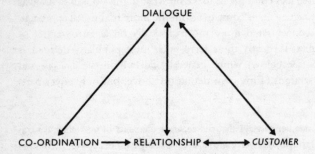

The three key elements of marketing are:
- *Dialogue* – to establish customer needs and to negotiate suitable solutions to these;
- *Relationship* – investment in the effective external exchanges necessary to optimize these solutions, in practice, to the benefit of both sides;
- *Co-ordination* – management of internal operational resources across the whole organization in order to deliver these solutions.

The difference between marketing theory and practice – such as that evidenced in the four Ps – is not necessarily due to academic bloody-mindedness, even though the real-life practice is there for all to see. But that practice, if less than perfect, is clearly what managers employ – with some degree of success! Indeed, for several decades, as marketing theory was being developed from practice, the process of learning marketing was essentially by apprenticeship; it was, and in many respects still is, a very practical craft. At the other end of the spectrum, however, the leading academics soon were, and still are, attempting to provide the theory which, in as simple and academically elegant a fashion as possible, explained the key factors involved. The essence here was simplification and abstraction. On the positive side, this theoretical work has produced a number of genuinely useful theories which have helped to explain specific aspects of marketing practice, and have thus led to improved practice.

On the negative side, problems have often emerged when these quite specific theories have been extended to a much wider use by rather less able academics. The theories have, in particular, been used to provide general frameworks for whole sections of undergraduate courses – and to justify the high fees charged by a whole host of consultants – on a scale far beyond what their originators would have realistically claimed for them or indeed would have thought wise.

It is the over-inflated body of false theory which, at one extreme, this book aims to bring to your attention in order that you may be able to avoid its seductive simplifications. At the other extreme, the book recognizes that the best of marketing theory – coupled with sound marketing practice – can provide a most effective framework for at least some of the more important marketing activities. In this context its role, therefore, is to identify just what is that 'best of marketing theory', and to encapsulate this in the most practical 'rules of thumb'.

The complexity of marketing theory is perhaps best summed up by one of the three 'I's from the Preface – 'Individuality'. The only marketing theory which matters is that which applies to the unique circumstances facing the marketer in the individual situation. The latter part of this first chapter now concentrates on some techniques which can help managers, such as yourself, judge which is the most appropriate theory to use.

G **Rule G3 – *The Critic's Charter***

The practical steps in evaluating a marketing theory for use in a given situation are:

1. Is it directly relevant to the specific needs of the situation? (*if not, discard it*)

2. What other theories attempt to explain the same phenomena? (*check for alternatives*)

3. Does it offer the (most) productive framework for meeting your specific needs? (*discard any explanations which are clearly less effective*)

4. How does it complement the theories you are using to examine other phenomena? (*if it clashes with the main techniques to such an extent that it could cause confusion then discard it, after checking to see that it is not the only one 'in step'*)

5. What reliance can be put upon it and what evidence is there of its effectiveness? (*discard all techniques which have no substantial, proven backing*)

6. Is it 'original' or has it been distorted by later interpretation? (*discard all theories which have been stripped of their meaning by popularization, or go back to the original*)

7. Does it match with your own experience, and does it make sense? (*discard anything which does not make sense, but only after you are sure you understand what it is trying to say*)

8. Then, and only then, use it – but only as a starting point (and as a framework) for further investigations to find the solution which best matches the unique needs of the specific situation. Unless persuaded otherwise by the facts, assume your own judgement is better than that of any experts (who cannot understand the specific situation as well as you can)!

It should be obvious, from the list above, that the most important feature of this approach is the rejection of anything and everything which does not directly help you solve your specific problem. This may sound trivial, for why should anyone think of offering solutions which are irrelevant or simply do not work? But, in their enthusiasm to help, many marketing experts will rush to do just that! As we saw earlier, the recognition of the *individuality* of each situation is normally a key requirement for sound marketing practice.

This process will inevitably discard most of the theories and techniques on offer. Even so, there is a reasonable chance that there should be at least one idea which can offer some new insight into the problems at hand. The most important advice is to use it as no more than a starting point. Indeed, its main value may be in terms of the new insights it stimulates, which may in turn suggest new solutions. More generally it should offer a productive framework within which answers may more easily be worked out.

However you use theory, though, you should only use it as an aid to your own judgement. In marketing you cannot delegate important decisions to outsiders. No matter how expert they are, they cannot have the degree of experience, of the matter in hand, that you do!

The rules later in this book should all be approached in the spirit of the above charter. Their practicality, rather than their academic elegance, should be the acid test they must pass. As far as possible I have already applied these principles. Thus, each of the existing models has been evaluated (based on almost half a decade of research across hundreds of managers, and three decades of practical experience) in terms of its value for marketing practice.

The rest of this chapter concentrates on just two general applications of marketing theory. The first offers one general suggestion as to how you may best apply your own judgement to any given marketing situation. The second is an introduction to **Realistic Marketing**, another set of basic philosophies which lies behind the collection of rules which makes up the rest of this book.

The **Analytical 4-Step** simply outlines the stages which may help you to deploy your own judgement in any given marketing situation.

G **Rule G4 – *The Analytical 4-Step***

Step 0: START with nothing more than a blank sheet of paper.

Step 1: SEARCH without any preconceptions as to the outcome and, based upon your own knowledge and experience, write down what you think are the key factors involved.

Step 2: SELECT, then progressively discard the least essential until you have reduced the number to six.

Step 3: PRIORITIZE these six factors.

Step 4: SYNTHESIZE the relationships and patterns that exist, if necessary returning to Step 1, in order to reduce the six factors to no more than two 'prime directives' which encapsulate these.

This process, which may be used in a variety of management situations but is especially suited to handling the complexities and uncertainties to be found in marketing, is deliberately kept as simple as possible. The hallmark of effective marketing practice is often simplicity.

T **Rule T3**

If you don't understand exactly what is happening you cannot hope to control it!

The most powerful starting point for analysis is often the simplest: a *blank sheet of paper*! Without any preconceptions about what to expect, without any artificial frameworks to bias your views, without any tick-lists to limit your horizons, you simply write down the *key factors* about the situation which faces you. This may be the simplest approach, but it is not necessarily the easiest of starting points! Many managers feel threatened by the lack of guidance. Later in the book you will find a number of techniques which may help you over this first hurdle. In any case, this is a search process, so these factors should already have emerged from your previous desk research (which we will be looking at in a later chapter) or more likely will already have been known to you as a result of previous experience.

Then start the *selection process*. Following much the same process as in the 'Critic's Charter', delete all those ideas which will not be absolutely crucial to the marketing strategy or tactics you are planning.

Be ruthless and progressively discard the least essential until you have no more than six factors left.

Then *prioritize* these six factors (from one to six, in descending order of importance) and note why you have chosen these priorities (since, at a later stage and as conditions change, you may want to change the order of these items).

Finally, try and identify what relationships exist between these factors. Some may be trade-offs (price against quality, say), some may be complementary (support levels and image, say). This is also a stage when the 'rules' to be described later in the book may help. But, whatever aids you use, simply try to see what patterns emerge. At one extreme, this is a process of *synthesis* – trying to combine the components to produce something bigger and better than the individual parts. Ideally, you should reduce the six factors to no more than two 'prime directives' (the concepts or philosophies on which managers are able to focus, but which still encapsulate the key elements). At the other, it revolves around 'dilemmas', where there are several options which are apparently in conflict with each other. The management of the dilemma, so that apparently conflicting options may need to be simultaneously applied – with synergy rather than friction – is the route to success in these cases. The classic example is that of the Japanese, who simply did not accept that raising quality standards would cost more; and who went on to show that in practice it actually reduced overall costs.

Depending upon the outcome of this final stage it may then be necessary to return to the first step – to add in the extra factors which this has suggested might be relevant. The whole process is then repeated. In many marketing planning activities iteration is the key to progressively optimizing the final output.

This, then, is the 'Analytical 4-Step' approach to analysis, although there are actually five steps and Step Zero is perhaps the most important of all! In the present context this is referred to as 'Zero Level Marketing'. It is a commitment to approach each new activity afresh – a blank sheet of paper – without the prejudices derived from previous exposure to theories. The one great virtue of the 'Analytical 4-Step' is that it is totally under your control – you know exactly where you are.

The final section of this chapter outlines the basic philosophies of 'Realistic Marketing' which shape the theories and rules described in the rest of the book.

T **Rule T4 – *The Basic Philosophies of Realistic Marketing***

a) PRAGMATISM – above all, any theory claiming adherence to these philosophies must offer valuable, practical support for the marketing practitioner.

b) SUBSERVIENCE – but it must clearly limit itself to being just an aid to the manager's own marketing (decision-making), never a replacement for it.

c) COMMON SENSE – and it must be explained in terms which mean that it can be fully understood by, and supported by, all those implementing it.

d) INDIVIDUALITY – it should normally be seen only as providing support for the specific elements of marketing currently under consideration, and should not be derived from irrelevant generalizations.

e) OPTIONALITY – and it ideally should signal that it is only one of a number of options, one of the alternative approaches to the specific topic.

f) INCREMENTALISM – an especially important point is that its action should usually be capable of (and usually be seen to be) operating incrementally upon the factors involved.

g) ITERATION – and this action should generally be repeatable until an optimal outcome is reached.

h) RESOURCING – but it must take account of the reality of the resources – human and technical as well as financial – available to the organization.

i) INTEGRABILITY – indeed it should, as far as possible, make clear what role it also plays, if any, in co-ordinating the operational resources across the organization as a whole.

j) INVESTMENT – the time dimension, which means that marketing decisions must be viewed as investment decisions affecting the long-term as well as the short-term, must be allowed for.

k) ZERO LEVEL – finally, in summary of a number of the above factors, any theory, such as it is, should be directly relevant to the situation in hand, in line with the discussions earlier in this chapter.

From this very long list, the first factor is normally the most important since it encapsulates the 'realism' which is the definitive feature of this form of marketing. It also leads naturally to most of the other factors listed, including multiple, alternative approaches to marketing topics (best handled by the Zero Level approach), as well as the very real constraints imposed by limited resources, and previous history, and it highlights (at least in this version) marketing's central role in co-ordinating the organization's resources overall.

2 / *Competition*

Competition has always been a preoccupation of marketers, since, over time, relative advantage usually translates into absolute success and the influence of competitors is one of the most important factors determining the performance of an organization. These competitors, though, need not be commercial competitors. They might just as easily be other departments, within government, say, which are competing for attention and resources. Any exploration of marketing needs, therefore, to take on another dimension, that of the relationship to competitors.

The 'conventional' theory which now dominates this aspect of marketing has mainly been developed over the past two decades, notably by Michael Porter. The following long section summarizes the most important elements of the current thinking:

Competition – the Industry

According to this dominant theory, the first factor in the competitive environment is that of the 'industry'. This may seem trivial, since presumably you will already know what the level of competitive activity is in your industry/market. But, on the other hand, if you unreservedly accept this theory (and this is a commitment I myself do not necessarily make), then what you are seeing may only be a short-term deviation and the inherent 'industry' characteristics will ultimately determine what longer term developments you should expect.

The 'industry' is defined quite broadly, as a group of firms (or organizations) which offer products (or services) which are near substitutes for each other. According to the theory, the 'character' of that industry will often largely determine the competitive activities taking place within it, and the profits of most of the participants. Some of the factors which may contribute to this overall 'character' may be:

• *Size of market* – the larger the market the more attractive it will generally be to new entrants, and the more competitive it may become. On the other hand, looking at the theory critically, it is just as likely that the larger the market the more likely it will be that it will be segmented. This is a process which will be discussed in a later chapter, but in this context it means that the market is broken down into a series of smaller markets. This will allow 'niche' marketing, thus reducing competition.

• *Number of organizations competing and concentration of business* – the greater the number of organizations in a market the more competitive it may be, if the brands are of roughly the same size. But, again taking a more critical view, this may also be related to the pattern of concentration of the overall business into the hands of the major players; clearly a monopoly or oligopoly will significantly reduce competitive forces! The most stable and profitable market (apart from a pure monopoly) is usually that with one or two dominant brands and a few smaller brands.[1] If the range of comparable brands, say four or five, are all of the same size, on the other hand, then the market may be viciously competitive as each brand strives to make the breakthrough to the dominant position.

• *Product differentiation* – the most sophisticated marketers will aim to differentiate their product or service from the others in the market. In general, the more that products or services are differentiated the less direct the competition will be. This is, indeed, the main limitation on this theory of competition, since most sophisticated marketers have very deliberately differentiated their brands to remove them from such competition (and the industry theory accordingly holds relatively few lessons for them).

• *Economies of scale* – it is often considered that economies of scale are the main features of any market. The theory is that the greater the economies of scale, the greater will be the benefits coming to those with large shares of the market, and hence the greater the competition by offering incentives to 'buy' market share in order to become the lowest cost producer. Conventional competition theory has tended to focus on this aspect (which is, in some respects, the antithesis of marketing theory which would favour differentiation) and to a degree the whole industry theory tends to stand or fall by the extent to which this factor predominates – in most markets, I would argue, it falls!

1. D. S. Mercer, 'A Two Decade Test of Product Life Cycle Theory', *British Journal of Management*, Vol. 4 (1993) pp. 269–74.

T Rule T5 – *Experience Curve*

In many markets, the more that is 'produced' the more is learned, and the more experience is available to reduce costs. This element of economies of scale relates to experience over the total production run, not just the current production levels, so its effect is cumulative, potentially offering the early leaders a major competitive advantage – and creating substantial barriers against late entrants.

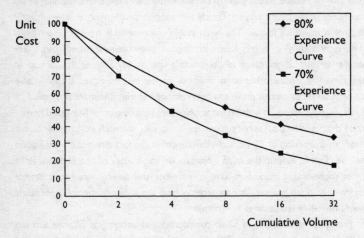

The definitive support for this theory was given by the Boston Consulting Group[2] when it proposed (in 1970) a general observation, based upon its consultancy work, that the characteristic decline in the unit cost of value added 'is consistently 20 to 30 per cent each time accumulated production is doubled. This decline goes on in time without limit (in constant prices) regardless of the rate of growth of experience. The rate of decline is surprisingly consistent, even from industry to industry.'

On the other hand, the evidence is that many markets are moving towards a significantly increased variety, in terms of the ranges of products or services offered. This is a requirement imposed by consumer demand, and is the very reverse of that favouring economies of scale – once a viable level of mass production has been reached. Benetton in the early 1980s, for example, had a product line with more than 500 colour and style combinations. In the 1980s,

2. Boston Consulting Group, *Perspectives on Experience* (1970).

as well, the Japanese manufacturers moved to 'flexible manufacturing', which enabled them to increase the range they offered without dramatic reductions in efficiency.

The evidence[3] does seem to show that a clear brand leader – in most consumer goods markets at least – holds a significant advantage over the other brands, typically holding twice the share of the second brand, and three times that of the third, and able to employ marketing activities which do enjoy substantial economies of scale. It is arguable, therefore, that the 'experience curve' may also reflect the cumulative marketing investment – where marketing is essentially an investment activity:

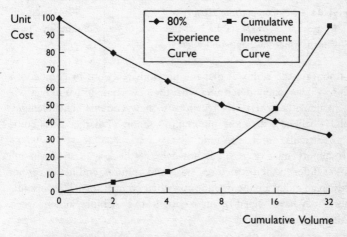

Cumulative Volume

• *Legislative barriers* – it has long been the case that sitting tenants in large markets have managed to persuade government to enact legislation to govern the competitive behaviour of the main players. Pressure groups used to redirect this process can often offer the most profitable form of investment, and can erect near insuperable entry barriers!
• *Control of distribution channels* – if the distribution channels can be denied to competitors then competition can be limited.
• *Over-capacity* – perhaps the most sensitive indicator of price competition, and one which is genuinely important, is the degree of over-capacity. Beware those markets, particularly those with economies of scale, where there is a significant amount of spare capacity. If it exists you can be sure that everyone will be

3. D. S. Mercer, *Intimations of Immortality: Death of the Life Cycle* (ADMAP, 1993).

focusing on sales (and hence production) levels, almost regardless of price, and that almost inevitably leads to low, commodity-based prices.

• *Age of market and rate of change* – dynamics of a market will have an impact on the players within it. According to life-cycle theory the older markets should be more competitive, as growth slows down and the competitors look for growth at the expense of each other. On the other hand, the evidence[4] suggests that this has not happened in at least some consumer goods markets – even though, according to most theory, these should have been most susceptible to this effect.

 Rule T6 – *Competitive History*

In most stable markets the best indicator of *future* competitive positions is what has happened *before*.

In this way, the reality is that the previous reactions of competitors will to a large extent determine what the new competitive moves will be, particularly in terms of reactions to new entrants. This element, which I believe is the most important in almost all markets, may come as no particular surprise to you!

Instability may be created, however, if the organizations in the market differ in their structures, goals and cultures, and hence cannot easily 'read' what are the intentions of their competitors. This 'inscrutability' may have helped Japanese entrants to destabilize some markets to their eventual benefit.

Susceptibility to outside factors

All the above factors may pale into insignificance if there are key factors outside the market which determine its future.

The good and the bad

In a rather more practical contribution, Michael Porter[5] suggests that there are good and bad competitors. 'Good' competitors play by the rules the industry has tacitly recognized: they typically limit price competition, help to expand the industry and do not aim to destroy other competitors. 'Bad' competitors, on

4. D. S. Mercer, 'A Two Decade Test of Product Life Cycle Theory', *British Journal of Management*, Vol. 4 (1993) pp. 269–74.

5. Michael E. Porter, *Competitive Strategy* (Free Press, 1980).

the other hand, usually do the opposite: they break the rules, buy brand share (often by starting a price war) and upset the equilibrium. To optimize their results, 'good' competitors should, within the very strict legal guidelines, aim to (co-operatively) constrain the 'bad'. Which type you have facing you makes a quite dramatic difference to your prospects.

Porter takes competition on to an even wider canvas when he identifies five key actors engaged in extended rivalry:

* *Industry competitors* – the rivalry amongst existing firms.
* *Potential entrants* – the threat from new entrants, which may change the rules of competition, but against which 'entry barriers' can be built.
* *Suppliers* – the bargaining power of common suppliers, which can change the structure of industries.
* *Buyers* – the bargaining power of the customers.
* *Substitutes* – the threat of substitute products or services, which may destroy the whole industry, not just the existing competitive positions.

Entry barriers

One answer to the very dangerous threat of 'potential entrants' is for the 'sitting tenants' to erect 'entry barriers':

* *Economies of scale* – as discussed above.
* *Positioning* – one advantage the existing brand leaders have, which is often overlooked, is that they usually occupy the prime positions in the market. This makes it very difficult for a newcomer to find any product advantage save price.
* *Structural* – the industry may be constrained by its structure, which works against newcomers who are fighting for the few very scarce resources which are not already owned.
* *'Switching costs'* – Michael Porter[6] also identifies the fact that customers may face significant costs in switching to new suppliers; costs which keep them locked to the old ones.
* *Political* – again as mentioned earlier.

Exit barriers

In passing, it is worth mentioning that there may also be cost penalties which work to prevent companies leaving an industry. The net result is that such firms are often forced to stay in the market, and engage in destructive rivalry.

6. *Ibid.*

I differ from Michael Porter, in that I believe that – at least for the market leaders – it is the organization itself, rather than the market it is in, which determines the competitive position. The smaller organizations may, of course, be dominated by the competitive positions taken by the market leaders. Even the leaders may, over time, be influenced by outside views as to what the overall position should be; and these become self-fulfilling predictions (aided and abetted by experts such as Michael Porter). There is, however, always the opportunity to break away from the disabling history of 'bad' competition – a possibility which Michael Porter's followers tend to downplay.

Simplifying matters somewhat, but not quite as much as Michael Porter, I would suggest that competitive power can be built on four main fronts to make up the 'power diamond':

S | **Rule S2 – *The Power Diamond***

Two of the factors, 'Differentiation' and 'Scale Advantage', are those at the heart of Michael Porter's work, described below. The other two, 'Market Position' and 'Brand Investment' (or, from the other side of the relationship, 'Customer Franchise') are not usually considered in competition theory – though they are explored in considerable detail later in this book.

It is the total area between these fronts (which reflects the overall power of the brand), and how the cutting edges (the corners of the diamond) are deployed in practice, which indicate how much competitive leverage the brand may be able to generate.

Competitive Strategies

Having taken care of the rather arid topic of 'industry', which you must recognize simply because it is so influential (so much so that your competitors may come to believe in it and it will then be a self-fulfilling prophecy!), Michael Porter,[7] again, moves on to more productive ground when he states that there are just 'three potentially successful generic strategic approaches to outperforming other firms in an industry:

1. overall cost leadership
2. differentiation
3. focus'

As we have already seen, the first alternative has come to prominence in recent years, and organizations have invested vast sums to achieve economies of scale. The second and third alternatives, however, rely on using factors other than price to contain competition. Product differentiation, particularly 'branding', is a key device since it removes the product from some of the most direct elements of competition (particularly from price competition). Segmentation and product positioning, which will be discussed in a later chapter, are also particularly effective devices for containing competitive pressure. They allow the marketer to concentrate, to 'focus' in Michael Porter's terminology,[8] resources to best defend his or her offering within a small segment of the market.

Leaders and followers

Michael Porter's work is undoubtedly the most influential in this area, but there are other commentators with contributions to make. Some emphasize a different competitive split – that between those ('leaders') products or services which have a substantial market share (typically 40 per cent or more), with a very strong position, and those ('followers') which have minor shares, with marginal positions. The approach each of these organizations adopts may be very different:

7. *Ibid.*
8. *Ibid.*

Leaders

In this case, the 'competitive thrust' may not necessarily be the only, or even the main, objective, since they stand to gain significantly from market expansion, and their promotional effort will often include elements directed as much to this end as against their competitors. In terms of competitive activity, it is normally expected that companies with major 'brand leaders' will concentrate their effort on advertising. Sometimes such strategies are described in military terms (especially by Kotler and Singh).

Defending (leader) market share:
• *Position defence* – making the brand position impregnable.
• *Pre-emptive defence* – launching an attack on a competitor before it can be established, while it is still vulnerable.
• *Counter-offensive defence* – attacking the competitor's home territory so that it has to divert its efforts into protecting its existing products.

Followers

On the other hand, in these cases, the whole strategy is likely to be fiercely competitive, aiming only to grab the largest share possible of the existing 'cake'. Their main competitive device is likely to be 'below the line' promotion and, in particular, price competition.

Again in military terms, the strategies might be:
• *Frontal attack* – where the challenger takes on the market leader in its own territory and attacks the opponent's strengths rather than its weaknesses. For this, considerable resources are needed.
• *Flank attack* – a segment (or geographical region) where the market leader is most vulnerable is chosen. This is the most usual approach.
• *Encirclement* – this involves 'launching a grand offensive against the enemy on several fronts . . . where the aggressor has, or is able to muster, enough resources to break the opponent's will to resist'.
• *Bypass attack* – this is most prevalent in high-technology markets, where a challenger puts its efforts into bypassing existing technology and winning the battle for the next technology to be brought to the market.

So much for the theory! It is meant to be enlightening, and in some specific situations it might be – which is one reason I have given so much space to it. The main reason, though, is the one I mentioned earlier, that so many managers have been indoctrinated into this very fashionable belief that it does begin to have a life of its own! In particular, the aspect of economies of scale (which is, in practice,

central to much of this theory) is widely believed in and many strategi
are written around this basic assumption. It is one with which, you
will have gathered, I do not feel altogether comfortable, at least not
when it is presented as a general principle.

So what do I see as the most important elements of competitive
strategy?

T **Rule T7 –** *Know Your Competitors*
By far the most important aspect of effective competitive strategy is
that you get to know your competitors personally!

I mean this in two senses. In the first, quite literally you should
meet with your competitors and get to know them. I will discuss this
below, but for now absorb the startling fact that the qualitative research
undertaken by myself and my colleagues has revealed that many, if
not most, managers believe they already operate in a competitive
situation where informal (but not illegal) cartels dominate!

The second aspect is rather different. It is getting to know all about
your competitor's organization just as if it were a person – so that
you can predict his or her response to your own actions, and to those
of others.

Competitors' Response

One of the aptitudes which marks out great generals, as much as chess
masters, is the ability to get under the skin of their opponents; to
understand them in such a way that they can predict what their
responses to different situations might be. So probably the most important, but often neglected, aspect of any competitor research is to
determine how each of the competitors may respond to future changes.
In a very general sense, there are four main categories of possible
response:

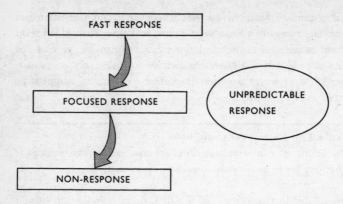

• *Non-response* (or slow response) – this competitor will not respond directly to any changes in the environment, or at least will not do so in the short term. It may be a dominant brand leader, or it may be a competitor in a particularly weak position, which cannot resource any reaction.

• *Focused response* – some competitors will only respond to certain types of challenge (typically on price).

T **T8 – *Fast Response***
A consistently fast response to competitive actions is usually the most (cost-) effective strategy.

• *Fast response* – there are a few organizations which have a policy of immediate and substantial response (often a deliberate 'overkill'), as a deterrent to future challengers as much as to the current threat. If this strategy can be resourced it usually is the most effective – and the most cost-effective – since the sooner the threat is removed the sooner high profits can be generated again. It is recommended that this is your own strategy (if you can afford it and are not forced into either of the first two categories).

• *Unpredictable response* – the most difficult to deal with and the most dangerous (to themselves as much as to others), however, are those organizations whose responses cannot be predicted at all! You should never adopt this strategy, unless all else has failed.

Of course, you will also need to understand not just what the competitor might want to do, but also what it is capable of doing. Again, like a good general, you will want to know what is the disposition of the enemy's forces before you enter battle. This analysis should use all the techniques of 'desk research' described in a later chapter, but in particular it should ideally be motivated by a genuine interest, indeed a fascination, about everything a competitor does or says – that way nothing will be missed!

Let us now move on to the practical actions you can take in relation to your competitors.

Michael Porter[9] states that 'Perhaps the single most important concept in planning and executing offensive or defensive competitive moves is the concept of commitment.' He goes on to explain that such commitment can 'deter retaliation', can 'deter threatening moves' and can 'create trust'. The key element of persuasion is seen to be that the decisions are 'binding and irreversible'. In other words:

T **Rule T9 – *Competitive Conviction***

By clearly staking out your position, you can signal to the opposition exactly what your competitive strategy is, and thus pre-empt moves by them which might destabilize your position or that of the market as a whole.

In the earlier figure this would have come under 'Fast Response'. Conviction or commitment marketing, which is described in its more general sense later in the book, is based upon believing in your product or service with such a degree of blinding conviction, of almost an evangelical fervour which carries over to your relations with the outside world, that the obvious degree of conviction itself becomes the main message.

Such conviction marketing, when undertaken by the most powerful marketers, can go much further. It can force the competitors to fight the battle on ground of your own choosing. At times it may almost seem as if such competitors are mesmerized by the degree of your conviction – if it is strong enough. It is a device normally only available to market leaders, but strong second brands, with aspirations to lead, can also sometimes use it. This approach, although not featured

9. *Ibid.*

in most competitive theory, comes close to the aggressive, almost military-based tactics, which are at the heart of traditional theory.

A much more radical approach in terms of conventional theory, but one which seems to be more prevalent in practice, is collaboration.

Collaborators and Cartels

As you will have observed, it seems to be a requirement of managers that they swear an oath of 'death to the enemy'; few will publicly admit to anything less. We have christened this the 'Warrior' approach. It wins battles in war, but produces few profits in the commercial arena. In any case, according to our research, the opposite would appear to be true in business practice. Indeed, in group discussions, when the participants realized that the majority of those present collaborated, they admitted that they did the same. We eventually had a majority (in these small groups) who even said that the organizations in their industry operated almost as an informal cartel!

T **Rule T10 –** *The Siege Ramp*

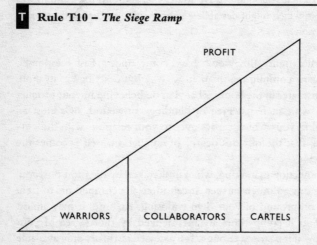

- *Warriors* – these brave individuals, with their militaristic approach, win the war – though not necessarily the peace – and all too often pay a high price for their achievements; the industry has been destroyed in the course of their battles.

• *Collaborators* – on the other hand, work together to stabilize their industry; in Michael Porter's terms they are the 'good' competitors. They do not engage in destructive rivalry, and avoid price battles.

• *Cartels* – these go one step further, to work positively together to develop the future of the industry, with mechanisms for collaborating on joint industry projects.

T **Rule T11 –** *The Three Paired Codes of Positive Collaboration*

Code 1, part one: POSITIVELY OUTPERFORM YOUR COMPETITORS, by as large a margin on as many fronts as possible. Collaboration does not in any way mean that you stop competing – collaboration is not the same as surrender, and competitors respect the organization which is simply better than the rest.

Code 1, part two: NEVER INDULGE IN NEGATIVE ATTACKS, on any front. Do not, even temporarily, pursue campaigns which might be seen as destructive (price wars, dirty advertising or whatever).

Code 2, part one: UNDERSTAND YOUR COMPETITORS. I have previously recommended that you understand your competitors in order to beat them, here I suggest that you understand them in order to recognize why they take the actions they do, and so not to read into those actions hostile intent where there is none.

Code 2, part two: BE STRAIGHTFORWARD AND TRUST-WORTHY – in turn, if your competitors understand you and trust you, they will even tolerate actions they don't like. When trust breaks down, however, beware; some of the most destructive industry wars have come about because of misunderstandings.

Code 3, part one: TALK INDUSTRY NOT ORGANIZATION – the one thing you have in common with your competitors, and the thing you both want to promote, is the industry you share. Always emphasize your commitment to maintaining and developing that industry.

Code 3, part two: JAW-JAW NOT WAR-WAR – above all, talk to your competitors whenever you can. When you meet them, at industry conferences or socially, say, go out of your way to be positively friendly towards them, and to positively discuss the future of your shared industry.

T **Rule T12 – *Three Additional Codes for Cartels***
Code 1 – JOIN, OR SET UP, AN INDUSTRY FORUM, so that you have positive ground on which to discuss your shared objectives and, if necessary, to debate those which divide you.

Code 2 – RUN INDUSTRY CAMPAIGNS, which may be good for the industry in themselves, but more important force all the collaborators to think positively.

Code 3 – THINK COLLECTIVELY, so that you can, within the constraints imposed by law, jointly act in the common interest of the industry, even while competing strenuously within it.

These positive approaches are the most productive of all, if your competitors will support them, and the indications are that, in the great majority of cases, they will. They are so clearly in everyone's best interests that only a fool would think otherwise. Unfortunately, there are still some fools around! If they are merely foolish, and not dangerously insane, one of the best strategies for teaching them the lessons of good (competitor) manners is 'tit for tat'.

T **Rule T13 – *Tit for Tat***
This is a very simple approach to a competitor's actions. If your competitor makes an aggressive move you respond with one, but as soon as the other's aggressive moves cease so should yours.

This has the virtue that the competitor is not rewarded for 'bad' behaviour (since you immediately undermine any gain that might have been made) and is rewarded for 'good' behaviour (by the immediate removal of your matching action).

Most important of all, it very clearly shows your rules of engagement: you are a 'good' competitor – but will not tolerate bad behaviour.

3 / Product:Service Strategy

As we saw in the first chapter, there is a broad consensus of opinion which holds that marketing is focused on the customer. In general, this consensus also supports the view that the first thing to be considered, in any marketing situation, is that customer. Why, then, does this book talk about the product or service before it investigates customer needs?

The main reason is that before you can hope to know your customer you must know yourself. It is not sufficient to approach your customer with a general, bland interest. Rather, if your investigations are to be productive, you must focus on those aspects of the customer's needs which are most relevant to your, and your organization's, specific interests. We will see in a later section that even your understanding of yourself, in the context of your marketing needs, has, ultimately, to be informed by the customer's viewpoint; but that the first point of departure has to be an exploration of the product or service itself. This approach also happens to be the one which most managers intuitively adopt!

A word of warning, though. The product or service, in the marketing context, is almost certainly not what it appears to be; or, at least, it will be rather more than this. This concept is popularly known as the **product package**, and it applies just as much to the service industries and non-profit sector. Any such package is a complex mix of product and service (of tangible and intangible elements) which I will refer to as the **Product:Service Package**.

The Product:Service Package

This 'package' embraces all the aspects of the product, tangible or intangible, which matter to the customer. Thus, for that simplest of products, the soft drink, it will encompass far more than the main ingredient itself; for the water it contains comes, free of charge, out of the nearest tap, and even adding some sugar and carbon dioxide doesn't stop it being one of the cheapest of commodities. The flavouring may be proprietary, but in physical terms it is probably the distinctive packaging – which promises far more than flavoured fizzy water – which first starts to justify the premium price. The overall package also contains a range of intangible elements. The advertising promises more still and, invested in by the supplier over several generations, now manages to persuade the consumer that this is no ordinary fizzy water, but is Coke or Pepsi – which is something totally different. Even in the case of the most basic of commodities, the intangibles – especially image – may be all!

Some of the most important elements of the package are the ones which may not be at all evident to the consumer. In particular, distribution, the chain which eventually brings the product or service to the consumer, may be a critical factor. If the product is not easily available when the consumer wants to purchase it then it will probably not be purchased. In the case of complex products (and services) the list grows even longer. Service and customer support may well become the most important factors in building customer satisfaction.

As a reminder, then, here are some of the elements which may be important in the overall package:

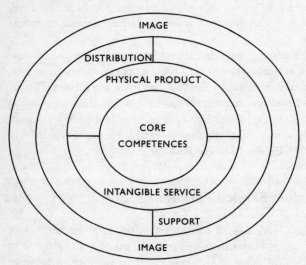

Rule T14 – *The 'Product' Iceberg*
The first rule of product strategy is that you MUST recognize ALL
the hidden elements of the Product:Service Package. Like an iceberg,
90% of what matters in any such package is hidden from view.

One way of examining this Product:Service Package is to see what
the organization itself does at each stage of the process of producing
and delivering the product or service. One popular approach, very
effectively promoted by Michael Porter, is that of the 'value chain':

Value chains

Michael Porter[1] divides the elements of this value chain into nine parts:

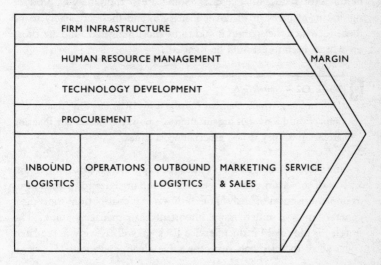

Each of these is to be investigated separately, to optimize the value it adds to
the product/service – though he also suggests you look at the links between
them.

Although he carefully stresses that the investigation should look at added
value in terms of 'differentiation' (his word for those activities which improve
the customer's perceived value of the product or service, by making it seem

1. Michael E. Porter, *Competitive Advantage* (Free Press, 1985).

different to its competitors) as much as in terms of reduced costs, it is the latter aspect (of 'cost reduction') which tends to dominate his work – and that of many of his followers.

Sensitivity Analysis

The focus on costs can, however, be very illuminating. One especially enlightening approach is to take the cost(s) in each of these areas (or part of an area) separately, and see what happens (in percentage terms) to the overall margin when each of these individual costs is reduced by 10 per cent. Reductions in some areas will have little impact on the overall margin (and hence can be safely treated as of lower priority, in this cost reduction exercise). Some areas, though, will produce significant changes in the overall margin; and these are likely to be those to which the margin is said to be most 'sensitive', and are those on which attention should be focused.

---

o **Rule O2 –** *Sensitivity*
    Determining which element (changed by 10%) has the greatest (%) impact on the overall organization is a powerful device for focusing attention on key issues, especially cost issues.

One great advantage of the value chain approach is that it highlights aspects of the chain which are critical to the organization's work. For example, this form of analysis often shows that distribution (in its most general sense) is much more important than managers think. The search for the total Product:Service Package will, as we will see later, cover all of the elements from the value chain, and more.

Practical Value Chains

The main problem is that Michael Porter's approach may sometimes be too restrictive. A more practical approach is to split the activities of the organization into those characteristic groupings which are natural to its specific operations (in line with the philosophy of 'individuality'), rather than the theoretical nine categories described by Michael

Porter. In addition, his upper set of cross-organization activities should be ignored, since – in our experience – they only tend to confuse managers trying to use this approach.

○ Rule O3 – *The Practical Value Chain*

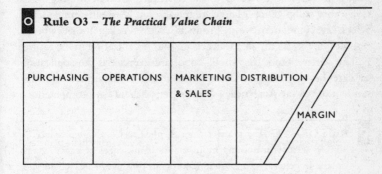

As can be seen from the diagram above, the visual presentation is also made more meaningful if the size of each segment of the value chain reflects its importance (on whatever basis – volume, added value, sensitivity etc. – you decide is most useful).

Another type of diagram looks even more directly at the added value (where this can simply be in financial terms, or in terms of customer value or perceived value):

○ Rule O4 – *Added-Value Diagram*

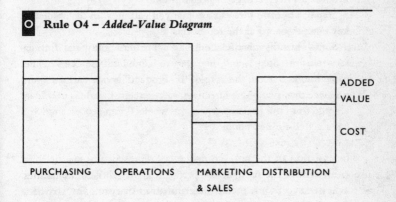

Core Competences

First and foremost, however, is the need to determine the organization's core competences. These are the absolutely essential ingredients,
which are unique to your Product:Service Package, that will be
responsible for the sustained success of your organization in the future.

The starting point for this all-important exercise is the application
of Zero Level Marketing, described in the first chapter, and the subsequent use of the Analytical 4–Step to derive these core competences:

O   **Rule O5 –** *The Analytical 4-Step Applied to Core Competences*

Step 0: start with nothing more than a blank sheet of paper; try to
isolate, in general terms, what makes your product or service unique,
what special 'competitive advantages' it, and your organization, have.

Step 1: then, without any preconceptions as to the outcome, write
down what you think are the key factors involved – those key factors
which best describe what you have found in Step 0, but also including
those from other inputs (such as existing corporate strategies).

Step 2: then progressively discard the least essential until you have
reduced the number to six – the least essential in this context being
defined as those least important to the long-term survival of the
Product:Service Package or organization.

Step 3: prioritize these six, so that you end up with the absolutely
key competence(s) at the top of this list.

Step 4: identify what relationships and patterns exist, and if necessary return to Step 1, and then start to combine these competences
to define, in outline, the core of the Product:Service Package (with
no more than two prime directives: key concepts), and (as new ideas
emerge from this process) repeat the whole 4-step process until you
have a well-formed outline.

The isolation of the core competences represents by far the most
productive use of the Analytical 4-Step across the whole of marketing.
We will need to return to this determination of core competences a
number of times, to ensure that, in the wider context of the customer
viewpoint and the even wider one of the external environment, they
are correct, and then to optimize their positioning in the light of

this new information. Remember, from the principles of Realistic Marketing, iteration and incrementalism are central aspects of the strategy process.

Honing down the *key* competences is, initially, a daunting task. It is often easier, initially, to write down a much bigger list of possible 'competences' (without having to determine how important they are) and then progressively refine these down by iteratively applying Step 2 of the 4-Step.

Even then it is quite possible that you will need some help to get you going, so we have developed the concept of the **Core Competences Pie** – four separate segments of the organization's internal and external environment which are used to stimulate separate approaches to the overall problem. Using this intermediate approach, you first develop your wider list of competences within these initial, broad categories. Focusing your thoughts in this way may stimulate your imagination to unearth competences which, blinkered by the more conventional approaches, you might not have considered. Perhaps more important, it will also show you which competences appear in a number of slices and, since they have wider impact, are more likely to be the crucial ones. The segments we find most useful in this context are:

• *Historical resources* – this slice of the pie represents the traditional, inward-looking view of the organization. It reflects what the organization sees as being most important to itself: typically those competences in which it has most pride; the activities it believes it does better than anyone else; and, in general, what has succeeded in the past is an especially good indication of what will succeed in the future.

• *Competitive position* – this slice, however, requires you to look more dispassionately at its position, in relation to its 'competitors' (who are defined in the widest possible sense, including government departments in the public sector just as much as commercial competitors in the private sector). Which competences give the organization a sustainable competitive advantage over those competitors? The key word here is sustainable. In this context short-term advantage means little – to be a genuine core competence it has to be sustainable over the long term.

• *Customer benefits* – we will explore the customer viewpoint in much more detail in a later chapter of the book, but at this early stage it is sufficient merely to introduce the competences which relate to this slice of the pie, and to consider those which you (the supplier) think offer most to (or are most wanted by) that customer.

• *Future developments* – this is the aspect most often neglected, since most managers tend to look backwards rather than forwards. Put in a nutshell, it simply asks which competences will be important in five or ten years' time. This often turns out to be the most powerful contributor of all, because our experience shows that managers find it easiest to widen their vision if the timescale they are talking about is (in their terms) very long – this freedom acts as a potent stimulant for their, and your, imagination.

S   **Rule S3 –** *The Core Competences Pie*

It has to be remembered that the whole point of the Core Competences Pie lies in integrating the slices – the reverse of what might be expected, but we hope this will, yet again, make it that much more memorable.

Matrices

The Core Competences Pie might look like a matrix, but where possible I have deliberately avoided the use of matrices, which many other academics recommend, because in general we have found that such matrices tend to distort the messages they are set to contain.

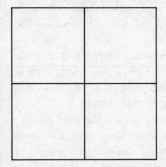

No matter how sophisticated the claims made for them, all matrices are essentially simple. Most often the pigeon-holes are given 'explanatory' titles. In the Core Competences Pie these would be:

HISTORICAL RESOURCES	CUSTOMER BENEFITS
COMPETITIVE POSITION	FUTURE DEVELOPMENTS

The items they contain are then also ascribed certain performance or action characteristics – depending upon which of the four boxes they have been allocated to.

Criticism of matrices

The reasons we avoid the use of matrices are:

• *Limited factor inputs* – for a 2 × 2 matrix there can only be two true dimensions, and these are usually so generalized that they can offer only very limited analytical power.

• *Subjective allocation* – which box to put a product into is often a very subjective decision. Once the product is in the box, however, its given characteristics acquire a gloss of respectability which the original judgement would not have had and often deludes users (not least into a false sense of security).

• *Black and white outcomes* – probably the worst feature is that outcomes are limited to just four categories and are black and white, with no shades of grey. A hair's breadth to one or other side of the dividing line and the strategy for a product, say, changes totally.

• *Most matrices were originally quite limited in their ambitions* – which is understandable when the gross simplifications they contain are taken into account. Their inventors, who were usually sophisticated academics, recognized these limitations. Unfortunately, much wider reaching claims, which have typically come from later 'evangelists', are often made for them that hide some important flaws.

How to use matrices

The above criticisms should not discourage you from using matrices; but they should persuade you to use them properly. Matrices should only be used to obtain a different view – which should be combined with all the other information available to build an overall, balanced picture.

As it is, I must issue one stern warning about the use of even a 'pie' in the case of core competences. That is, that the ultimate aim of the Core Competences Pie is to condense the number of core competences and to prioritize them. There is no virtue, and much vice, in lengthening the lists in each slice of the pie; and considerable danger in trying to balance them with those in the other slices. If you simply cannot think of anything to put under 'Future Developments', say, then leave it blank!

The immediate outcome of all this work is a list of, and hopefully an understanding of, what is central to the current work and the future of the organization: its core competences. The reason for this work will now begin to emerge.

One of the most important keys to success, in almost all walks of life, is to concentrate resources where they may be most productively deployed. Resources, even in the richest of organizations, are never boundless, and are rarely sufficient to meet all the demands which might be placed upon them. Resources have, therefore, to be allocated – even rationed – between groups of competing activities. In practice this often appears, at least to outsiders, to be a remarkably random process.

Thus, to formalize this process, and to help concentrate resources where they can be most effectively used, a number of rules have been developed. Below I group together some of the most useful of these under the overall banner of the 80:20 Rule:

G **Rule G5 –** *The 80:20 Rule*
The most general and powerful rule of all is this one. It simply states that, across a wide range of situations, 20% of the contributors (customers, say) will account for 80% of the performance (sales volumes, for instance).

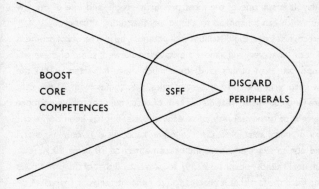

BOOST
CORE
COMPETENCES

SSFF

DISCARD
PERIPHERALS

T **Rule T15 – *Support Success Forget Failure (SSFF)***

This rule has much the same message, but in a more specific context. It asks only that you abandon the tendency of managements to throw good money after bad, trying to rescue projects which can never succeed, and instead put these resources behind the proven successes.

T **Rule T16 – *Discard Peripherals***

This works from the other extreme, and is even more ruthless. It demands that you do not just ignore the weaker elements of your operations, which some define as anything which is not central to the core competences, but that you actually discard them.

T **Rule T17 – *Boost Core Competences***

This is the most positive statement. It merely says that, in this reallocation of resources, these should be diverted to those activities which have the most beneficial impact on the development of, or application of, the core competences.

The 80:20 Rule itself has been in use for more than a century. First enunciated by an Italian, Pareto (hence its alternative title, the Pareto Rule), it is just as relevant today. It is still one of the most productive tools, and one of the few general ones which can be applied to almost any marketing situation.

It simply recognizes that the distribution of potential, be it in terms of products or customers or whatever, will almost inevitably be skewed; some of these will be more important than others (and some much more important). That the typical skew is so large that 80 per cent of sales, say, comes from 20 per cent of customers (and conversely that 80 per cent of customers contribute no more than 20 per cent of turnover) may come as a surprise, but has been borne out by countless practical examples. On the other hand, as it is only a general principle and not an exact equation, the outcome may be 70:30 or 90:10 (but, by definition, it will almost never be 50:50). Its power, and that of the other rules listed, comes from the fact that it enables you to concentrate your resources on just that 20 per cent, confident that these are the important ones, responsible for 80 per cent of your 'business', and you can safely limit any investment in the other 80 per cent.

A very practical device which assists this process is ABC Analysis:

Rule O6 – *ABC Analysis*

This could not be simpler. When you (or more likely your computer) are listing the results of any analysis you just print the output in descending order of importance: most important first.

In this way, the key items are always at the top and receive your immediate attention. Conversely, the minor ones are at the bottom and it does not matter if they are ignored. This may sound trivial, but by itself it may revolutionize your view of the world. No longer will those customers and products whose names start with the letter 'A' dominate your life!

Core competences are sometimes described as the 'focus' on what the organization does best, but to me the term 'core competences' simply encapsulates what is needed for corporate success. In this context it is not resources which need to be concentrated, but the *attention* of management in general, and yourself in particular, which must be focused on those core competences.

Deciding just what are these core competences is a long process which demands constant review. If you are using the Analytical 4-Step as a device to aid this analysis then these stages are Steps 2, 3 and 4, where you have ruthlessly to cut back to no more than six competences (though these may be portmanteau categories), prioritize them, and then reduce them to no more than two prime directives.

These core competences are, then, a distillation of what gives your organization its distinctive character or, to be more precise, that which positively distinguishes it from other organizations in the same field (in the commercial field this is now often referred to as 'competitive advantage'). This must, though, be looked at in the context of the longer term; it must also represent *substantial* competitive advantage.

Your Product:Service Package

The next step, having searched your own (organizational) soul in this way and drawn up the outline, is to determine what the detailed features of your Product:Service Package should be. Despite the work which has already been undertaken, this may not be as easy as it

. You may know what you expect – and want – to sell,
cornflakes for instance, but the consumers may have very
ideas. You know what goes into those cornflakes, the highest
ingredients you can afford perhaps, but the consumers will
ently pose different demands. They may first of all want reassurance that it is a healthy food for the family, something that may
possibly be difficult to justify (when at least one critic claimed that
the cardboard box they came in contained more nourishment!). Indeed
they may even purchase the product because of an image – waking
up happy and full of life, say, which may be somewhat easier to convey
in the world of perfect families which inhabit television commercials!

The overall content of the Product:Service Package is ultimately
determined by the customer, by design or by default. You may provide
the physical framework but they (aided, of course, by what you
say in your advertising and promotional output) will read into it
the wider offering which they want to see. Most of the rest of this
chapter is devoted to exploring what this Product:Service Package
might be.

The first of these explorations looks at a definition of the 'market'
in which this product or service exists:

What is a market?

To a producer or service provider, the most practical feature of a market is
that it is 'where' the product or service is sold or delivered, and the profits
generated. It can also be described in terms of the 'physical' definition of the
product or service, and this is the framework favoured by many economists. It
can be defined geographically. It may even be defined demographically.

*The key for a marketer, however, should be that the market is always defined in
terms of the customer.* Thus, Philip Kotler[2] sees buyers (actual and potential) as
constituting the market, where sellers constitute the industry. The concept even
applies to non-profit organizations, every one of which has clients, or 'customers'
in the conventional marketing terminology. Their 'markets' are ultimately just
as powerful a force on their strategies.

---

2. Philip Kotler, *Marketing Management*, 6th edn. (Prentice Hall, 1988).

Who is the market?

In the long run it is the customers who decide what the market really is, by their buying patterns. They set the boundaries, and by their purchases choose what products or services will remain in the market. Inevitably, then, to understand the market, the producer must understand the customer.

Because of the more traditional views of producers, and despite marketing theory, in the shorter term the practical definitions of markets tend to revolve around the following factors:

- *Product or service category* – this says what is bought, as defined in the 'physical' terms of the producer.
- *Geography* – where the product or service is sold or delivered is another clearly understood concept.
- *'Physical' customer groupings* – producers do recognize obvious groupings of customers; teenagers versus senior citizens, for instance.
- *Intangibles* – the only intangible which is widely recognized, and then only as differentiating commercial markets, is price.

Customers, prospects and penetration

Taking the producers' myopia about markets one stage further, they mainly see markets in terms of their own participation in those markets:

- *Customers* – they are defined quite simply as the buyers of your brand, but the dividing line is often not quite so clear and may need to be further defined by marketing research.
- *Users* – this may be a fine distinction, but users are often not the same as purchasers.
- *Prospects* – the term 'prospects' is most often used in face-to-face selling, 'potential customers' more often being used in mass markets, but the meaning is the same; those individuals in the market who are not the organization's customers. Again, the boundaries need defining for each situation.

The important fact is that some of the individuals in the market buy the producer's brand and some don't. The measure of this difference is often given by brand 'penetration':

- *Penetration* – this is the proportion (%) of individuals in the market who are users of the specific (brand) product or service.

The measure of 'penetration', though, does not allow for the rate of usage or purchase by different individuals. The most commonly used measure, therefore, is market share or brand share:

- *Brand (or market) share* – this is the share of overall market sales taken by each brand. Even then, there may be further complexity, since the share can be of volume or of value – depending upon what the producer wants to measure. This can sometimes lead to two producers claiming to be market leader, one in terms of volume and one in terms of value – though the latter is usually judged to be the more important measure.

These are the classical definitions of markets and the various actors within them, and the shares they hold. However, life may be much more complex: for example, Andrew Ehrenberg, formerly of the London Business School, says that consumers buy 'portfolios of brands'; they switch regularly between brands, often simply because they want a change.

> ### ○ Rule O7 – *Consumer Portfolios*
> 'Brand penetration' or 'brand share' reflects only a statistical chance that the majority of customers will buy that brand next time as part of a portfolio of brands they favour! It does not guarantee that they will stay loyal.

Influencing the statistical probabilities facing a consumer choosing from a portfolio of preferred brands, which is required in this context, is a very different role for a brand manager compared with the much simpler one traditionally described, of recruiting and holding dedicated customers. The concept also emphasizes the need for managing continuity– by rules such as the Competitive Saw (see Rule S4 below).

On the other hand, one of the most prominent features of many markets is their overall stability – or inertia, whichever description you find most useful. Thus, in their essential characteristics they change very slowly, often over decades – sometimes centuries – rather than over months. This stability has two very important implications. The first is that if you are a clear brand leader you are especially well placed in relation to your competitors, and should want to further the inertia which lies behind that stable position. This will, however, still demand a continuing pattern of minor changes, to keep up with the marginal changes in consumer taste (which may be minor to the theorist, but will still be crucial in terms of those consumers' purchasing patterns – markets do not favour the over-complacent!). But these minor investments are a small price to pay for the long-term profits which brand leaders usually enjoy.

T **Rule T18 –** *Cash Cows*
Only farm-hands make a career out of milking cows, and only fools jeopardize the investment contained in an established brand leader!

The second, and more important, implication is that if you want to overturn this stability, and change the market (or significantly change your position in it), then to succeed you must expect to make massive investments.

T **Rule T19 –** *The Investment Challenge*
Before challenging a brand leader make sure your pockets are deep enough to sustain the decade or so of investment this may demand!

T **Rule T20 –** *The Inertial Balance*
Stability is the natural state of a market, but there is still a risk of sudden and dramatic change – which is compounded by myopic management:

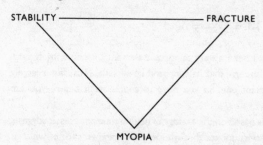

Even though stability is the natural state of markets, sudden changes can still occur, and the environment must be constantly scanned for signs of these fluctuations:
• *Stability* – although this 'steady-state' may be the natural state it will often require significant investment to maintain it.
• *Fracture* – albeit occasionally, outside events can destroy that stability, sometimes so radically that the market's most important characteristics

are changed completely (and it is overturned – hence the precarious balance shown above).

• *Myopia* – despite this omnipresent threat, many organizations are short-sighted and never see beyond the minor changes taking place in the stable, steady-state universe which seems to protectively surround them. They may not even recognize a fracture when it is actually upon them, and destroying the very foundations of the organization.

Few organizations, however, seem to be able to recognize this even when the foundations of their business have been destroyed; most suffer from terminal myopia! Paradoxically, the very few which do see what is coming often emerge strengthened by what has happened to them. It may be painful at the time, but a 'fracture' provides an excellent environment in which to learn about what is really important to your organization, what are its real core competences.

Awareness of change is, therefore, a vital aptitude – to be cultivated by the managers of any organization. Traditionally, it has only been approached from the viewpoint of the minor ups and downs which afflict the stable market. It is not wholly surprising, therefore, that tradition leaves this management of change to a concept as limited, and of such dubious value, as the Product Life Cycle:

The 'Product' Life Cycle

The 'life cycle' has long been a very important element of marketing theory. You should be aware, though, that its supposed universal applicability is largely a myth,[3] but an important one. So you need to appreciate it before you can dismiss it!

Its 'intuitive appeal' is based on the analogy of natural (human) lives. It suggests that any product or service moves through identifiable stages, each of which is related to the passage of time (as the product or service grows older) and each of which has different characteristics:

3. D. S. Mercer, 'A Two Decade Test of the Product Life Cycle Theory', *British Journal of Management*, Vol. 4 (1993) pp. 269–74.

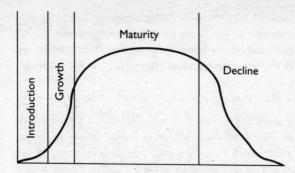

Introductory stage

At this first stage of a product's life, the supplier can choose from strategies which range from 'penetration', where the supplier invests to gain the maximum share of a new market, through to 'skimming', where the maximum short-term profit is derived from the 'innovation'. In either case, the main task is to create awareness of the brand. In general, the 'pioneer' who invests can expect to retain the highest market share; usually double the share of later entrants, even over the longer term.

Growth stage

As a result of awareness having been largely established, and in the light of growing competition, the emphasis at this stage may well be on promotion of the 'brand' – on establishing the correct attitudes to the product. Promotion is still heavy, and suppliers often have to make further, substantial investments. In recent years, another feature of this phase has been the battle for distribution.

Maturity

No product or service can grow forever; and eventually all the significant potential uses will have been developed. The sales curve will flatten, and it will have reached maturity. The majority of products or services currently in the marketplace are at this stage, and much of the theory and practice of marketing revolves around this 'steady state' – building groups of loyal users, and attracting those of competitors.

Decline stage

Eventually the whole market may decline or other, newer products may be introduced which are themselves a substitute for the established product. The product or service thus goes into a terminal decline which can last for years.

Lessons of the life cycle

Every product or service must, almost by definition, have a life cycle. It is launched, it grows, then it dies. As such, it offers a useful 'model' to keep at the back of your mind. Indeed, if you are in the introductory or growth phases, or in that of decline, it perhaps should be at the front of your mind, for the predominant features of these phases may be those revolving around such life and death. Between these two extremes, it is salutary to have that vision of mortality in front of you.

The most important aspect of product life cycles is that, to all practical intents and purposes, they often do not exist! In most markets the majority of the major (dominant) brands have held their position for at least two decades. The dominant product life cycle, that of the brand leaders which almost monopolize many markets, is therefore one of continuity!

In the most respected criticism of the product life cycle, Dhalla and Yuspeh[4] state: '. . . clearly, the PLC is a dependent variable which is determined by market actions; it is not an independent variable to which companies should adapt their marketing programs. Marketing management itself can alter the shape and duration of a brand's life cycle.'

So, the life cycle may be useful as a description, but not as a predictor, and usually it should be firmly under the control of the marketer. The important point is that in many, if not most, markets the product or brand life cycle is significantly longer than the planning cycle of the organizations involved. It thus offers little of practical value for most marketers. Even if the PLC exists for them, their plans will be based just upon that piece of the curve where they currently reside (most probably in the 'mature' stage); and their view of that part of it will almost certainly be linear, and will not encompass the whole range from introduction to decline.

The above section on the Product Life Cycle is long, despite the fact that – as you no doubt detected – I think that it has little value in

4. Nariman K. Dhalla and Sonia Yuspeh, 'Forget the Product Life Cycle Concept', *Harvard Business Review* (1976) January–February.

practice. Indeed, I believe that its use may be positively dangerous for many organizations since it tempts managers of successful, mature brands to prematurely anticipate their move into decline. But it is probably the most widely known, and taught and respected, piece of marketing theory. It is imperative, therefore, that you appreciate the problems that its use, in any form, might pose.

How, then, might you manage change? At one extreme, seeing fractures in advance, or even recognizing their implications after they have occurred, is very difficult. This is best handled by 'scanning', described in a later chapter. Responding to them once they have been detected is perhaps best ensured by undertaking the most effective possible marketing – better than that of other organizations which might also attempt to take advantage of the fracture – and, most important of all, reacting much faster than those competitors.

The Competitive Saw

Handling the less dramatic changes which regularly occur in the stable market is a different matter. These are dealt with especially poorly by the PLC. The technique which has accordingly been developed, as a positive alternative to ineffective use of the PLC in this ('mature') range, is called the 'Competitive Saw':

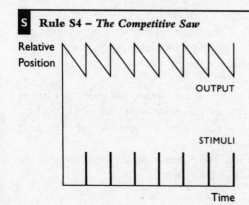

S   Rule S4 – *The Competitive Saw*

Relative
Position

OUTPUT

STIMULI

Time

The principles involved are very simple, as is indicated by the chart above. The first is quite simply that every 'stimulus' (every investment, be it an advertising or promotional campaign or a new feature added to the 'product') results, after a short delay, in a rapid improvement in 'output', raising the product or service's position (typically directly in terms of its competitive position, and indirectly in terms of sales levels).

The second is that this advantage is then steadily diluted as competitors invest in their own activities, and the performance level (the competitive advantage or sales) slowly drops until the next stimulus is applied. Because of the competitive aspect and because it largely removes variations due to seasonality etc., the measurements are usually in terms of relative share (though absolute figures may also be used).

This is a very simplified model of what actually happens, though something approaching it can be observed in practice (in the way that, for instance, advertising agencies routinely track the impact of advertising campaigns on awareness levels), which is not the case with the Product Life Cycle. Despite its simplicity, it offers a number of significant benefits:

• *Intimations of mortality* – it very effectively replaces the one important function of the Product Life Cycle, that of reminding managers that there will be no future if they do not look after their brands, and continue to invest in them – but it does this more directly and practically, and without the major drawbacks inherent in the PLC model.

• *Timescaling* – on much the same theme, it is an ever-present reminder that you cannot neglect your brands, or stop investing in them, for too long – especially during the very extended 'maturity' phase of a successful brand.

• *Linkage of inputs and outputs* – it encourages, and provides a framework for, managers to actively plan what inputs are needed; when, and what the outputs will be; and what the efficiency of conversion of inputs to outputs is.

• *Surfacing of investment* – it makes very clear the need for, and the results of, investment policies on brands.

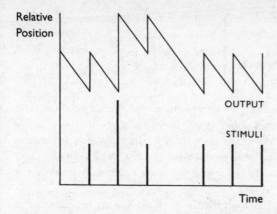

This becomes even more clear in the 'Stepped Saw' (see above). This looks at the effect of major inputs, major investments (such as new products or significantly increased promotional spending). These may have the effect of raising the average level of the 'saw teeth'; though, as shown above, later neglect (or a comparably strong competitive response) can just as easily result in a step down to a lower average level.

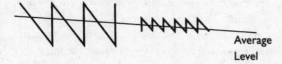

   As the above illustration shows, there are two elements to performance. One is the average level – averaged over longer periods than the short timescales that normally are reported on by the Competitive Saw. This is strategically most important since it shows longer term trends (a slowly decreasing average might be hidden by the variations in the short-term saw). The other is the pattern of the saw itself, the time intervals and the performance variation per cycle, which determines the tactical approach.

   The idea of the saw should not lull you into expecting regularity. Different stimuli will have different impacts, and will be more or less efficient, so the saw will be a jagged one.

As the saw is primarily an illustration of the impact of short-term investments, the main criterion will be which of the stimuli available will result in the most efficient investment pattern (which, advertising or new features, say, will produce the greatest impact for the same amount of money), though a mix of stimuli will usually produce the highest efficiency overall.

The three main lessons of the Competitive Saw are the importance of relative performance, the time-related nature of this, and the investments which lie underneath. Adopting the long-term perspective implied by the third of these observations reveals another important implication. Thus, following the implied principle of the fixed asset, the shorter term sawtooth maintenance pattern can be overlaid on a gradually declining trend in performance, notionally equivalent to depreciation in financial accounting. Over time there may be a slow drift away from the ideal position as the customers' needs and wants change and/or competitive positioning improves. Your own response to this may take two forms. The first, and perhaps the most effective, is that of 'dynamic repositioning'. The need for change is regularly tracked and the brand's position readjusted – in much the same way that an autopilot's feedback mechanisms ensure that an airliner follows the correct flightpath. The emphasis here is on the dynamic approach to (current) change – whereas most of marketing theory revolves around decisions based upon static (historic) positions.

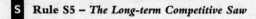

S Rule S5 – *The Long-term Competitive Saw*

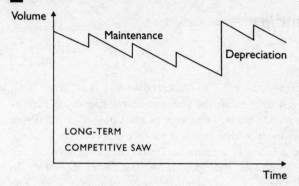

If such dynamic repositioning is not possible, perhaps because the necessary product changes come in discrete steps, then periodic readjustments may be needed. This is where the second form, the concept of depreciation, is especially valuable. It allows the build-up of reserves to cover the significant costs of such repositioning exercises.

Encouraged by PLC theory, which seems to emphasize the futility of long-term investment, the long-term asset investment aspect of brand performance is largely ignored by traditional marketing theory. We believe, on the contrary, that it should represent the main element of marketing strategy and, in view of the dangers it poses for the unwary, that the PLC should be dropped from the marketers' vocabulary!

T Rule T21 – *Marketing Depreciation*

The investment in a successful brand needs to be maintained both in the short term, by regular marketing programmes funded from annual budgets, and in the longer term, by (less frequent) major investments (in repositioning and relaunching) which require reserves provided by a depreciation fund.

4 / *Branding*

I have mentioned the topic of 'differentiation' a number of times now, and it is usually by far the best way of avoiding direct competition. Quite simply it means that your product or service is different to its competitors or, perhaps more important (but easier to achieve), it is *seen* to be different by consumers. Traditionally, this has been one of a number of possible strategies (as Michael Porter suggested). In particular it has been the main alternative to 'economies of scale'. The choice between these strategies is best approached by the use of the Boston Advantage Matrix:

Boston Advantage Matrix

The Boston Consulting Group is best known for its cash-flow matrix (usually known just as the Boston Matrix, of which more later), but it subsequently developed another, much less widely reported matrix which approached the economies of scale (described by them as 'competitive strength') versus differentiation (described as 'a number of strategic options') decision rather more directly. This is its Advantage Matrix:

T Rule T22 – *The Boston Advantage Matrix*

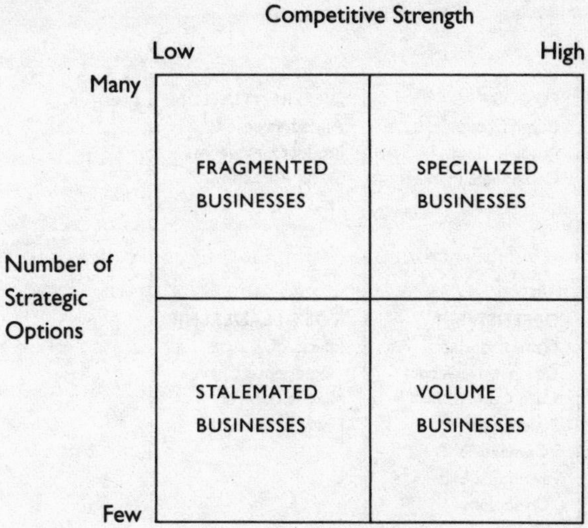

Competitive Strength

	Low	High
Many	FRAGMENTED BUSINESSES	SPECIALIZED BUSINESSES
Number of Strategic Options	STALEMATED BUSINESSES	VOLUME BUSINESSES
Few		

This takes as its axes the two contrasting alternatives: Economies of Scale against Differentiation. The result is the four quadrants shown above:

• *Volume businesses* – in this case there are considerable economies of scale but few opportunities for differentiation. This is the classic situation where organizations strive for economies of scale by becoming the volume, and hence cost, leader.

• *Stalemated businesses* – here there is the opportunity neither for differentiation nor economies of scale. The main means of competition, therefore, has been reducing the 'factor costs' (mainly those of labour) by moving to locations, indeed to different countries in the developing world, where these costs are lower.

• *Specialized businesses* – these businesses gain benefits from both economies of scale and differentiation (often characterized by experience effects in their own, differentiated segment). The main strategies are focus and segment leadership.

• *Fragmented businesses* – these organizations also gain benefit from differen-tiation, particularly in the services sector, but little from economies of scale. Competition may be minimized by innovatory differentiation.

The strategies which can be developed on the basis of this matrix are illustrated by Rowe et al.[1]

Competitive Strength

	Low	High
Many	**FOCUS** Buyer Groups Product Lines Geographic Markets	**DIFFERENTIATION** Added Value Product Uniqueness Skilful Marketing
Few	**DEFENSIVE** Gamesmanship Competitive Tactics 'Cash Cow' to milk Stalemated Competition Favourable Exit Conditions	**COST LEADERSHIP** Effects of Experience Curve Market Growth Financial Strength

Number of Strategic Options

The key point to emerge from the above analysis is that the most powerful combination is economies of scale and differentiation together. As we will see below, if you are successful in achieving differentiation then economies of scale may well follow.

There are a variety of means of achieving differentiation, not least those of segmentation and positioning, which I will introduce in the next chapter, but at this point I want only to talk about **branding**, which has traditionally been the vehicle by which differentiation is conveyed.

Branding Theory

The epitome of differentiation is 'branding'. The product or service (now including those of non-profit-making organizations) is given a 'character', an 'image',

---

1. Alan J. Rowe, Richard O. Mason, Karl E. Dickel, Neil H. Snyder, *Strategic Management* 3rd edn. (Addison-Wesley, 1989).

almost like a personality. This is based first of all on a name (the brand), but then almost as much on the other factors such as the packaging and, in particular, advertising. The aim is to make the brand so unique that it effectively has its own separate market.

Brand monopoly

In economic terms the 'brand' is, in effect, a device to create a 'monopoly' – or at least a form of 'imperfect competition' – so that the brand owner can obtain some of the benefits which accrue to a monopoly, particularly those benefits related to decreased price competition. Most 'branding' in this context is established by promotional means. But the monopoly position may also be extended, or even created, by patents and intellectual property rights.

In all these contexts, 'own label' brands (the brands of a retailer, for example) can be just as powerful; and indeed some of these are already perceived by consumers as the 'brand leaders' in their markets.

Branding policies

There are a number of possible policies:
• *Company name* – often, especially in the industrial sector, it is just the company's name which is promoted.
• *Family branding* – in this case a very strong brand name (or company name) is made the vehicle for a range of products.
• *Individual branding* – is where each brand has a separate name, which may even compete against other brands from the same company.

In terms of existing products, brands may be developed in a number of ways:
• *Brand extension* – the existing strong brand name can be used as a vehicle for new or modified products. This appears to be the most prevalent form of development, which is understandable since it maximizes the use of the investment in the brand name.
• *Multibrands* – alternatively, in a market that is fragmented amongst a number of brands, a supplier can choose to launch totally new brands in apparent competition with its own existing strong brand(s).

Branding has traditionally been seen as the almost exclusive territory of consumer goods companies, but it has much wider application than that. All organizations, whether they sell to consumers or industrial users, whether they offer products or services, whether they are profit-making or non-profit-making, have at least one brand, which is usually the name of the organization.

This may come as a surprise, or even as a shock, to those organizations whose focus in life is the product or service they produce, and who think brands are only for goods which appear on supermarket shelves. Nothing could be further from the truth. The brand encapsulates the Product:Service Package. Because this package is usually so complex, and almost always contains a range of intangibles in addition to the physical elements, it has to be denoted by some form of symbolic representation – a tangible peg on which to hang all these other elements. Sometimes that actually may be a symbol, the logo, the design of which can cost a small fortune, and which is meant to enshrine the character of the brand. More generally, and often just as effectively, it is simply the name of the product or service, or – most often of all – that of the organization.

Many would argue that the (brand) name in itself is critical. Certainly, when you are launching a brand name it helps considerably if the name describes the product in some way or other. International Business Machines very clearly described what the company was about, as did Alka Seltzer. But most suitable names have long since been claimed and these days you are likely to be limited to neutral names which are deliberately selected to be inoffensive worldwide, e.g. Kodak, Exxon. The owners of the very successful 'Sweat' soft drink brand in Japan may have difficulty in bringing it to the West!

On the other hand, it is what you manage to associate – over time – with that brand name which represents the real strength of the brand. IBM, as it is now called, is meaningless as an English word yet it resonates with very powerful associations, and this is just as true of McDonalds (and I don't even have to say what the product is here – the brand is so powerful). Coca Cola, perhaps the most powerful brand of all, would have quite negative connotations if its buyers took the name seriously and associated it with the drug which was essential to its original medicinal properties, but which has long since been dropped from its formulation!

The most powerful brands, then, encapsulate a bewildering array of elements.

◉ Rule O8

It is best to think of BRANDS in human terms, as if they had the complex physical characteristics, overlaid with a rich personality, possessed by any of your friends.

It may often be just as true of the way that the consumers think about the brand: their favourites are their friends, they're the ones they feel comfortable with, the ones they can take home knowing they will fit in with their lifestyle, and so on.

Personalization of your brand(s) also helps you develop them. If you can think how they could be changed to become better friends to the consumers – much as you would change to fit in with your circle of friends, wearing suitable clothes, talking about the things which interest them, doing the same things together – then you are on your way to developing a successful brand. This is just as true of the serious brands, those in capital goods (like IBM) or medicine. The personality they need to establish may be a professional one (like a doctor or engineer, say) but the rules still apply.

This should force you to recognize – and deal with (from planning through to controlled implementation) – all the intangible elements which go to make up a large part of this personality. These are the elements which are too often neglected in the concentration on the more obvious tangible elements.

Perhaps the most important fact, and one which is sadly neglected in most organizations, is that the brand is the most important and valuable property that, with very few exceptions, any organization owns. It contains all the value which has been added to the organization by its investments in service to the customer over the years: image, reputation, loyalty, trust, etc. These are assets which are normally worth far more than the stocks and equipment which feature on most balance sheets. On the few occasions when a brand valuation actually has been added to the balance sheet it has dwarfed everything else.

Yet most organizations treat their brand(s) as if they were worthless. They gratuitously damage them by constant changes in strategy, by confusing switches in image, by employees offering poor service, etc. If anyone in their organization vandalized any piece of capital equipment in such a manner they would be instantly disciplined! Even the largest organizations are not exempt from this criticism. Recent research has shown that they also fail to establish brand strategies and their senior managers do not know what their brands stand for (or sometimes what they are!).[2]

Therefore, the most important aspect of the brand is that it must be recognized as offering the organization's most important investment potential.

This has two major implications. The first is that this is a long-term investment, that will typically take a number of years to pay dividends. The second is that the development and use of that investment should be carefully planned and, most important, it should be zealously safeguarded from damage. Paradoxically, the worst damage is usually inflicted by the owners – by neglect, by cavalier changes in direction (often brought about by marketing departments wanting to do something new), by focusing on short-term solutions, etc.

S **Rule S6 – *Branding Practice***

The brand is simple in concept but normally represents the most powerful device offered by marketing practice *to all organizations in all fields*. WITH VERY FEW EXCEPTIONS, IT EMBODIES THE MOST IMPORTANT AND VALUABLE INVESTMENT THAT ANY ORGANIZATION CAN HOLD. It must be developed over the longer term – not milked for short-term results – and above all it must be safeguarded. IT ENCAPSULATES THE WHOLE PRODUCT:SERVICE PACKAGE and is the means by which the richness of this is conveyed to your customers in a personified form. It offers the best way of integrating (and protecting) all the intangible elements which contribute to the power of the Product:Service Package. IT MUST BE POSITIVELY TREATED AS THE MOST IMPORTANT INVESTMENT THE ORGANIZATION HAS.

This investment may also be seen, from the other side of the fence, in terms of the relationship with the customer.

---

2. J. Sheerman and S. Parkinson, 'Critical Success Factors in the Management of Brands in the 1990s', paper presented at the UK Marketing Education Group Annual Conference (1993).

Usage and loyalty

The customer's response to the brand may be most directly observed in terms of purchasing patterns:

- *Usage status* – Philip Kotler,[3] recognizing that this is quite a complex issue, conveniently groups 'users' into 'non-users, ex-users, potential users, first-time users and regular users'.
- *Usage rate* – most important of all, in this context, is usually the rate of usage. 'Heavy users' are likely to be disproportionately important to the brand, where the 80:20 Rule applies.
- *Loyalty* – a third dimension, however, is whether the customer is committed to the brand. Philip Kotler, again, defines four patterns of behaviour:
1. Hard-Core Loyals: who buy the brand all the time.
2. Soft-Core Loyals: loyal to two or three brands.
3. Shifting Loyals: moving from one brand to another.
4. Switchers: with no loyalty.

Volume of business

In industrial markets organizations will categorize the 'heavy users' as 'major accounts', and put senior sales personnel and even managers in charge of these; the 'light users' may be handed to a general sales force or to a dealer.

Customer Franchise

One of the most positive ways of consolidating the consumer as the most important focus of the organization is to look on this relationship as a prime asset of the business, one that has been built up by a series of marketing investments over the years. As with any other asset, this investment can be expected to bring returns over subsequent years. On the other hand, also like any other asset, it has to be protected and husbanded.

This 'asset' is often referred to as the 'customer franchise'. At one extreme it may come from the individual relationship developed face to face by the sales professional. At the other it is the cumulative image, held by the consumer, resulting from long exposure to all aspects of the product or service, and especially to a number of advertis-

3. Philip Kotler, *Marketing Management*, 6th edn. (Prentice Hall, 1988).

ing and promotional campaigns. In some markets the customer franchise may be so strong as to be exclusive; in effect, giving the supplier a monopoly with those customers.

As we saw from the earlier reference to Andrew Ehrenberg's work on brand portfolios, consumers may regularly switch brands – for variety – but they may still retain an image of the brand which will swing the balance when their next purchase decision is taken. Thus it may still have a value (upon which the advertiser can build) even if the current purchasing decision goes against it. A later decision may, once again, swing in its favour.

The customer franchise is, therefore, a very tangible asset, in terms of its potential effect on sales, even if it is intangible in every other respect. It is based, though, on an accumulation of impressions over time. Unfortunately, too many marketers, particularly those in creative departments within advertising agencies, signally fail to recognize the importance, and long-term nature, of this investment. They treat each new campaign as if it could, and should, be taken in isolation – no matter how it meshes with previous messages which have been delivered to the consumer. The evidence is that consumers, on the other hand, do not view the advertising and promotion in such lofty isolation; instead they incorporate it into their existing impression – to good or bad effect, depending on how well the new campaign complements the old.

All of this may sound very familiar, and you may be asking what happened to the brand which just a few paragraphs ago was also said to be the major investment. You will be reassured to learn that there is no contradiction in this. The consumer franchise is, to all practical intents, the external *alter ego* of the brand. The brand is how the producer typically sees the (internal) investment. The customer franchise is the outcome of that internal investment; the counterbalancing entry with the customers.

Rule S7 – *The Customer Franchise*

This is the prime asset of the organization. It is the external *alter ego* of the brand.

It may come from the individual relationships developed face to face by the sales professionals. It may also be the cumulative image held by the consumer, resulting from long exposure to all aspects of the product or service over a number of advertising and promotional campaigns.

The customer franchise may be so strong as to be exclusive, in effect giving the supplier a monopoly with those customers. Alternatively it may have a particularly strong position amongst a portfolio of brands being purchased making it, on average, the first choice.

As an investment, therefore, it must be seen in the long-term context. It has to be protected and husbanded. It must not be squandered by short-term approaches such as inappropriate advertising or promotional tactics.

Rule O9 – *The Customer Franchise Curve*

The special characteristics of this investment are shown by the curve below:

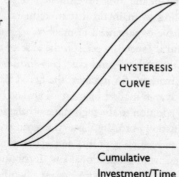

This curve – which is indicative of what might happen rather than an exact measure – shows how the value, which is notional (since it is very difficult to put an exact figure to this), grows slowly at first and then rapidly before it finally saturates (albeit probably after a number of years). Similar processes are at work when the value drops off after investment is stopped (note that the bottom axis is the cumulative investment over time). This means that in the first instance the fall in value is slow (and sales, for example, may not show any significant impact), but then the value drops very rapidly indeed, faster than it rose over the same intervals. The most important aspect, however, is that the curve shows 'hysteresis' (a scientific term describing the extra work which results – and the inefficiencies thus created). When reinvestment occurs it has to be raised to the higher curve again. The result is that there is a significant gap between the curves. That gap represents the cost of failing to sustain the investment. In the short term there is very little penalty (at the level of the Competitive Saw, for example, it can be assumed that investing in bursts of activity is no more expensive than continuous activity). In the longer term, however, extended periods of little or no investment can prove to be very costly indeed.

In view of my earlier strictures about theory, I will emphasize that you should not be fooled by the graphical 'accuracy' into thinking that this curve has been measured. It has not as yet, for it would be very difficult indeed to put anything other than notional figures to the customer franchise values at each stage. It is simply intended as a model to help you understand the sort of forces at work. It nicely illustrates the main features of the long investment process and then the very real costs of failing to maintain that investment, which all too many organizations have experienced in practice.

The power of the brand is especially seen in the case of the brand leaders; those in the top three slots – and especially the brand leader itself. In consumer goods markets, for instance, the brand leader often holds 40 per cent of the overall market or more. This level is usually highly profitable, since in addition to the high value of sales generated, its strong position in the market normally allows the setting of a higher price (and hence significantly higher profit) and economies of scale are possible (not least in terms of promotional and distribution costs).

The profitability that a brand leader commands usually offers, therefore, ample justification – especially over the longer term (where such brands can easily maintain leadership for decades) – for the high levels of investment which are needed to achieve this position. The Japanese corporations, who are willing to make such long-term investments in markets, have been especially well rewarded for their efforts.

S Rule S8 – *The Rule of 1:2:3*

The most competitive markets are typically dominated by 2–3 brands. Between them they account for around 70% of total sales.

For maximum stability the ratio of share should typically be that the BRAND LEADER SHOULD HOLD TWICE THE SHARE OF THE SECOND AND THREE TIMES THAT OF THE THIRD.

The brand leader usually has around 40% of the overall market; and is correspondingly profitable – justifying the investment needed to reach this position.

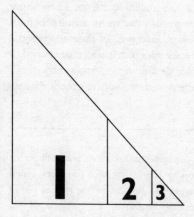

The exact ratios vary from market to market, and even the average may vary somewhat, depending upon what parcel of products is examined. The Boston Consulting Group,[4] for example, also suggest that the brand leader should hold twice the share of the second brand, but they differ in detail when they suggest that it should hold four times that of the third brand (giving a rule of 1:2:4!). But the general principle of the Rule of 1:2:3 seems to hold.

4. Bruce D. Henderson, 'The Rule of Three and Four' (Boston Consulting Group, 1985).

5 / Segmentation and Positioning

Segmentation

The substantial advantage enjoyed by the brand leader is, by definition, only available to one brand in a market. On the other hand, it is often possible to break the larger markets into smaller segments. These larger markets may contain within them distinct groups of customers with quite different detailed needs and wants, and each of these represents a different 'segment', with different consumer purchasing characteristics. This process is called **segmentation**, or sometimes 'target marketing', because the supplier carefully targets such a specific group of customers.

S **Rule S9 – *Segmentation***

The value of discovering separate segments, each with rather different characteristics, is that they allow producers to offer products which target the needs of just one segment, and hence are not in direct competition with the overall market leaders.

This process represents, therefore, the most important practical application of marketing for most organizations.

Segmentation is, thus, a strategy used by vendors to concentrate, and hence optimize, the use of their resources within an overall market.

One focus may be that of consumer behaviour. An alternative may be the product or service itself, but this follows much the same rules, from a different perspective. In the context of the consumer, the traditional factors are often grouped as follows:

- geographic: region, urban or rural, etc.
- demographic: age, sex, marital status, etc.
- socio-economic: income, social class, occupation, etc.
- psychological: attitudes, lifestyles, culture, etc.

Segmentation by benefit

Using such general factors has its limitations. Indeed, there is some evidence[1] that these conventional factors may not offer significant differentiation between meaningful segments. It is much more productive to relate segmentation to the specific characteristics of the market for the product or service.

Different customers, or groups of customers, look for different combinations of benefits; and it is these groupings of benefits which then define the segments. It is these differences which the producers can most effectively use to target their brands, or the public service providers their offerings; to position them where they most clearly meet the needs of the consumers in that segment.

Segmentation by consumption profile

Recently a number of research agencies have started to characterize consumer segments in terms of the buying choices of the consumers in them. Thus, they are characterized by their purchases of a range of key products and, in particular, by a range of media read and television programmes watched.

Segment viability

There is a pure, customer-oriented, marketing reason behind segmentation. By designing products or services which are narrowly targeted on the needs of one specific segment, whose consumers are looking for very much the same thing as each other, it may be possible to offer them the best match to their needs. In practice, however, producers usually target segments rather than the overall market because this allows them to concentrate their resources on a limited group of consumers. The brand can then be made to dominate that segment, and gain the benefits of segment leader, albeit on a smaller scale than if it were the overall market leader.

For this to happen, the segment has to be viable, has to be worthwhile, say, in terms of revenue generated against the costs involved. It therefore needs to meet a number of broad criteria:

- *Size* – the first question to be asked is simply whether the segment is substantial enough to justify attention; will there be enough volume generated to provide an adequate profit. In general, it is best to choose the smallest number of segments into which you split the overall market, and hence the largest average

---

1. K. Hammond, A. Ehrenberg, and G. Goodhart, 'Brand Segmentation: A Systematic Study', paper presented at the UK Marketing Education Group (MEG) 1993 Conference.

size (including the one you are targeting), that still allows the resources to be productively concentrated and head-on competition with the market leaders avoided.

• *Identity* – the segment has to have characteristics which will enable it to be separately identified (and measured by market research), by both the producers and the consumers. It must be recognizable to both as a cohesive entity.

• *Relevance* – the basis for segmentation must be relevant to the important characteristics of the product or service; it must be 'actionable'.

• *Access* – finally, the producer must be able to get at the segment which has been found. If tapping that segment is too difficult, and accordingly too expensive, it clearly will not be viable.

If all these criteria are met segmentation is a very effective marketing device. It can allow even the smaller organizations to obtain leading positions in their respective segments – often then described as 'niche' marketing – and gain some of the control this offers. It is worth repeating, yet again, that the most productive bases for segmentation are those which relate to the consumers' own groupings in the market and not to the artificially imposed producers' segments.

 Rule O10 – *Practical Segmentation*
Practical segmentation must be based on characteristics or dimensions that are significant to the CONSUMER rather than the supplier.

To discover – and utilize – these 'natural' (consumer-based) segments requires a number of steps:

a) **Market research** – the basis for almost all effective segmentation must be sound market research. This is described in more detail in a later chapter. The critical consumer characteristics which are to form the basis of the segmentation must be determined, and this demands that all the related characteristics are measured (including customer attitudes and their perceptions of product attributes as well as their 'demographic' characteristics and usage patterns).

• *Background investigation* – the first stage is to undertake the desk research which will best inform the researcher, and the marketer, as to what the most productive segments are likely to be. This leads to the 'hypotheses' to be tested.

• *Qualitative research* – the 'dimensions' which are important to these consumers, and the 'language' which is used by them, should be first investigated by qualitative research, such as 'group discussions'.

• *Quantitative research* – the next stage is to conduct the quantitative research, using the dimensions identified in the previous stage, to try to measure attitudes to the brand (and its competitors), as well as the consumer's 'ideal brand'.

b) **Analysis** – this is the most important stage of segmentation. It is now almost invariably dependent upon the use of considerable computing power: this is needed to undertake the complex analyses on the large number of variables involved. Usually some form of 'factor analysis' is used to group together those variables that are almost interchangeable in the consumers' eyes. Then 'cluster analysis' is used to create the specified number of groups/segments of consumers. Each of these clusters of consumers should be as similar within itself, but as different from other clusters, as possible.

The typical outcome will be a set of prioritized position maps, delineating these segments, preferably limited to the 6–8 most important dimensions – which is usually all that the average marketer can handle!

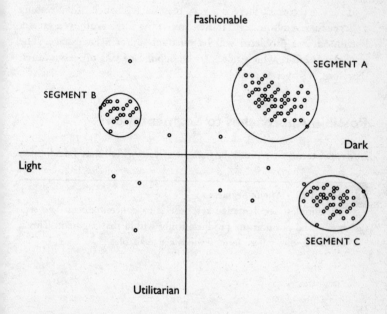

c) **Implementation** – these clusters (typically no more than half a dozen in number, where more than this would probably fragment rather than segment the average market) then need to be described in terms of the key characteristics which differentiate them. Then, and only then, can the supplier's products (and the competitors') be mapped onto these dimensions, and the product 'positioning' exercise (described below) begun.

d) **Segmentation/positioning** – the marketer must then use these 'maps' to decide exactly what his or her plans should be, taking into account the resources available as well as the competitive and consumer positioning on the 'map'. Which will be the target groups, which will be the chosen segments? Where will the products or services be repositioned (if this is needed) to compete most effectively and/or to be most attractive to consumers?

S   **Rule S10 –** *Segmentation and Positioning*
These are probably the most important decisions any marketer has to make. From them most other decisions will emerge naturally.

If they are correct there is a very reasonable chance of developing a successful overall strategy. If they are wrong there is an even greater likelihood that problems will be encountered at a later stage. The intellectual effort which needs to be applied to this process cannot, therefore, be overestimated.

Possible Approaches to Segmentation

In overall terms there are four main strategies which may be adopted:

T   **Rule T23 –** *Single Segment*
The simplest segmentation response is to concentrate on one segment, and position the product firmly within that segment. This is often the case where limited funds are available.

This is a very effective form of marketing, especially for the smaller organization, since it concentrates resources into a very sharply focused campaign. It is, perhaps, more risky – since there may be a greater likelihood of a single small segment disappearing.

O **Rule O11 –** *Customized Marketing*

In recent years two trends have combined to allow for ever narrower segments or niches:

Increasing Variety Demanded – consumers have come to demand that their 'exact' needs are catered for.

Flexible Manufacturing Methods – led by the Japanese, organizations have found that they can deliver a much greater variety of products, without reducing productivity to any significant extent.

The outcome has been that even some 'mass marketers' can now provide (at least to a degree) individually customized products.

O **Rule O12 –** *Multiple Segments*

One complex response to segmentation is to address several major segments with one brand, or to launch several, possibly related brands each targeted against different segments. This technique may also be adopted by an organization which is intending, ultimately, to achieve full coverage but is approaching this segment by segment – probably in order to reduce the demands on its limited resources, but possibly also to limit competitive responses.

Cross segment – some, probably most, suppliers resolutely ignore the segments and pattern their marketing on other factors.

O **Rule O13 –** *Full Coverage* (or 'mass marketing'). In this case, limited to those organizations which can afford the strategy, the intent is to address the whole market.

Full coverage can come in two forms:
Undifferentiated – a few organizations attempt, sometimes successfully, to address a whole market (including its segments) with a single product or non-segmented range.

Differentiated – alternatively it may be to an extent differentiated where the organization covers the market with a range of products or services (under the one brand) which are more or less individually targeted at segments.

○ Rule O14 – *'Niches'*

A specialized, and indeed extreme, version of segmentation is that of creating 'niches' – practised especially by some organizations in the retail sector. In this form the 'niche' (the segment) chosen is barely viable for one 'supplier'. The organization then sets out to capture this segment (and possibly to expand it), confident in the knowledge that no competitor will subsequently be able to (profitably) follow. The danger is that competitors based in other segments may still be able to draw sales from the niche market and, in the process, reduce the viability of the niche operation itself!

○ Rule O15 – *Counter-Segmentation*

Segmentation has been a very popular strategic marketing device in recent years. There is an argument that it may have been taken too far in some areas. The response could, accordingly, be to consolidate several segments; launching a brand (or repositioning a brand or integrating several existing brands) to cover several segments. This may allow economies of scale, without major reductions in benefits, and, on balance, increase competitive advantage.

Segmentation is a time- and resource-consuming process, but the benefits to be derived far more than outweigh this. Tony Lunn[2] reports, for example, that 'In all cases . . . marketing men volunteered the information that the benefits more than justified the time and expenditure involved. In some cases the findings were held to have contributed to substantial gains in market share, in others to arresting decline in share in the light of fierce competition.'

---

2. Tony Lunn, 'Segmenting and Constructing Markets' in *Consumer Market Research Handbook*, 3rd edn., ed. by Robert Worcester and John Downham (McGraw-Hill, 1986).

Positioning

The final stage of the segmentation process above introduced the concept of positioning. This is, though, a separate technique – albeit that it works most effectively in conjunction with segmentation. Unfortunately, there can sometimes be confusion between 'segmentation' and 'positioning'; and indeed, as we have seen, the two processes often overlap. The key difference is that *segmentation applies to the market itself*, to the customers who are clustered into the 'natural' segments which occur in that market. The *positioning relates to the product or service within the market*, and to what the supplier can do with these 'products' to best 'position' them against these segments.

A further complication is that 'positioning' can sometimes be divorced from 'segmentation', in that the supplier can choose dimensions on which to position the brand that are not derived from research, but are of his or her own choosing. Indeed, such positioning can be applied (to differentiate a brand, for instance) even when segmentation is not found to be viable! This is the practical 'positioning' of products or services so that they are recognizably different from their competitors – as measured in terms of their positions on the 'map' of competitive brand positions (ideally along the dimensions which matter to the consumer!) – and positively gain a competitive advantage as a result.

S **Rule S11 –** *Product (or Service) 'Positioning'* is, following segmentation, the most important activity in the whole of marketing. Carried out effectively by design, or poorly by default, it determines every other element of marketing.

In practice positioning typically uses many of the sophisticated techniques applied to segmentation, but in its simplest application it only requires that you decide 'where' you want your product or service to be, alongside the critical dimensions (or variables) which are determined by its market/customers.

Easiest of all to use are graphical 'maps' which show the position(s) in terms of these dimensions. Conventionally, such product positioning maps (sometimes described as 'product space') are drawn with their axes dividing the map into four quadrants. This is because most of the parameters upon which they are based usually range from 'high' to 'low' or from '+' to '−' (with the 'average', or mean, or zero position in the centre, where these axes cross).

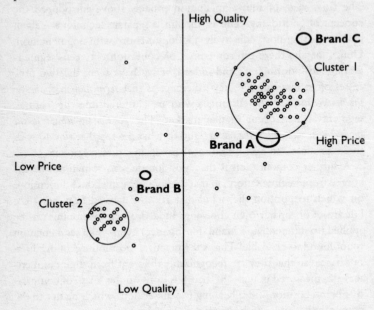

The value of each product's (or service's) sales (or 'uptake'), as well as that of each cluster of consumers, is conventionally represented by the area of the related circle.

In the above case there are just two clusters of consumers, one buying mainly on the basis of price (and accepting the lower quality this policy entails) and one on the basis of quality (prepared to pay extra for this). Against these segments there are just two main brands (A and B), each associated with a cluster or segment. There is also a smaller brand (C), associated with cluster 1, offering an even higher quality alternative (but at an even higher price).

Real-life product positioning maps will, of course, be more complex, involving a number of such dimensions, and drawn with less certainty as to where the boundaries might be. But they do, once more, offer a very immediate picture of where potential may lie, and which products or services are best placed to tap this. They also offer a sound basis for 'repositioning' existing products (or launching a

complementary new product), so that they better match the requirements of the specific 'clusters' on which they are targeted. In the
above example, Brand C might be content to remain a 'niche product'.
Alternatively, the positioning map shows that if it were reduced in
price slightly (and were backed by sufficient promotion) it might
become a very competitive contender for Brand A's market
share.

If the positioning research is carried out regularly, over a period of
time the map can also show how these positions are changing.
Tracking changes in position is a very powerful marketing tool.

There are alternative graphical approaches which try to produce
just one diagram which contains all the information which would
otherwise be contained in the various dimensions. It is my belief that
these often add to the confusion rather than remove it, and the basic
approach offers a better picture – one which is inherently more understandable.

Because of its importance, I will repeat my earlier statement, suitably
modified. Based on effective segmentation, positioning is the most
important activity in the whole of marketing. Carried out effectively
by design, or poorly by default, it determines every other element of
marketing.

This technique completes the set of rules which I am suggesting are
most useful for helping to define the Product:Service Package. We
finish this chapter with a review of the 'Learning Loop', encapsulated
in the diagram that follows:

◉ Rule O16 – *The Learning Loop*

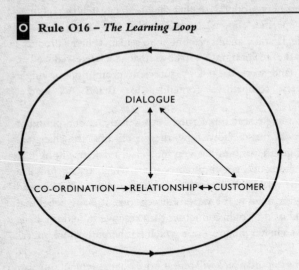

The essence of Realistic Marketing is that it is an ongoing process. More specifically, it is iterative; the processes are repeated so that the lessons learned at the later stages are fed back to influence the earlier stages in the decision-making process. This should also be an incremental process, so that there are small (incremental) improvements at each iteration.

We call this the Learning Loop, since the value is the learning which is progressively accrued.

6 / *The Customer*

We now know something about ourselves, or at least about our organization and its products or services. The next step, then, is to find out about the customer; for he or she is, as I have already stressed a number of times, the focus of marketing practice.

There is one relatively easy way of finding out about customers – and that is to ask them to tell us about themselves. That is what both marketing research and selling are largely about. But before we can even do that we need to know what questions to ask, for the process is very much like one of those games where you have to discover the mystery object by asking the least number of questions. This is not because the customers are secretive. It is simply that, just as you do not yet understand them, so they do not understand you – and, as helpful as they want to be, they cannot answer questions which you do not ask!

To know literally everything about your customers would require such vast volumes of information that you would never be able to make practical use of it. In the more traditional forms of marketing the search is therefore narrowed down to those facts which are of most direct use, by using models (theories) which map just the purchase process. This approach focuses on the aspect of the customer's life which is of particular interest to the marketer. There are a range of alternative models, but of these I believe that AIUAPR, which most directly links up to the steps in the marketing/promotional process, is the most generally useful.

◉ Rule O17 – *AIUAPR*

AWARENESS
↓
INTEREST
↓
UNDERSTANDING
↓
ATTITUDE
↓
PURCHASE
↓
REPEAT

• *Awareness* – before anything else can happen the potential customers must become aware that the product or service exists. Thus, the first task must be to gain the attention of the target audience. All the different models are, predictably, agreed on this first step. If the audience never hears the message they will not act on it, no matter how powerful it is.

• *Interest* – but it is not sufficient to grab their attention. The message must interest them and persuade them that the product or service is relevant to their needs. The content of the message(s) must therefore be meaningful and clearly relevant to that target audience's needs, and this is where marketing research can come into its own.

• *Understanding* – once an interest is established, the prospective customer must be able to appreciate how well the offering may meet his or her needs, again as revealed by the marketing research. This may be no mean achievement where the copywriter has just 50 words, or ten seconds, to convey everything there is to say about it.

• *Attitude* – but the message must go even further; to persuade the reader to adopt a sufficiently positive attitude towards the product or service that he or she will purchase it, albeit as a trial. There is no adequate way of describing how this may be achieved. It is simply down to the magic of the copywriter's art and the strength of the product or service itself.

• *Purchase* – all the above stages might happen in a few minutes while the reader is considering the advertisement in the comfort of his or her favourite armchair. The final buying decision, on the other hand, may take place some time later, perhaps weeks later, when the prospective buyer actually tries to find a shop which stocks the product.

• *Repeat purchase* – but in most cases this first purchase is best viewed as just a trial purchase. Only if the experience is a success for the customer will it be turned into repeat purchases. These repeats, not the single purchase which is the focus of most models, are where the vendor's focus should be, for these are where the profits are generated. The earlier stages are merely a very necessary prerequisite for this!

This is a very simple model, and as such does apply quite generally. Its lessons are that you cannot obtain repeat purchasing without going through the stages of building awareness and then obtaining trial use – which has to be successful. It is a pattern which applies to all repeat purchase products and services, industrial goods just as much as baked beans.

This simple theory is rarely taken any further: to the series of such repeat purchases. The consumer's growing experience over a number of such transactions is often the determining factor in the later – and future – purchases. All the succeeding transactions are, thus, inter-dependent, and the overall decision-making process may accordingly be much more complex than most models allow for.

In the single dimension which the original model inhabits, from top to bottom there is a growing involvement of the customer with the product or service. The 'Enhanced AIUAPR Model' takes this and adds a further dimension which specifically reflects, on one side, the attempts by the vendor to influence the process. This was implicit in the original model. It shows, however, the way in which the vendor's involvement changes from the most impactful advertising at the start of the process to the highest quality support at the end – a progression which is not fully described in less complex models. On the other side, though, it also shows the involvement of the customer with his or her peer group – this is not even hinted at in the original version.

○ Rule O18 – *Enhanced AIUAPR*

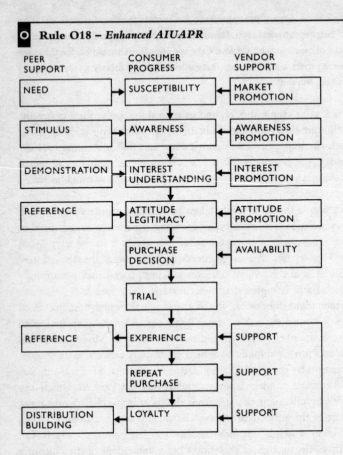

PEER SUPPORT	CONSUMER PROGRESS	VENDOR SUPPORT
NEED	SUSCEPTIBILITY	MARKET PROMOTION
STIMULUS	AWARENESS	AWARENESS PROMOTION
DEMONSTRATION	INTEREST UNDERSTANDING	INTEREST PROMOTION
REFERENCE	ATTITUDE LEGITIMACY	ATTITUDE PROMOTION
	PURCHASE DECISION	AVAILABILITY
	TRIAL	
REFERENCE	EXPERIENCE	SUPPORT
	REPEAT PURCHASE	SUPPORT
DISTRIBUTION BUILDING	LOYALTY	SUPPORT

The starting point is, in this case, earlier than in the original model:

• *Susceptibility* – even before you can build awareness, the consumer's mind has to have been opened up to the concept behind the product or service. In line with the theories we will look at later, this acceptance of a new need may have emerged from the workings of the opinion leaders in the consumer's peer group. This is also the stage where the supplier has to accept some form of market- (or segment-) building role, often making use of public relations as much as advertising.

It should be noted that the seemingly distinct steps usually overlap. Thus, some sections of the population – the opinion leaders say –

could be well into the repeat purchasing stage while other sections are only just beginning to perceive the need. Accordingly, promotion and advertising often will have to meet the requirements of a number of stages at the same time – one reason why very successful advertising campaigns are so rare!

• *Awareness* – you have already seen how this works in the original model, though the role of high-impact advertising (or prospecting in industrial markets) was implicit rather than being a formal part of the model as here. The main difference, though, is that research shows that the stimulus is as likely to come from an opinion leader in the peer group. These offer a hidden, and potentially very powerful, 'sales force' on behalf of the product or service, albeit that they in turn have been recruited by advertising (or by public relations activities – often a neglected medium, which is especially important in reaching this group).

• *Interest/understanding* – these two are coupled together, since it is difficult to conceive of one happening without the other being at least in part also involved; but they may offer very different challenges to the advertiser. Again it is members of the peer group, already users, who may be most likely to proffer a 'demonstration' of the product (or the results of the service) to the prospective consumer.

• *Attitude/legitimacy* – although one further stage is added, that of 'legitimacy' (persuading the prospective purchaser that, backed by his or her favourable attitudes, a purchase may be justified), this is merged with the attitude-building process, and both may be dependent on the 'reference' support from members of the peer group who are already loyal users as much as traditional advertising.

• *Purchase decision* – this should be, by this stage of the process, almost automatic and, for once, the consumer is probably alone in making this particular decision. A key element, also featured in the original model but often (wrongly) taken for granted, is that the product or service must be easily available for the consumer to make the purchase.

• *Trial/experience* – one stage ignored by the original model is what happens when the consumer tries the product or service for the first time. This may, or may not, be a favourable experience, but at whichever end of the spectrum it lies it still represents a major discontinuity in the model. At this point, the nature of the accompanying processes changes. In the case of the vendor's promotional activities the emphasis switches abruptly from recruitment to support (perhaps still involving advertising, but mainly by conventional support services). This is perhaps best illustrated by the switch from new account selling before to account management afterwards, in face to face selling. At the same time, the consumer switches from being a recipient of advice to one who can, from experience, advise his or her peer group. We hope this is of a positive nature, since a bad experience is typically reported to many more peers than a good one!

• *Repeat purchase* – in this development of the original model this becomes almost a technicality.

• *Loyalty* – the final step, that of creating a loyal user, is more important and based upon successive positive experiences (backed by sound customer support). These loyal users become, in turn, the 'references' for new users (or even the 'opinion leaders' which feature so strongly in this enhanced model).

Having made the model necessarily complex in order to explain the underlying processes, I will now offer a much more practical, condensed version:

S **Rule S12 – *The Three Pillars of the Purchasing Process***

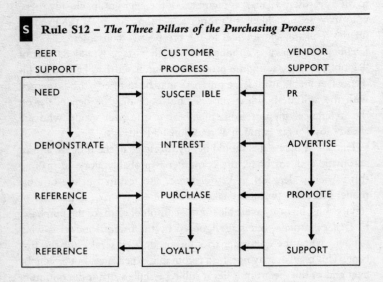

This embodies, in a much simpler form, the key stages in the process. Thus, the central pillar (the customer's progress) highlights the tentative nature of the first stages as the customer moves from 'susceptibility' to the actual 'purchase', and then the subsequent stages as confidence builds into loyalty, which are just as important.

The break point, at the time of the first (trial) purchase, is reflected in the vendor's pillar by the switch from promotion to support (though this aspect is rarely emphasized in theory). It is even more obvious in the 'peer' pillar in the switch from the 'taker' (of advice), before first purchase, to 'giver' (as a loyal referee) after purchase.

Whilst this model is especially useful in providing a framework to handle the new consumer's progress over time, it does not really do full justice to the richness of the interaction between the individual consumer and the whole community, not just the direct peer group, and the 'inertia' which this may lead to. Added to this is the wealth of personal and community experience built up over time, which multiplies the problems of access by the marketer, and often slows down the rate of structural change so that it occurs over the decades measured by the sociologist rather than the months in the marketer's plan. The model which best demonstrates this complementary aspect is that of the 'Peer Pyramid':

◯ Rule O19 – *The Peer Pyramid*

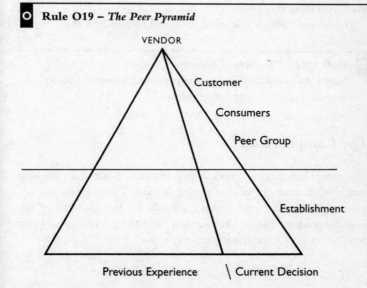

VENDOR

Customer

Consumers

Peer Group

Establishment

Previous Experience \ Current Decision

The pyramid deliberately represents the customer as being topmost of a layered set of influences. Not least amongst these influences are the consumers, the family for consumer goods and services, and the users in an organization. Their views are frequently decisive – perhaps, over the longer term, even more so than those of the direct customer. But beyond them, and beyond the peer group which was so influential in the 'Pillars' model, are the whole range of 'establishment' forces, which regulate what may happen, as do a range of government bodies, or which control the processes of communication, as do the various media. It is these longer-term 'structures' in society which marketers often fail to see (though, as already suggested, sociologists do track the slow movements of these over the decades).

The vertical/diagonal split in the diagram is normally even more important. That large part to the left represents the great body of past experience that the customers, along with all those involved in the various layers of the pyramid, have already built up by the time they come to the current decision. Most recent experience may indeed be at the forefront of the customer's mind but need not necessarily outweigh that body of previous experience (despite the fervent hopes of the vendor – and the lack of reference to such past experience by most marketing theory).

The simple message that vendors should recognize is that:

O **Rule O20 –** *The Drag of History*
Significant investment is needed to overcome the inertia which comes from accumulated (purchasing) history.

The Complex Sale

This complexity of interaction, with many participants and stretching over time, is most evident in the complex sale. This is typically a sale to an organization rather than an individual – though some of the lessons it holds may also be profitably applied to the seemingly simpler demands of consumer goods markets.

T Rule T24 – *The Complex Sale*

The complexity of the changing influences in a complex sale over time can be shown in the model below:

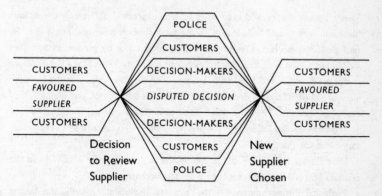

Here, in the period of the 'disputed decision', when the supplier is changing, there are three main groups involved:

• *Customers* – these are the people who actually use the product or service and who, for most of the time, are the main contact with the supplier.

• *Decision-makers* – those in authority who have the formal responsibility for decision, and who may be quite separate from the customers.

• *Police* – the various departments (such as purchasing and quality control) who can veto the decision if certain standards (such as price limits or quality levels) are not met.

This diagram overstresses the time devoted to such decision-making. For most of the time, probably more than 90 per cent of the total, the winner of the disputed purchase decision becomes the 'favoured supplier'. It then proceeds to deal only with the 'customers' in the diagram above, usually the direct customers or end users who make use of the product or service, with no serious challengers in sight over long periods of time. Perhaps the best way of looking at this simple ongoing relationship is through the picture provided by the **Competitive Saw** – which also provides the necessary incentive to keep that relationship fresh. That is, until something undermines the customer's confidence in the arrangement (most usually as a result of a significant failure on the part of the supplier). Then, as shown above, the more complex decision-making phase is entered upon. In that phase the other two sets of actors enter the scene:

Decision-makers and influencers

There is much theory, and even more opinion expressed, about how the various 'decision-makers' and 'influencers' (those who can only influence, not make, the final decision) interact. Decisions are frequently taken by groups, rather than individuals. Often the official 'buyer' does not have authority to take the decision.

Robert B. Miller and Stephen E. Heiman,[1] for example, offer a more complex view of industrial buying decisions (particularly in the area of 'complex sales' of capital equipment). They see three levels of decision-making:

1. Economic Buying Influence – the decision-maker who can authorize the necessary funds for purchase.

2. User Buying Influence – the people in the buying company who will use the product and will specify what they want to purchase.

3. Technical Buying Influence – the 'experts' (including, typically, the buying department) who can veto the purchase on technical grounds.

An important aspect of the organizational buying process, in particular, is the balance of influence between these three sets of people:

◯ Rule O21 – *Balancing Under the Influence*

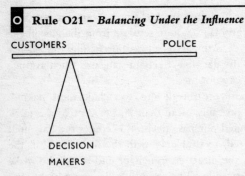

CUSTOMERS   POLICE

DECISION
MAKERS

The customers, in this context usually the users of the product or service, are typically the real decision-makers; the formal decision-maker has no option but to support their decision. Indeed, it is very

1. Robert B. Miller and Stephen E. Heiman, *Strategic Selling* (Kogan Page, 1989).

unusual for permission to be refused, unless it is controversial, or especially important, or cannot be resourced. But always waiting to pounce are the 'police'. These are the individuals (or departments) with veto power which, if brought into play, may outweigh even substantial customer protest. They may sometimes become an unexpected stumbling block; even a minor resource decision is likely to be policed by the finance department, not the formal decision-maker. You should be aware, though, that there are many other forms of 'police' waiting to see if you overstep the mark (sometimes 'secret police', whose involvement you do not even know about until they veto your pet project). They may range from the experts checking the technical specifications to those charged with guarding labour practices. The rule is, accordingly, that the widest possible range of customer contacts should be made. They may turn out to be the 'secret police' themselves (or they may be able to warn you who these are). If you recognize who they are it is often easy to defuse potential problems in advance, but not so easy after the event.

This simple principle is a general one, but is especially applicable to complex sales.

O Rule O22 – *Safety in Numbers*

In a given sales situation, the more people you can recruit to your side from the group who will decide or influence (or police) the purchase decision the higher your chances of winning that decision (and securing your position).

It is a basic fact of marketing life, as we will see elsewhere, that the amount of business which can be generated is proportional to the number of prospects which can be recruited ('the numbers game'). **Safety in Numbers** is a rather more specific principle. It simply says that the more people who are recruited to your side in advance of the decision the safer are your chances of winning. This is true in the consumer goods situation where there are a number of consumers of a product or service who make their wishes known to the purchaser. Hence the more of these consumers who vote for your product the greater the chance of its being bought. It is especially true of the complex sale where, by definition, there are a number of powerful inputs to the decision-making process.

There is one very important caveat to this simple philosophy, and that is the need to recognize the decision is not dependent upon a majority vote among equals. For one thing, the voters will have different weights attached to their votes. The direct users (consumers) will often have more influence than the supposed senior decision-maker.

Most important, however, is the existence of veto power in general (not just in the special case of the 'police' which we examined earlier). Even the most junior member of the decision-making group may, if he or she feels strongly enough about the issue, outweigh all the votes of the others (and in effect have a veto). Unless the rest of the group feel almost as strongly about your offering they will be tempted to switch to a less controversial decision – and there will usually be a number of other offerings almost as good (in their eyes) as yours. It is rare indeed that a supplier has a virtual monopoly which will overcome such resistance.

◯ Rule O23 – *Defuse the Veto Bomb*

All members of the group must be canvassed for their support – and for information as to whether there are any unseen vetoes in the offing. If a possible veto is unearthed then the person involved should either be converted to the majority view, or isolated so that their (veto) power is taken away from them.

It is an onerous chore, which often demands very sensitive detective work, but once more all the bases must be covered.

Partnership

The most important aspect of handling the complex sale is understanding how a partnership may be built. We will return to this later in the book, but at this stage we will focus on finding out how the customer's organization can, in effect, be fused with your own. Shared elements of identity or values, or shared group membership, or simply shared business interests are often what makes such partnerships work; the emphasis is on 'shared'. It is important to recognize these synergistic components, which often revolve around intangibles such as the organizational cultures or even personal relationships between the key participants. It is also important to adopt the right perspective, the right frame of mind. 'Partnership' best describes this approach, which should be adopted from the very start of any business relationship.

T **Rule T25 – *Partnership Triangle***

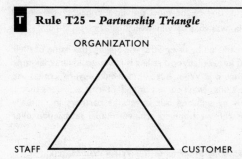

This diagram usefully emphasizes several of the key elements in such a partnership:

• *Three way involvement* – the customer is formally involved with the organization as a whole, and the relationship with that corporate body (typically enshrined in the formal relationship with the sales professional who is the formal contact) is clearly important, especially in terms of the mutual trust. But the customer's contacts overall are mainly informal ones, with the sales professionals but also with a range of staff throughout the vendor's organization. It is often these 'staff' relationships which are most important to that customer, and have the most impact. This is an aspect of the relationship which is often forgotten.

• *Internal stress* – in turn, the tension between these formal (organizational) and informal (staff) relationships often leads to tension within the vendor organization – which may be communicated to the customer, with distinctly unwanted results.

• *Power lies at the base* – it is no accident that in the diagram the most direct relationships, and the heaviest weighted ones, are at the bottom of the pyramid, between equals who interact on various issues from both sides. It is they, and not the senior management, who will ultimately make the partnership work or fail.

Win–Win Matrix

In selling theory, such as it is, one of the most powerful concepts, developed by Miller, Heiman and Tuleja, was that of 'win–win':

> Those of us who have prospered by using Strategic Selling [the name of their technique and their book] know that good selling is never an adversarial game in which Buyers' Losses are our Wins, but ... in which Buyers' Losses are our Losses too, and their Wins always serve our self-interest as well as theirs. We understand that only by enlisting our buyers as partners in mutually supportive joint ventures can we hope to achieve mutual satisfaction over time.

They conceptualize this philosophy in terms of the **Win–Win Matrix**:

SELLER (I)

I WIN YOU WIN	I LOSE YOU WIN
I WIN YOU LOSE	I LOSE YOU LOSE

BUYER (YOU)

In practice, this is something of a gimmick since their comments show that the two remaining 'win' quadrants tend to be unstable; and degenerate into the lose–lose situation. Even the I lose–You win situation degenerates, since it sets up unrealistic expectations for the future. The authors stress '... let the buyer know it ... the most serious mistake you can make in playing Lose–Win is failing to tell your Buyers that they're getting a special deal.'

On the other hand, the concept of win–win is a very powerful concept and the only real alternative of lose–lose serves to highlight this. Partnership, or win–win, is what must always be looked for.

If you substitute a triangle for a matrix, however, the message is conveyed even more forcefully, since it demonstrates how unstable the relationship may become if you adopt the wrong approach:

⬤ Rule O24 – *Win–Win Triangle*

SUPPLIER   CUSTOMER

The main lesson of this rule is the stress it places on sharing the 'win'. If either side loses in the short term then the triangle immediately becomes unstable and topples over – so that, in the long run, neither side wins. As we saw above, 'win–lose' and 'lose–win' are ultimately unstable and degenerate into 'lose–lose'. The 'Win–Win Triangle' simply shows this more directly.

7 / Marketing Research

Continuing to focus on the customer, we address the theme of marketing research. How do you find out about the outside world in general and about the consumer in particular?

There will be rather fewer practical rules here than in the other chapters, since the intention is that the reader understands what lies beneath the surface of sophisticated research programmes. The practice should normally be that the work itself should be subcontracted to the best available research agency.

O **Rule O25 – *Marketing Research is the province of the specialist. The skill is in choosing the most suitable, not the cheapest, agency.***

First, then, let us look at how such a marketing research process generally works. To keep the explanation simple I will concentrate on just one project: a piece of conventional doorstep survey research. Much the same features can be found in all such research, in desk research, for example, but in these cases it is complicated by the number of such individual pieces of work running at the same time, so it is more difficult to see where one begins and ends. Such research projects have a characteristic shape:

S Rule S13 – *The Research Diamond*

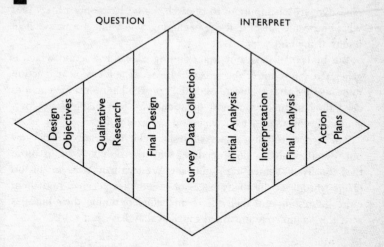

In broad terms the horizontal dimension indicates the passing of time as the project progresses, and the vertical one the number of people involved at each stage.

• *Hidden time* – the main message that emerges from the horizontal progression is that the more obvious elements where you might expect time to be taken, especially those involved in the seemingly complex and relatively lengthy process of data collection, only represent a minor part of the overall process. If the research is to be fully productive then the periods at the beginning, when it is designed, and at the end, when it is used as the basis for action plans, must be allowed to progress at their own pace. Rushed research is too often wasted research. Sometimes you do need answers very fast, but you must then recognize that, in such a situation, the questions had better be very simple.

• *The bulge in the middle* – it is in the middle of the diamond where the main manpower resources are eaten up (and the major costs incurred). But this is usually a matter of relatively menial legwork. Getting the first, design stage right can often reduce this bulge to a more manageable size. Time spent at the early stage, on design, can often save money and sometimes time as well if this means the later stages are better planned.

• *The cutting edges* – the diagram is well named the 'Research Diamond' since its most important features (albeit the least well recognized) are the cutting edges at the beginning and end. Design objectives are all-important to research. If you have only a fuzzy idea what you want out of it at the beginning, you will get a fuzzy set of results at the end.

But by far the most important cutting edge is the action which is generated as a result of the research. Indeed, the focus on that action must begin with the objectives. If the research has no planned actions depending upon it you must question why it is being done. But, above all, you must act on what you eventually find.

The Japanese often seem less sophisticated in the research they carry out, but they always do something with the results. What is more they usually do something significant. Western marketers are all too prone to look at the many pages of results they receive, find them quite interesting and then file them before resuming their business activities, completely untainted by what they have just read!

Environmental Analysis

As with all good rules, there must be exceptions, and environmental analysis in general, or scanning – which starts the whole information-gathering process – in particular, certainly falls into this category, since it is not required to result directly in action. Environmental analysis is a very wide-ranging activity. In its broadest sense it encompasses all those activities which the organization uses, formally and informally, to keep abreast of those changes in the external environment which will affect its future. At its widest, as in scanning (the horizon), it can include all the actual (news and documentary) material to be seen on television or read in the newspapers and periodicals. Certainly you should not rely on just one newspaper (even the *Wall Street Journal* or the *Financial Times*), which will almost inevitably be biased in one way or another, but take a range.

Rule O26 – *Scanning*

The widest approach to environmental analysis is characterized by a general lack of awareness of what is likely to be found (an open mind is the most basic requirement). The sources of information will be many and varied, and the volume of data relatively great. Its purpose is to forewarn you of changes to come. HERE THE SIMPLEST, AND BEST, ADVICE MUST BE TO MAINTAIN THE MAXIMUM EXPOSURE TO THE WIDEST RANGE OF MEDIA.

This is sometimes called undirected viewing.[1] If it is carried out formally, it can represent a major expenditure of resources. But it also offers the most important benefits in terms of long-term survival (though it is typically neglected by many organizations).

The one further requirement is expertise in your subject. This will not help you if your viewing is not wide enough, but with such expertise you are more likely to recognize what items are most likely to bear upon the future of your organization. There is no easy answer, but this 'attitude of mind', which I call 'informed viewing', is the best that is generally available.

Rule O27 – *Clippings File*

Using various media sources, you should build up a 'clippings' file, as a basis for environmental analysis. This may literally contain newspaper clippings, but it should ideally also contain photocopies of relevant extracts or even whole articles.

To be most useful, you should have a number of clippings files in your filing cabinet, arranged by groups of the subjects which you are currently studying. In the first instance, these groups will need to be very broad, because undirected viewing by definition covers a very wide scope. Slowly but surely, though, a few of them (less than one in a hundred perhaps) will start to develop a focus, as you gather more information and patterns start to emerge: this is the whole essence of scanning. Recommended practice might be to collect the clippings as

1. Francis Joseph Aguilar, *Scanning the Business Environment* (Macmillan, 1967).

you find them and then file them once every two weeks: once a week is probably too often and once a month too infrequent. When you do this filing you should ruthlessly discard, before you file them, those clippings which, with the hindsight of the two or more weeks, now seem to be a flash in the pan. At the same time, you can weed out those already in the file which now seem outdated and, most importantly, see if any new trends are emerging.

O **Rule O28 – *Team Scanning***
Even on a limited scale the resource demands of scanning imply the necessity for a team approach.

One of the most interesting suggestions for handling this came from an organization which asked all its employees (shop-floor workers as well as its managers) to clip any news item (found in the newspapers and magazines they regularly read) they felt might be relevant to the future of the organization. All of these clippings, from the most sensational tabloid newspapers to the serious press, were then 'scanned' by the environmental analysis group. When a pattern emerged, of a phenomenon being reported across a number of such sources, it was reasoned that these particular 'weak signals' possibly indicated an important underlying trend, and it was thereafter tracked in more detail. This seems to offer a particularly comprehensive approach to such coverage. It may be beyond the culture of most organizations, but it could be adapted to work across a smaller group (for example, those in the marketing department, including a range of personnel from secretaries to senior managers).

There has been a considerable amount of discussion about 'weak signals', which are small items of information which signal important changes as yet unrecognized, since their main impact has still to come. The comment, largely by academics, has concentrated upon retrospective analysis. Thus, for example, the 'signals' that Japanese manufacturers were coming to dominate certain industries (the motorbike industry, for instance) are, once you look for the related 'weak signals', obvious to see, and yet they were totally overlooked by the existing suppliers in these markets. This is an important message to convey to those conservative organizations that have settled into a comfortable rut, and may not be able to, let alone choose to, read these danger signals.

The problem, which most of these academics tend not to address, is that whilst it is easy to see these patterns with the benefit of hindsight it proves very difficult indeed to detect them in advance. They are, by definition, weak signals. There is no obvious evidence of their special importance and they are buried amidst large amounts of similar data which acts as 'noise', drowning them out. As mentioned earlier, the only generally recommended answer is that the 'reader' should be an 'informed' observer, who knows rather better than most (because he or she is an expert in the industry, for instance) which of these weak signals is most important. Indeed, the term 'weak signals' is a bad one, since it implies, by analogy with electronic communications, that you can use some form of scientific 'device' to amplify the signals. This is not the case.

There is, in fact, a whole range of approaches to the general topic of environmental analysis.

S Rule S14 – *The Viewing Funnel*

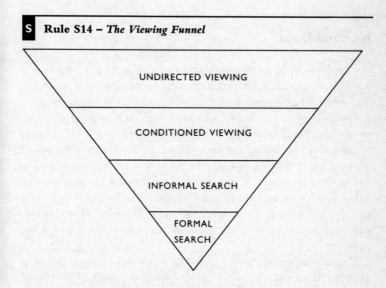

As can be seen from the above diagram, the range of approaches starts with the very wide approach of undirected viewing and progressively narrows until an increasingly tightly focused 'search' activity is employed. We will look at this later (informal search is typically associated with desk research and formal search with that and survey research). In the present context, however, we are concerned with 'conditioned viewing'. To a degree, at least as defined by Aguilar, this overlaps what I have described as 'informed viewing', but in essence it is narrower than that. It takes the more clearly defined areas where relevant information is most likely to be forthcoming (such as the industry sources, including journals and personal contacts) and concentrates on the types of information which are likely to be the most productive. In this way it narrows the scope of the research down so that it becomes a much more practical proposition for most organizations to resource. The one major drawback is that it will not find those 'fractures' which originate outside of this field of interest. These are potentially the most dangerous (precisely because they are the most unexpected) but, as some consolation, it is quite probable that even the wider (and much more expensive) 'undirected viewing' would also fail to identify many of these.

Internal Data

We now move on to discuss what specific marketing information is available for the marketer, and how it can be retrieved and processed. The first, and often the most important, element is the information held within the organization. In recent years, and in particular since the increased availability of computerized databases, the whole process of collecting and distributing internally held management information (including that relating to marketing) has become systematized. The system which handles these processes in a controlled and co-ordinated fashion has come to be called the Management Intelligence System (MIS). In this context, however, it is just the systematic collection and organization of the data which is relevant to the needs of the marketer.

In most organizations the key data on company performance is likely to be already available on computer databases. This should include accurate sales data, split by product and by region. In this electronic age it should even be possible to obtain such up-to-date information via your own personal computer. The abstracted data can then be processed from a variety of perspectives and *ad hoc* reports or enquiries may be easily prepared. You should be aware, however, that the data collected by the average system is driven by accounting needs;

it records, even if the system is near perfect, only those transactions which result in the organization actually completing a sale. And furthermore, it will often reflect an unbalanced picture until the month-end procedures have been completed.

The next problem to address is how to deal with the potential torrent of data. The simplest starting point is the **ABC Analysis** we have already looked at. It is very easy, in this context, for all it means is that reports are sorted with the most 'important' customers (or products or whatever is the subject of the report) at the beginning. Typically this will be in terms of volume (or value) of sales, so that the customers are ranked in order of their sales off-take. As the **80:20 Rule** says, the top 20 per cent of customers on such a list are likely to account for 80 per cent of total sales, so this approach can be used to reduce the data to be examined by a factor of five.

A more sophisticated approach, if you are primarily interested in using the data for control, is:

O **Rule O29 –** *Variance Analysis*
In this approach performance criteria (typically budgets or targets) are set, against which performance of each of the products or customers is subsequently monitored. If performance falls outside the expected range this is highlighted.

This means that only those items where there are 'variances' need be reviewed. The performance data described above has the great advantage, in terms of analysis, of being numeric. This makes abstraction and manipulation much easier where arithmetical operations are commonplace. Much of the remaining data within an organization is, however, available only in written form as memos or reports, of which perhaps the most useful to marketing are the sales reports.

The reliance on words rather than figures may seem to make the manager's job easier, but precisely because this verbal data seems so approachable, there is an unfortunate tendency to accept it at face value. In addition, the 'data' is often difficult to analyse, where writers of such reports tend to use the same words to mean different things, and the importance they attach to events more often reflects their own enthusiasm rather than any absolute measures. Collating a number of such reports and distilling these into a coherent impression therefore becomes a matter of judgement rather than simple analysis, and all too often is used simply to bolster the manager's own preconceived ideas.

Often, access to the key data is limited to a few people; the traditional system requires that the recipient (say, the regional sales manager) recognizes the importance of the data and then incorporates it in his or her own reports to higher management. The message thus travels through the hierarchy of the organization, becoming filtered and distorted at each stage. Delays are then inevitable and, more important, it becomes necessary for a number of intermediaries to recognize the significance of the data. If just one of them ignores it (because he or she does not see its relevance, or even because he or she doesn't want it to go higher) that data is lost to those in the chain above.

In contrast, the increasing use of electronic mail should have a dramatic effect on the availability of such information. This way it is almost as easy to send a memo to a hundred recipients as to one. Indeed, if, as is the case with most such systems, standard distribution lists are available, it is even easier. The data is available to everyone immediately and may be distributed to ten times as many managers, providing them with data they previously might have missed and yet need for their work. Equally important, it provides them with a better perspective on what is happening throughout the organization and there are now specially developed computer programs for storing and retrieving vast quantities of written information. However, if you are still reliant on written material circulating in the traditional ways, here is one suggestion for coping with it:

O **Rule O30 –** *Facts Books*

One very simple and especially effective solution to data overload (at least in terms of the top level of key facts) is to create a series of 'facts books'. These collect together (preferably in the simplest possible form – usually just a ring binder) all the key data.

External Data

As the term implies, this is data which does not come from within the organization, and for which the main source is usually that offered by desk research. This is based on published data (in its widest sense), often referred to as secondary data (because it has been generated in response to someone else's questions). Once such data has been located, its handling follows the same processes as for internal data. It is the 'finding' that is different, and provides the key to sound desk research.

Sources of information

Some useful sources of data which might be considered in this search (by managers in general, not just those involved in marketing) are:
• Libraries
• Directories
• National and local agencies
• Databases
• Trade associations
• Exhibitions and conferences
• News media.

The widest ranging source of published data (on everything from details of ancient civilizations through to the latest stock market prices) is usually a library, typically a public library. The reference libraries, which are usually part of the central library, will hold even more data. More important, though, is that these libraries have access to national libraries. As a result, if you can find sufficient information to specify the book not available at your local library (usually author, title, publisher and date of publication – though often just the author and title will suffice) it can usually be retrieved from elsewhere. Much of the published data is located in journals, often specialist periodicals, and the best source may then be one of the more specialized libraries, such as those run by trade associations.

The most important directories will also be available in your central library, but, again, the more specialized ones may only be found in those of trade associations. National and local government departments and agencies are often major providers of data, especially to support specific initiatives – but they may still be useful for other purposes.

A growing amount of information is being made available (mainly by commercial information providers, but also by government bodies) on computerized databases. These cover almost every subject, with vast quantities of information on technical subjects, such as patents, as well as the marketing information with which this book is primarily concerned. Data can be particularly easy to access, though the cost of doing so may be high. On the other hand, there is now an increasing amount of information becoming available on the Internet. This is, as yet, usually free. It is more difficult to access – though the specialized web browsers and indices help – and is of uneven quality.

One of the best sources of data, not least the 'informal' data acquired during conversations at meetings, is that of trade associations. There is usually a fee for membership, but this is frequently very good value in terms of what may be learned from these sources.

Once more, though, the most important source of external data is likely to come from face-to-face contact. In the case of members of the sales force this will largely be part of business-as-usual, in the form of sales calls. Elsewhere, such opportunities have to be created. In most organizations perhaps the most fruitful sources of such new material are those likely to be found at exhibitions and conferences.

Finally, there is a range of consultants who will take the whole information-gathering process off your hands, for a fee (usually quite a large one – so that this is, understandably, the most expensive solution).

It's worth noting that the most prevalent, but unrecognized, source of external data for all managers (and the one which 'scans' the widest perspective) is that of the news media (especially the morning newspaper and the television news and current affairs programmes). The amount of information these provide is probably much greater than that received from any other source, albeit that the coverage is so much wider. The choice of newspapers in particular thus becomes important. The quality papers are likely to be of more value than the tabloids, but ideally a range of newspapers should be read to judge the bias each almost inevitably imparts to even the simplest news item.

Survey Research

The most generally recognized aspect of marketing research is the surveys conducted on consumers/customers. The stereotype is the market research interviewer standing on the street corner accosting passers-by or walking the streets, clipboard in hand, knocking at closed doors. As we have already seen, this probably represents only a very small part of the data available to any organization. It is, though, particularly important data, since it often provides the only true 'listening' part of the dialogue with the consumer. In the main, it is a process undertaken by consumer goods companies.

The starting point for obtaining such survey research is the specialist organizations which offer market research services; for few organizations will have the resources to handle all aspects of their own research. The suppliers who offer the easiest and quickest solution are the providers of syndicated services. They typically have on-going standard research programmes, the results of which they sell to a number of clients. Shared cost is one advantage of such an approach, but another is that these services are usually sold on the basis of quality, rather than (as much of other research) only on the basis of price. In addition, some researchers will sell 'space' (or more accurately interviewer time) on the back of their omnibus surveys, so that you can ask one or two simple questions at the end of the main survey.

Retail audits, such as the A. C. Nielsen store audits, are the most sophisticated of such syndicated operations. The concept, though, is simple. In the traditional approach, an 'auditor' regularly visits each retail outlet on the panel and by means of a physical stock check on the lines being surveyed, combined with the information on deliveries, determines the rate of consumer sales. Most recently the data has been taken from the EPOS (Electronic Point of Sale) data captured by the tills, though this requires greater cooperation by the retailer, who may – correctly – see this data as valuable property. Such retail audits are generally believed to offer the best results in terms of accuracy of the volumes of consumer sales and, in particular, of the value of such sales, for brand share calculations, as well as for the all-important figures of prices and distribution levels. This information is, needless to say, invaluable to any consumer goods company wishing to control its sales through retail outlets.

Customer research is, however, the staple diet of the market research industry. The research organization is commissioned by a client to undertake a specific piece of research. The research company then accepts responsibility for all aspects of the research, including planning and designing. But it may then appoint a sub-contractor to do the detailed fieldwork and analyses. The client company does not see these sub-contractors, and does not need to; all it needs to see is the outcome (and to be happy with the validity of this).

Because this is a very important process, I will now describe the five stages which are most generally followed in conducting survey research:

⊙ Rule O31 – *Stages of Survey Research*

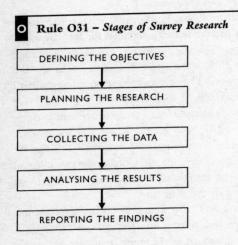

```
┌─────────────────────────────┐
│   DEFINING THE OBJECTIVES   │
└─────────────────────────────┘
              │
              ▼
┌─────────────────────────────┐
│    PLANNING THE RESEARCH    │
└─────────────────────────────┘
              │
              ▼
┌─────────────────────────────┐
│     COLLECTING THE DATA     │
└─────────────────────────────┘
              │
              ▼
┌─────────────────────────────┐
│    ANALYSING THE RESULTS    │
└─────────────────────────────┘
              │
              ▼
┌─────────────────────────────┐
│   REPORTING THE FINDINGS    │
└─────────────────────────────┘
```

Defining the objectives

As was indicated by the 'Research Diamond', the most important stage of almost all market research, and the one at which the research is most likely to be misdirected, is defining the objectives. Only the client can know what he or she wants the research to investigate and although an expert from the market research organization is usually involved before the research itself takes place, the objectives need to be clear, and clearly stated (so that the researcher understands them), and unambiguous. Most market research fails because it is merely asked to confirm the existing theories of the commissioning organization.

● **Rule O32** – *Research Errors* can result from errors of COM-MISSION: where the questions are slanted to produce the answers that the organization expects or wants. A good market research agency should, however, detect such bias and remove it. More diffi-cult to deal with are the errors of OMISSION, where the key questions are never asked, and this is a problem which few market research organizations would be in a position to detect.

It is at this stage that the initiative passes to the research agency to undertake the detailed planning, though the more sophisticated client will still want to remain involved.

Planning the research

Before the main, quantifiable survey research can start, it is almost invariably necessary to undertake some qualitative research to find out exactly what are the questions to be quantified. Only if you ask the right questions will you get the right answers, and in practice it is remarkably difficult to decide what those questions should be. It is not enough to think that you know them, for if you did you probably would not need the research – and the great benefit of marketing research is that it explores what you do not know. Too much research is expensively undertaken to justify a prejudice which the manager already holds.

So, the first step is to find out in as open-ended a way as possible what the customer thinks the questions should be. This poses almost as big a problem as the manager's prejudice. Customers, unfortunately, do not spend their time thinking through their complex buying motiv-ations. That is the brand manager's job. All the customers want to do is get on with the enjoyable occupation of buying things. It requires considerable skill and sophistication, therefore, to unlock their minds and start to understand what really motivates them. This is, generally speaking, the province of the expert psychologist, not the friendly door-step interviewer. Accordingly, qualitative approaches to research revolve around the very sophisticated skills of such psychologists.

There are a number of such approaches in use, but the one which is used in the great majority of cases is group research, where the psychologist or specially trained interviewer leads a discussion amongst a group of customers, often called group discussions or focus group research.

---

o **Rule O33 – *Group Discussions***
Obtaining QUALITATIVE data from a selected group of participants (typically containing 6–10 members, sharing similar interests) who are encouraged to discuss the topics the researchers are investigating.

The interviewer ('group leader' or 'moderator'), who has to be skilled in the technique and often is a trained psychologist, carefully leads the discussion, ensuring that all the group members are able to put forward their views. The interviewer's role is essentially a passive one, where his or her prime concern is to foster group interaction (and to avoid any one individual dominating the group). The essence of such group discussions is that the participants can develop their own ideas in an unstructured fashion, interacting with, and stimulating, others.

The whole session is usually captured on a tape recorder for later analysis in depth. This approach allows insights which may be hidden from the pre-conceived questions posed in questionnaire surveys and in particular it allows the customers' own language to emerge so that the subsequent survey questions can be phrased in ways which are meaningful to them. It is an excellent method for generating hypotheses when little is known, and is thus a particularly productive approach to piloting the first stage of larger research projects. It is, though, increasingly being used as a cheaper and faster alternative for those organizations which cannot afford the full-scale research and, in line with the move towards low-cost research, even for those which can. This is arguably better than nothing, but the client should beware of attributing too much significance to it. The sample sizes are usually far too small to allow any statistical conclusions to be drawn. Unfortunately, some of the less reputable agencies commissioning this research may still try to attribute something approaching statistical significance (or at least an unjustifiable degree of importance) to the results. In this case, it must be the client who has to recognize the very real limitations of the information which can be derived from them.

One especially powerful method of starting the process of unearthing the customer's deeper motivations is:

O **Rule O34 –** *Repertory Grids*

By removing interviewer (and questionnaire-designer) bias, whilst allowing the respondent free rein to his or her own ideas (and indeed 'forcing' this process), this questionnaire-based technique can give a very clear picture of what really motivates respondents. It is, though, a very sophisticated and expensive process.

The precise aim of this technique, often called Kelly Grids after the name of the inventor, is to discover what are the key dimensions of the respondents' attitudes towards the product or brand – typically as part of a positioning exercise. In an individual interview, each respondent is presented with a list of items. These items (around 15–20 being the recommended number) are normally presented in simple word form, for example, the names of products or brands, or statements about them. Three of the items ('triads') chosen at random from the list are presented to the respondent at a time. The respondent is asked to choose the two most alike. He or she is then asked to say why these two are similar, and are different to the third. The remaining items on the list are then sorted on the same basis. The process is repeated with three further stimuli, again selected at random, and the respondent is asked to give another way in which the selected pair are the same, and different to the third. The whole process continues until the respondent cannot find a further new reason for the similarity/difference (which typically occurs after ten or so triads, depending upon the complexity of the subject being studied). A number of such interviews (from 10–50) are conducted and the output analysed, usually by computer, to see which factors can be clustered. The output is a set of dimensions by which the customers themselves would describe the situation (usually something like a product/brand position). Its great virtue is that it forces the market researcher subsequently, in the quantitative survey research which is the second stage of all these pilot investigations, to research dimensions which are meaningful to the consumer rather than to the supplier. Using Repertory Grids is relatively expensive (at least in terms of pilot research) and, possibly as a result, they are rarely used in practice. This is a pity, since they offer one of the most valuable starting points for sound marketing research.

Collecting the data

The most widely used formal marketing research is, or at least should be, survey research. Typically, this may be designed to find out, descriptively, the participants' habits, attitudes, wants etc. It is simply based on asking the participant, the respondent, a number of questions. The classic device used on such surveys is the questionnaire: a pre-printed form on which the interviewer, or the respondent, fills in the answers to a series of such questions.

O **Rule O35 –** *Questionnaire Design*

As the key to survey research, the questions must be very carefully and skilfully developed.

In the first instance they must be COMPREHENSIVE.

Secondly, they will need to be in a language the respondent understands, so that the answers will be CLEAR AND UNAMBIGUOUS.

Finally, they should not be leading questions, leading to the answer preconceived by the researcher (or the client). The questions must be neutral, to encourage the respondent to reply truthfully.

If a key question is not asked it will not be answered. Even then, many words used by researchers and their clients, including those used in their daily language, may be strange to the respondents they are testing, particularly where these are less well-educated respondents. In addition, if the form of questioning is too complex (or, on the other hand, too vague) it may elicit confused answers. Above all, the most basic fault of much research is that, as a result of bad design, it plays back the answers that the researcher expects (or even wants) to hear.

The next stage of the research is when the army of interviewers descends on the unsuspecting public. There are a number of possible methods of contacting respondents. Mail is the cheapest solution and large overall samples can be used, allowing investigation of small groups – especially in industrial markets – still within acceptable statistical levels. But in many respects it is the least satisfactory one. The questions which can be asked are necessarily simpler and the questionnaire shorter; and it must be particularly well designed to keep the respondent interested and motivated to reply. More fundamentally, the response rates may be so low that their statistical validity may be questioned. It is worth noting, however, that response rates in fact may not be significantly worse than those for the typical face-to-face interview. The only difference is that in the latter case the 'non-responses' are not known (or at least are not recorded). Some – very carefully managed – mail surveys may, therefore, offer a viable alternative to face-to-face approaches.

Alternatively, the interviewer might use a telephone to contact respondents. It is a very fast survey technique and the results can be available in a matter of hours, and so it is often used now for those opinion polls where time is of the essence. On the other hand, the interview can only last a short time and the types of questions are limited. Even so, it is probably under-used as a technique, since it is relatively cheap and quite flexible.

Personal interviewing is the traditional (face-to-face) approach to marketing research, and it is still the most versatile. The interviewer is in full control of the interview, and can take account of the body language as well as the words. It is the most expensive, however, and is dependent on the reliability of the interviewer and on his or her skill. This means that the quality of the supervision provided by the field research agency is critical and may be a problem where so many organizations now place the emphasis on cost-cutting.

Samples

The basic principle of sampling (derived from statistical theory) is that you can obtain a representative picture of a whole 'population' (the term used by theorists to describe the total group of people, or objects, being investigated) by looking at a small sample. The number is usually, in this context, only a few hundred – but correctly handled it may still give an accurate picture of an overall population of millions. This applies to testing grain sold by the farmer just as much as it does, here, to market research. It is, needless to say, a very cost-effective way of obtaining information.

Samples are a somewhat academic subject. They are, though, important in terms of understanding the accuracy of the results which emerge and, as they represent a large part of the costs involved, offer a good indication of the quality of the work being carried out. There are two main ways such a sample may be chosen. The classically correct method is to select a sample at random. The list of the total 'population' to be sampled is chosen. Usually, for consumer research, it is the electoral register. This list is then used as the basis of selecting the sample, either by using tables of random numbers or simply by selecting every nth name.

The great advantage of random samples is that they are statistically predictable. Apart from any questions over how comprehensive the original lists are, they cannot be skewed (that is biased). The major disadvantage is that they are usually more expensive and, accordingly, they may be used less frequently for commercial work (except that based upon mail questionnaires).

Quota samples, on the other hand, aim to achieve much the same effect by asking the interviewers to recruit respondents to match an agreed quota of sub-samples. This is supposed to guarantee that the overall sample is an approximately representative cross-section of the 'population' as a whole. The interviewer, by means of knocking on doors or standing in a busy street, is required, for example, to select certain numbers of respondents in specified age and social categories. This clearly may be subject to 'skew' by selecting only the more accessible, those who make a habit of visiting their local high street for example. It is also difficult to apply rigorous statistical tests to the data. There is, in addition, a hidden problem of non-responses. The levels of these may be as high as in mail surveys but, as they are not recorded, they are out of sight (and hence ignored)! Quota samples are, though, significantly cheaper than using random samples; so they are the approach most frequently chosen for commercial research. It has to be said that, despite their apparent theoretical shortcomings, they often work well, and have done so, with documented results, for several decades. As quality does depend very directly upon the quality of the interviewer, and in particular on the quality of supervision, it is the approach most likely to suffer from the shaving of quality to achieve cost savings. At the worst level, if badly controlled, it may degenerate into 'convenience sampling', which is a polite phrase for interviewing whoever comes to hand.

There are some nice statistical calculations which will show you how many interviews you will need to conduct (in theory on the basis of a random sample, but the same figures are often applied to quota samples).

⊙ Rule O36 – *Sample Sizes*

As a very rough guide, if you want to achieve an accuracy of within 2 or 3 per cent, which is satisfactory for most occasions, you will probably need a sample of between 500 and 1,000 respondents.

Sample sizes as low as 300–400 are often found to be acceptable. The point to note is that you rarely need more than 1,000 and, much more important, you can equally rarely expect to get accurate results with less than 200 respondents.

Marketing research in the industrial goods area is typically less involved with survey research. On the one hand, the output of statistics about the 'average customer' may be less useful – where each customer's needs often have to be considered separately (the value of their business justifies this, and the contact with the salesperson makes it a possibility). On the other hand, the difficulty and cost of conducting such survey research on industrial customers is much higher. For one thing, the 'lists' (which define the population from which the sample is drawn) are often not available, or are inaccurate and incomplete. The result is that desk research is even more prevalent, and even more important, than in consumer marketing research, and this is often conducted by experts rather than by the individual manager. Much of the survey work which is done tends to revolve around in-depth (unstructured) interviews with relatively few respondents. In any case, the total population, the 'universe', may be just a few hundred organizations (especially if consideration is governed by the value of purchases). The interviews are usually conducted, by experts, on senior managers (and the views of the organization sought rather than those of the individual).

Analysing the results

The statistical data collected by surveys can be analysed in a wide variety of ways. Increasingly these analyses use the power of computers to see beyond the superficial results, but experts are then required to implement these techniques – and the confidence you place on the results accordingly reflects the confidence you place in their abilities.

Some examples of the techniques now being used include **multiple regression analysis**, which is a complex and sophisticated statistical (computerized) method which attempts to determine the structure of relationships between factors where there are more than two factors involved. It is concerned with establishing what contribution each of these factors – the 'independent variables' (for example, price and advertising) or 'dependent variables' (for example, sales or customer attitudes) – makes to the overall results. **Factor analysis** is another sophisticated technique which is used to group together 'related' variables (by the detection of related patterns in the data, usually concerned with buying behaviour). These may superficially appear to be independent but in fact can be shown to be highly correlated. That is, there is an underlying relationship which means that they behave in much the same way and have a similar impact on the final results. It is primarily a tool used to reduce a large number of possible variables to a smaller, aggregated or summarized, number, which can be more easily handled. On the other hand, using **cluster analysis**, factors can be found which strongly differentiate, for example, certain customer groups from others, so that each 'cluster' is isolated from other clusters, whilst being internally alike. It is a particularly important technique in the case of segmentation, where the aim is to split customers (and hence markets) into clearly differentiated groups. As such it is one of the most powerful analytical techniques available to the marketer.

Reporting the findings

The final stage is to report the results to all who need to know them. This requires some recognition of those personnel to whom the results may be useful – and, indeed, important results may have relevance to managers throughout the organization. Equally important, the language of the report may need to be translated for these different recipients. Very few of these managers will understand the terminology of market research or the limitations of the conclusions that may be drawn from the figures. The results will, therefore, have to be conveyed in terms which are meaningful to these particular individuals.

The favourite approach (at least in presentation to top management) seems to be to illustrate the dry statistics (which have probably already been considerably simplified) with verbatim quotes from individual respondents. The particular and very real danger here is that the senior management, being unversed in market research skills, will remember the most impactful comments (particularly the ones that reinforce their existing prejudices) rather than the boring statistics.

◯ Rule O37 – *Using Research Reports*

The key factors to be taken into account are:

* *Relevance*
* *Reliability*
* *Accuracy*
* *Bias*
* *Scope.*

Many managers find themselves on the receiving end of research reports, often those deriving from marketing research. Almost as many managers, on the other hand, are poorly trained in the skills needed to make sense of such reports. As a result, they tend to read the related conclusions uncritically, accepting (or sometimes rejecting) them at their face value.

To a certain extent the way you interpret the report must depend upon the specific circumstances: what is contained in the report, and what you want from it. Even so, there are a number of initial guidelines that might be helpful:

* *Relevance* – before you even look at the first page of the report, you should ask yourself whether the subject is relevant to your specific needs. Can you afford the time to study it? This can usually be deduced from a quick skim through the summary, coupled with an understanding of where the report has come from and why it was produced.

* *Reliability* – this is perhaps the most important question, but the one which is least often asked. How reliable are the results reported? What weight can be put on them and on the judgement of the researchers and, probably even more important, on the experts who are likely to be recommending some form of action to be taken on the basis of the findings. Be aware that personal reliability in a social context does not necessarily underwrite technical reliability in a business context (and, indeed, can blinker those involved). A more rigorous approach would be to examine the methodology (the questionnaire and sample design, say) since this is likely to give the best indication of the 'quality' of the work.

* *Accuracy* – having established that the material is both relevant and reliable, the next step is to assess the level of accuracy. The researcher should tell you this, but all too often this is a technicality which is buried deep in the technical appendices. As I have already indicated,

in marketing research, the answer can normally be deduced from the sample size. If the sample size is over 500 the results are likely to be accurate to within 2–3 per cent (always assuming the research has been well run). If the sample is over 1,000 it may be within 1 per cent. Below 100, though, as many of the more dubious pieces of 'quantitative' research may be, any statistical accuracy may be almost non-existent!

• *Bias* – most research reports contain some bias, conscious or unconscious. It is very difficult for even the most professional researcher to remove all of his or her biases and you would be wise to assume that the material still contains such elements of distortion. This bias may not be without value. The best research starts with a strong thesis as to what is likely to be found. Whilst this will inevitably colour the results it also ensures that the research is focused and provides meaningful insights. However, you need to know what assumptions (biases) are implicit in the work, and having recognized them you will then be much better placed to understand the real implications of the figures.

• *Scope* – the final question, before starting on the main body of the report, is what range of information it provides (often researchers only report the results that interest them – you may be able to ask further questions of the material about topics which interest you). This can be discovered most easily by looking at the questionnaire, to determine exactly what questions were asked.

It is only at this stage that you should start to read the main body of the report. The reason for this circuitous approach is that without it the writer of the report has probably gained your uncritical attention, and the opportunity to manipulate your judgement, as soon as you start to read his or her introduction.

The subsequent stages are:

• *Summary* – the first element to be read should now be the summary. This will provide the context for understanding the detailed results. It should, though, be read as such, not as a list of proven facts, and certainly not (if the research is important) instead of the detailed material.

• *Detailed results* – these should then be examined, preferably by looking at the original analyses (tables) as well as the written interpretation. They should, once more, be examined critically. Do you agree with what the researcher has deduced from them? Remember that although the researcher should be more experienced in the marketing research techniques involved, you are more experienced in the field being researched. So, don't hesitate to challenge the results! Most times you will find you agree with the researcher, but occasionally you will find new information which is worthwhile.

• *Think out your own summary* – only then can you think through (and put down on paper) the key results in terms of what affects your own work. It is a long process, but if the research is worthwhile then the effort you put into it should match its importance and, hopefully, your subsequent decisions will be correspondingly better informed.

Personal Research

So far, in the main, we have looked at the formal research systems; in this context even desk research can be seen as formal. On the other hand, informal contacts are the staple diet of management and probably represent the most important source of data available to any manager, particularly to one involved in the sales and marketing functions. Every meeting, be it a formal organized meeting of a group or an informal one between two individuals, is potentially rich with useful data. To take advantage of this a number of personal techniques need to be employed, which are normally not mentioned in the context of marketing research:

Questioning

As with formal research the key to personal research is questioning. Yet again, you only get the right answers if you ask the right questions. This might seem easy to achieve when you are asking the questions for yourself, but most people tend to ask very specific (closed) questions which narrow discussion or to confine the discussion to the areas set by their own personal preferences or prejudices. Much more useful are those open questions (of which the simplest – Why? How? What? – are the most powerful) which encourage the speaker to say what he or she considers is most important about the topic. The listener can then gain the most benefit from the speaker's knowledge and expertise. Later in the conversation, directive and then closed questions can be used to steer the conversation to the topics of greatest interest to the listener.

 Rule O38 – *Questions*
The most important, and productive, questions are the OPEN ones, which allow the person being questioned to ramble on.

They also seem to be the most difficult for a manager to ask, perhaps because they are not so obviously leading directly to the answer that is wanted. If the conversation proceeds with very short replies (and particularly just 'yes' or 'no'), it is likely that you are not using enough open questions, and may be missing the real issues. In practice, open questions come naturally if the questioner is genuinely interested in finding out what makes the respondent's business tick.

A particular technique, used by skilled researchers, is 'laddering'.

 Rule O39 – *Laddering*
The question 'WHY?' is repeated until the respondent cannot explain any further. It is a powerful technique for finding the underlying motives.

Unfortunately, in most normal discussions it is a very aggressive technique and must be used with great care.

A slightly less stressful and equally successful approach is 'rambling'. Eden, Jones and Sims[2] report that 'Probably the most obvious method for getting to know about the view a person has of the problem is to give him the time and space to "ramble" around his subject.' This can be an enormous strain on the listener, for it is difficult not to interrupt.

---

2. Colin Eden, Sue Jones and David Sims, *Messing About in Problems* (Pergamon, 1983).

◯ Rule O40 – *Rambling*

If the listener simply allows the speaker enough time – and does not interrupt his or her 'rambling' – the answers will emerge.

Even if managers do ask the correct open questions, they often undermine the progress by stopping the speaker in mid-flow. The natural accompaniment to an open question is silence. It can be a surprisingly aggressive technique, so it is best just to look very thoughtful. The person you are questioning will eventually feel obliged to talk, and usually what he or she then says is especially enlightening.

As indicated above, closed questions, typically requiring the answer 'yes' or 'no', have, justifiably, received a bad press. But it is still necessary to use them quite extensively to clarify points. As the discussion progresses, it is imperative that you establish whether or not you are taking the other person with you; or, as is all too often the case, whether he or she is politely acting out the role of audience to your orator.

Listening

Just as important a skill as questioning is listening. Many managers are too busy trying to put their own view across to hear what is being said in reply, and so they miss much of the key data.

◯ Rule O41 – *Listening* implies far more than hearing. It also involves the process of analysing what is heard in order to understand it – to make sense of it in general, and then to put it into the intellectual framework of the organizational activities being discussed. Listening is a very active pursuit, not a passive one.

It is conventionally reckoned that a good questioner should spend two thirds of the time listening and only one third talking. What is important, though, is how you use that time. The quality of the listening (which has much to do with how you analyse what you hear) is as important as the quantity.

Understanding

Hearing, and even listening, is still not enough. The key to questioning by managers is understanding, and that involves not only what the person being questioned says at the time but may also include what he or she said in a number of previous meetings. It will also include all the other evidence you have unearthed. Put it all together and, hopefully, you will be able to complete the jigsaw.

Understanding of informal communications is, therefore, a cumulative process; it is an important skill for managers, yet it is largely ignored by management educators.

• *Recording and organizing the data* – even before the advent of the Filofax and its electronic equivalents, managers used to carry notebooks in which to write notes on their various meetings and conversations. This is an excellent habit, and forms the basis of the process needed to convert these conversations into a retrievable form to go into the main filing system. As with the clippings file, it might be productive to file them every two weeks so that you can begin the process of editing them, and tracking new developments.

• *Prioritize and track change* – finally, as with all good marketing research, you should do something with these gems you have been collecting. The first step is (as it was with the clippings file) to group the ideas, then to prioritize them. Most important, though, is to query anything which emerges as different to what you might have expected. Why has it changed? It is all too easy to ignore such internal 'weak' signals, but much of management is about dealing with change, and the earlier you recognize that changes are emerging the better.

To complement these informal meetings and conversations, which fortuitously provide you with useful 'research' data, you can also use other informal sources. Not least of these is the **grapevine**; the collection of rumours and gossip which permeates most organizations. It is often better informed and more accurate than the formal information channels, so the tighter you can tap into it the better. It often runs in parallel with a network of **'fixers'** – managers who, perhaps because of their length of service or just their travels throughout the organization, seem to have contacts everywhere that matters. They know what is happening and what is to come, and in their spare time resolve the cross-departmental problems which others don't even know exist. The thoughts of these individuals should also be grist to your information mill.

The next technique in this section has the simplicity that is the hallmark of the Japanese, and it is their favourite approach:

O   Rule O42 – *Walkabout*

The power of the Japanese approach to marketing research is no more than going out and about, where the action is on the product or service in question, and experiencing what is happening. In particular, they meet their customers and distributors and talk through, at length, what is important to them.

It has none of the statistical validity which survey research enjoys, and even desk research can often lay claim to. Yet better than anything else it conveys the flavour, the essence, of what is being studied. If you want to understand Toyota you can spend months of desk research reading the hundreds of papers which have been written about its efficiency, or you can spend half a day watching the confident grace with which the workers on its production lines assemble cars.

The final technique brings together all the research data in the most practical form possible. For many, if not most, managers, the marketing research data remains just so much impersonal data in hundreds of pages in dusty files. Just a few managers, however, bring it alive by assimilating it into their everyday view of their business life.

O   Rule O43 – *Synthesis and Assimilation*

You should build an INNER model of the customers you are dealing with. Using the data you have received you should synthesize a multi-dimensional picture of them, and then assimilate it, almost as if absorbing it by osmosis through your skin.

In my opinion, the technique of walkabout is the most useful of all in this process, because it gives the best 'feel' for what the key elements are. Just as the actor who uses Stanislavsky's Method to bring the character he is playing inside himself, so the synthesizing manager should **live** the part of the customer. The great benefit of this is that the manager does not have to search through the vast collections of data to know what the customer's reaction would be to any of the several dozen decisions which may be made in a day. Instead, he or she can draw upon his or her inner model to instinctively 'feel' what the customer's response will be. This is a difficult process, especially when there are a number of different customer groups to assimilate in this way but, like the actor, the manager can – after considerable effort – usually achieve success.

Fractures and Marketing Research

One final note concerns areas where marketing research may not be particularly helpful. When there is a major discontinuity in the overall environment, described by Gareth Morgan[3] as a 'fracture', this changes all the factors to such an extent that market research may be largely useless.

In this situation most marketing research is meaningless since it essentially measures the historical position, and discontinuity means that the future will be different. Even consumer research will be largely valueless when this happens, since the consumers asked their opinions will not know enough about the new developments to answer the questions accurately, but will base their answers (incorrectly) on their existing perspective.

John Stopford[4] makes the point that the really significant new products have not emerged from incremental (and marketing-researched) changes, but have been genuine innovations. Perhaps more important for the readers of this book is his associated comment that the organizations which have survived such fractures (that is, major changes in their environment) have been the ones which have thrown out their standard operating procedures manuals. This may say relatively little about marketing research, but it says a great deal about the value of outdated theory as compared with practical flexibility in coping with change!

Fortunately, for most managers, such innovations are very rare,[5] though they have recently preoccupied some theorists. Some of these

3. Gareth Morgan, *Riding the Waves of Change* (Jossey-Bass, 1988).
4. John Stopford, personal communication (1989).
5. D. S. Mercer, 'A Two Decade Test of Product Life Cycle Theory', *British Journal of Management*, Vol. 4 (1993) pp. 269–74.

theorists have even suggested that the possibility of these discontinuities undermines the value of marketing research as a whole, but I believe that obtaining the best possible information about the outside world is still the key to the great part of successful marketing. The more you understand about the environment in general, and customers in particular, the more effective your marketing is likely to be.

8 / Advertising

We now move on to see what you can do with the knowledge you have gained about your customers. The most immediate application of this knowledge is in shaping the promotional programmes you will undertake. It is true to say, though, that almost all that is important about your promotional strategy should have been decided by this stage. The analysis you have already completed, determining the optimum Product:Service Package, will in effect have defined all the important variables, including those relating to the promotional components of the package. In particular, the positioning exercise(s) will have mapped out the factors which are the key to successful promotion. All that remains is to deliver that promotion to the customer.

Promotional Strategy

○ **Rule O44 –** *Promise What You Will Deliver, Brilliantly*
The offer you will be able to make in your promotional campaigns is already defined. All you have to do is to convey this information to your customers. The essence of this statement is that the promotional message is inherent in the Product:Service Package.

The promotional message is an integral part of the package. Often it may be the most important overall element, outstripping even the 'physical' elements.

At one extreme, the work which has been done so far should have very accurately defined what best meets the needs and wants of the customer, at least within the resources available to the organization. That product offer (the complete package, which includes the intangible elements such as image) should, itself, be the most powerful message you can convey to the customer. To try to add anything would not merely be to gild the lily but to reduce the impact of the main message.

O **Rule O45** – *Simplicity* is the key to successful promotion. Less is more.

At the other extreme, if the package is to be profitable this is not likely to be a one-time sale; profits are usually made from repeat sales. Thus, the message must not offer more than you can deliver in reality. It is said that satisfaction equals perception minus expectation.[1] If you raise the customer's expectations too high, his or her perceptions of the actual performance will almost certainly fall short of these, resulting in disappointment, and possibly a slight feeling of having been the victim of a fraud. On the other hand, if you don't raise expectations high enough you may not make the sale in the first place; you need to achieve exactly the right balance.

Having nailed down exactly what you can offer, the secret of great promotion is then to communicate that as brilliantly and powerfully as you can. This is where the all-important creative element should enter. The theory of promotion, especially that of advertising, was largely covered in the earlier chapters dealing with the customer. In describing that customer you also tend to specify how you should communicate with him or her. Thus, the advertising agencies have often been the main developers of the various models which try to explain the customer, and in particular the customer's buying behaviour. The lifestyle models have been especially attractive to these advertising agencies, since they offered a very attractive (often 'creatively' attractive) vehicle for their talents.

The practice of promotion is much more difficult to categorize. Apart from the rather mundane descriptions of the communication process, there is remarkably little suitable theory around. Practice is dominated by creative solutions (for the delivery of the message almost as much as for the message itself). This is inevitable where the task is to make your offering stand out from the many others, and then to make even detergents seem interesting and important.

Before we start to concentrate on the message, let us look at the range of delivery systems in the context of the promotional mix. As a very direct approach, there is face-to-face sales. There is the more

1. David H. Maister, 'The Psychology of Waiting Lines' in *Managing Services: Marketing, Operations and Human Resources* (Prentice-Hall, 1988).

indirect one, when it is too expensive to confront the customer personally, of advertising, or the even more indirect one of public relations. Finally, there is the very immediate one of sales (point of sale) promotion which, if the reports are to be believed, now accounts for the largest part of the spend on promotion as a whole. The 'Promotional Lozenge' sums this up in a more memorable way: shaped like a diamond, it does not have any clear cutting edges, however.

S   **Rule S15 – *The Promotional Lozenge***

ADVERTISING

PUBLIC RELATIONS (PR)   indirect   POINT OF SALE PROMOTION

direct

SALES

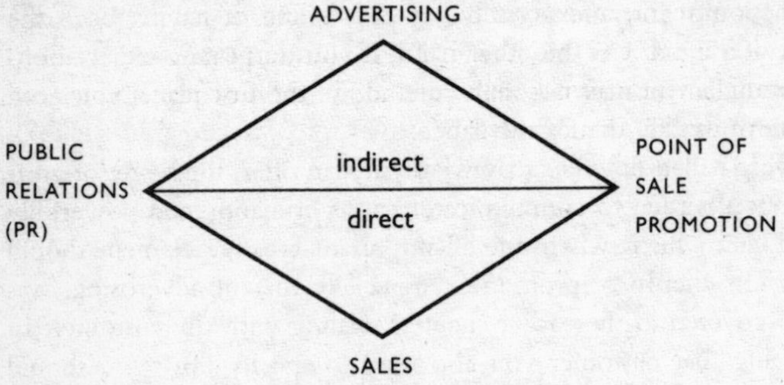

This lozenge is not as arbitrary as it may seem. It is actually organized along two dimensions. The vertical one is the move from direct (sales) to indirect (advertising) contact with the customer. Perhaps less obvious, but in many respects more important, is the horizontal dimension. This shows the flow over time, from the start with the establishment of a general interest via public relations (PR) through investment in image-building with advertising and much of the selling process, to the very immediate impact of sales promotional devices at the point of sale. It also demonstrates the gradation from the long-term investment in PR and advertising/sales to the very short-term effect of promotion.

The demands posed by your Product:Service Package determine the actual shape of the lozenge. If you need the face-to-face (sales) contact to explain a complex package, and the price of this is sufficiently high to cover the high costs this implies, then the lozenge becomes almost an inverted triangle:

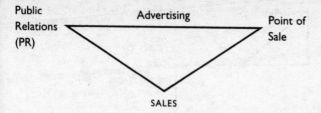

The advertising element is almost missing, though even in the sales environment there will remain some element of indirect contact, often in the form of direct mail, to generate prospects for the face-to-face contact. The point of sale here is a time (not a place), and the promotional element is usually only seen in the form of a price discount. Despite my earlier comments, sales professionals would argue that this does need to have a very sharp cutting edge.

Almost the exact reverse occurs for fast-moving consumer goods where the low unit price means that face-to-face selling is simply not an economic proposition.

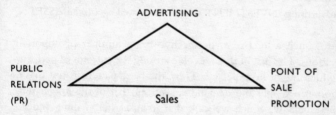

Here sales drops out of the picture, but not totally – for someone has to persuade distribution chains to carry the Product:Service Package to the point of sale (which here is a place not a time). Most of the effort, though, must by necessity be invested in the indirect communications. Once again, the promotion (here used at the point of sale) is very short term, usually in the form of some price reduction (either direct or indirect).

You can play many different games with the lozenge, but I will finish with one which distorts it to show, quite realistically, advertising, for, say, a consumer durable or a car, preceding face-to-face sales activity in the retail outlet.

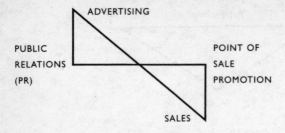

Advertising as a Fixed Asset

Traditionally, advertising and promotion have been treated as current costs with an immediate but short-term effect. Although this view is probably justified in terms of most forms of sales promotion it seriously distorts some important aspects of advertising and PR.

S **Rule S16**
   Advertising INVESTMENT should be treated as a fixed ASSET.

Adopting such a long-term perspective has a number of important implications. The first of these revolve around the patterns of performance which might be expected. Thus, the basic pattern is not that of the short-run supply and demand curves but that of the longer term Competitive Saw, which we looked at in an earlier chapter. Indeed, it is a level saw; its overall trend relatively flat but with the teeth representing the impact of the individual campaigns.

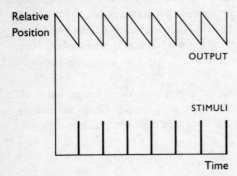

Following the implied principle of the fixed asset, this sawtooth maintenance pattern can be overlaid on a gradually declining trend in performance – notionally equivalent to depreciation in financial accounting. Over time there may be a slow drift away from the ideal position, as the customers' needs and wants change and/or competitive positioning improves. Your own response to this may take two forms.

 Rule T26 – *Dynamic Repositioning*
Change in relative positions should be regularly tracked and the brand's position readjusted to take account of this.

Dynamic repositioning is perhaps the most effective, working in much the same way that an autopilot's feedback mechanisms ensure that an airliner follows the correct flightpath. The emphasis here is on the dynamic approach to (current) change. In contrast, most of traditional marketing theory revolves around decisions based upon static (historic) positions.

If such dynamic repositioning is not possible, perhaps because the necessary product changes come in discrete steps, then periodic re-adjustments may be needed. This is where the second concept comes in.

 Rule T27 – *Advertising Depreciation* allows the build-up of reserves to cover the significant costs of major repositioning exercises.

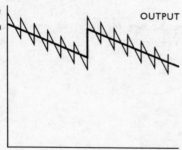

This long-term asset investment aspect of brand performance is largely ignored by traditional marketing theory.

The above pattern of responses assumes a complementary repositioning process which builds upon existing strengths. There are two exceptions to this: first is the new product launch, where the logistic curve (described in a later chapter) may be most effectively used to represent the relatively slow build-up of brand position which results from even quite high levels of investment. The key aspect here is the level of investment needed; to buy your way into a market is a very expensive process indeed. The main practical feature, though, is the level of risk. Most managements believe that risk is reduced if the levels of investment are minimized; in fact, the reverse is true.

T Rule T28

The more money you invest in a major change, the more you reduce the risk.[2]

If you want to make a major impact on a market (one that will, for instance, put you into the most profitable Rule of 1:2:3 slots) you must recognize that the level of investment needed will be correspondingly high; in practice, probably beyond the reach of all but the largest Japanese corporations where major markets are concerned. The second dimension is time. Any new penetration of a market takes far longer than is expected.

O Rule O46

The reality of new launches, even for successful introductions, is a mean of eight years to break even.[3]

---

2. Ralph Biggadike, 'The Risky Business of Diversification', *Harvard Business Review*, May/June 1979.
3. *Ibid.*

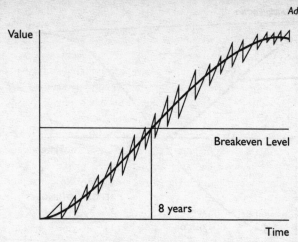

The second exception, a response which is rarely discussed, but is often encountered in practice, is that of combative repositioning.

T **Rule T29 – *Combative Repositioning*** aims for such a radically new position that it does not use existing strengths, but has to overcome them before it can even start to take effect.

Perhaps the most usual reason for this is that a change in advertising, say, incorporates a radically different message. This can often occur without management even realizing the implications for repositioning.

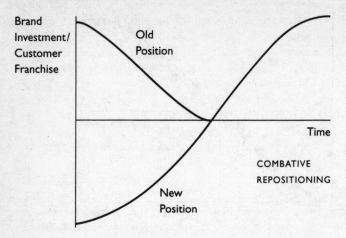

Brand Investment/Customer Franchise

Old Position

New Position

Time

COMBATIVE REPOSITIONING

As can be seen, the starting point of the combative repositioning is actually below the baseline, since the new investment has first to overcome the existing positioning before it can develop its own strengths. It should be obvious that this is likely to be a remarkably poor investment (even if it can retain some carry-over of the infra-structural investment – distribution, for example). It would often be more profitable to start a completely new brand.

Why then does combative repositioning happen so frequently? Sometimes the 'depreciation' simply cannot cope with all the changes needed, and a major repositioning exercise (incorporating essential elements of combative repositioning, since the new position is radically different) is needed; the necessity for the brand within the organiza-tion's portfolio is so strong that it justifies the extra investment. But this is usually just an excuse. Combative repositioning typically happens for two reasons. The first is simply that, while they do recognize the change in position implied, the perpetrators do not appreciate the level of investment which already exists in the brand's position. The second is less forgivable, and can most often be laid at the door of creatively ambitious advertising agencies or arrogantly insensitive brand managers. In this instance, they do not even understand what the current position is, let alone its strategic importance. In their anxiety to create an exciting new campaign they happily ignore what has gone before.

I would like to report that combative repositioning is the exception rather than the rule, but it is not. Only the really powerful brands seem to be safe in their managers' hands – but maybe that is why they remain powerful brands. Combine widespread ignorance about the levels of investment needed and the timescales involved, with the ignorance of the dangers of combative repositioning and it is easy to see why so few brand leaders are ever seriously challenged.

Having decided your promotional strategy, there are just two main aspects of the promotional task: the delivery vehicle and the message. Let us, therefore, start with the vehicle which will be chosen to carry the message. Here the single most important factor is the size of the budget. At one extreme, if you have a small budget you may be restricted to appearing in a range of very specialist media (possibly just in the small ads). At the other end of the scale, with a multi-million dollar budget, only television may be big enough to absorb it.

T Rule T30 – *The Media Ramp*

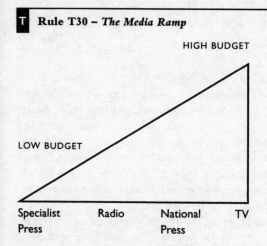

This basic cost equation may be moderated by the choice of advertising pattern.

◉ Rule O47 – *Advertising Bursts*

Most advertising is in practice concentrated into bursts, where it achieves the higher impact needed to overcome the customer's inertia, rather than being shown continuously.

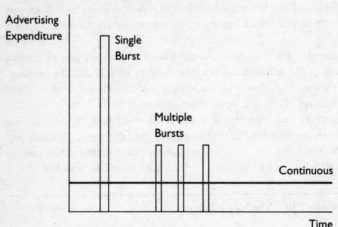

Even the heaviest advertisers use this approach, since the impact also depends upon the coverage relative to competitors; if your competitor's (current) exposure outweighs your own you may be in danger of losing the (current) competitive battle for the customers' hearts and minds. The optimal pattern therefore becomes a matter of sophisticated judgement – how many bursts are needed to retain the same impact as continuous advertising (that is, the trend under the saw is relatively flat, and there certainly is no hysteresis effect) versus the necessary minimal impact to be achieved by each burst.

Within the limitations set by the budget there are two criteria by which the pattern of delivery is judged. The most basic of these is coverage. Some consumer goods are targeted upon almost the whole population. In this case the level of coverage is simply a question of what can be afforded. The cost of reaching the last few per cent of the population grows exponentially. It is convenient to think of it as a variant of the 80:20 Rule – though in this case it becomes quite simply the 80 per cent Rule. Anything over 80 per cent coverage of any market or segment rapidly becomes prohibitively expensive.

⬤ Rule O48 – *The 80% Coverage Limit*

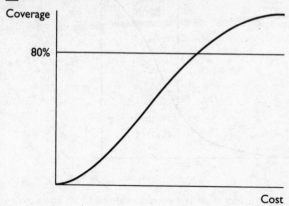

At the other extreme, the requirement for coverage of very specialized segments is selectiveness. There is simply no justification for coverage of those not in the target segment.

The other criterion is the degree of the individual's exposure to the campaign. It is generally agreed that the customers need to see any advertisement a number of times before it has any significant effect.

⬤ O49 – *5 OTS*

The usual rule of thumb is that 5 OTS (Opportunities To See) are needed to achieve adequate impact.

On the other hand there is a level beyond which saturation sets in and any further investment has no additional impact. The shape of the curve therefore is:

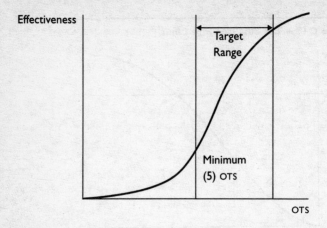

Perhaps the most useful chart is a combination of OTS and coverage, since this best demonstrates whether or not you are delivering your message to your chosen target audience with the optimal impact.

⊙ Rule O50 – *Sharpening the Cutting Edge of Media*

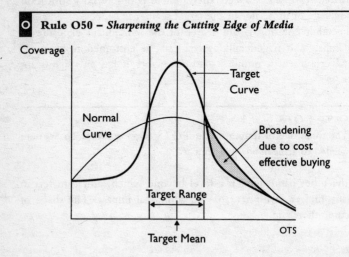

The ideal performance is represented here by the sharp peak, which closely matches coverage of your target audience to the optimal level of OTS. The reality is often closer to the much broader, diffuse curve, where large portions of the coverage receive inappropriate levels of OTS (either too low, which means that they are unlikely to recognize the message, or too high, where much of the exposure is wasted). Usually the best that can be hoped for is the more cost-effective curve, which is broader than the ideal but which takes advantage of the lower cost media and special deals to pull down the average cost per thousand while still using a core schedule which is quite tightly targeted.

To build the desired patterns a mix of specific media is often used. The broad performance of the main types along some key dimensions is shown below.

⬤ Rule O51 – *The Media Grid*

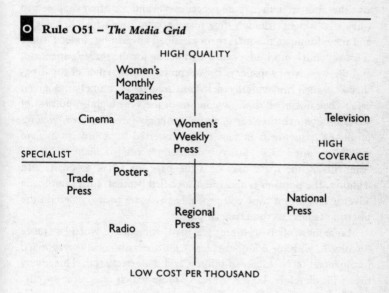

Advertising Media

In terms of overall advertising expenditures, media advertising is dominated by press and television, which are of comparable size (by value of 'sales'). Posters and radio follow some way behind, with cinema now representing a very specialist medium.

Spending in the press is dominated by the national and regional newspapers, with the latter taking almost all the classified advertising revenue. The magazine and trade/technical journal markets are about the same size as each other, but less than half that of the newspaper sectors. **National newspapers** are traditionally categorized, from the media buyer's viewpoint, on the basis of class, though this is of declining importance to many advertisers. They are obviously best matched to national advertisers who are happy with black and white advertisements (which can still carry quite detailed messages), although limited-quality run-of-the-paper colour is now available, and high-quality colour is available in some supplements. **Regional newspapers** may be dailies, which look and perform much like the nationals, or weeklies, but are rather more specialized – and are often supposed to carry less 'weight' (though they may be kept longer for reference) – and they dominate the market for classified advertising. Indeed, there is usually much more advertising competing for the reader's attention, and the weekly newspaper is fast becoming the province of the 'free-sheets', which are typically delivered free to all homes in a given area. They obtain all their revenue from the very high proportion of advertising which they carry, and accordingly have the least 'weight' of all. Advertisements in newspapers, referred to as 'insertions', are usually specified as so many centimetres across so many columns. Alternatively the space may be a full page, or a half or quarter. In addition, the position is also often specified, so that, for example, an advertiser of a unit trust will probably pay extra to make certain the insertion is next to the financial pages.

Magazines offer a more selective audience (which is more 'involved', with the editorial at least) and are traditionally categorized into general interest, special interest and trade/technical. The advertiser will, therefore, be able to select those which match the specific profile demanded by the advertising strategy. The audience is usually concentrated, containing only those with that specialist interest. The weight, or 'authority', of these specialist magazines is correspondingly high, and they may be kept for a considerable time for use as reference – as well as being passed to other readers (so that 'readership' figures may be much higher than 'circulation' figures). They can offer excellent colour, but the clutter of many competing advertisements may make the advertiser's message less impactful. In the trade and professional fields there are now a significant number of 'controlled circulation' magazines. These are like the 'free-sheets', in that they are delivered free to the recipients; but, at least in theory, those recipients should have been carefully screened to ensure that they are of value to the advertisers, and the circulation can, if properly controlled, represent a wide cross-section of the buyers, and influencers, in the advertiser's target audience. As with newspapers, the insertions are normally placed as full page, half page etc. The rates for positioning are usually more varied, with premiums paid for facing editorial matter (rather than buried in a mass of other advertisements) and, of course, for colour.

Television is the most important mass medium, albeit a rather transitory one. It is normally the most expensive medium, and as such is generally only open to the major advertisers (though some regional contractors offer more affordable packages to their local advertisers). It offers by far the widest coverage, particularly in the peak hours (roughly 7.00–10.30 p.m.), and especially of family audiences. Offering sight, sound, movement and colour, it has the greatest impact, especially for those products or services where a 'demonstration' is essential; it combines the virtues of both the 'story-teller' and the 'demonstrator'. To be effective, however, these messages must be kept simple – and have the impact to overcome the surrounding distractions of family life. The medium is generally unselective in its audiences, and offers relatively poor coverage of the upper-class and younger age groups, but as it is regionally based it can be used for regional trials or promotions (including test markets). The price structures can be horrendously complicated, with the 'rate card' (the price list) offering different prices for different times throughout the day, and this is further complicated by a wide range of special promotional packages, and individual negotiations! It is truly the province of the specialist media buyer. Satellite television is now supposed to be the medium of the future. Cable television was similarly supposed to represent the future a decade ago. This promise has been largely fulfilled in the US, where the average household can now tune into more than 30 channels. It has yet, though, to achieve comparable levels of penetration in other countries. In any case, it will still require much the same media buying, as well as creative rules, as the more earthbound channels.

Posters represent something of a specialist medium, and are generally used in support of campaigns using other media.

The use of **radio** has increased greatly in recent years, with the granting of many more licenses. It generates specific audiences at different times of the day: for example, adults at breakfast, housewives thereafter, with motorists in the rush hours. It can be a very cost-effective way of reaching these audiences (especially as production costs, too, can be much cheaper), though the types of message conveyed will be limited by the lack of any visual elements, and may have a 'light-weight' image.

Although the numbers in the national **cinema** audience are now small, this may be the most effective medium for extending coverage to the younger age groups – since the core audience is aged 15–24.

Finding out exactly who is the audience for a particular newspaper, or who watches at a given time on television, is a specialized form of market research – which is usually conducted on behalf of the media owners. The press figures are slightly complicated by the fact that there are two measures. There is that of readership, which represents the total number of readers of a publication, no matter where they read it (even in the doctor's waiting room). This is obtained from market research. There is also circulation, which is the number of copies sold (which is mostly independently validated), each of which may, of course, be read by a number of readers – typically around three per copy for a newspaper, but in excess of six per copy for some magazines. One particularly good measure of the effectiveness of press advertising, along with that of direct mail, can be implemented where the purpose of the advertising is to elicit a direct response, typically in terms of motivating the reader to ask for further information through a 'coupon' included in the advertisement or mailed material. Each such advertisement or mailing can then be given a code as part of the mailing address. The response obtained from each of the publications (or each of the mail packages) can then be measured accurately, at least in terms of the percentage coupon response rate. This, of course, may not be an appropriate measure if what is primarily being attempted is a shift in attitudes.

A more specialized form of testing is that relating to the content of the advertisement itself. This may take place at three stages: preliminary – where parts of the advertising (including 'concepts') are tested before being incorporated in the finished advertisement; pre-testing – where the finished advertisement is tested in its entirety (usually against its predecessor and/or its competitors) to ensure that it meets the objectives set by the advertising strategy; post-testing – the actual consumer results, researched after exposure to the advertising.

Media buying is a very sophisticated process, best left to the experts. It is to be expected that the final schedule will not look much like the planned one, since the deals which the media buyers obtain during their negotiations with the media owners usually distort the pattern in order to gain the best possible cost per thousand across the target audience.

○ **Rule O52 –** *Media Impact = Size × Position × Medium*

Impact is also an important element in the media selection equation. The reader or viewer does not react to all advertisements (even conveying the same message) equally. In part this may be as a result of the creative treatment, but it is also a function of the medium.

In terms of size, a full-page advertisement or a two-minute commercial may be more expensive (and increase the cost per thousand) but it may also have significantly greater impact. Research has shown that a full page may get 85 per cent more readership than a half page, and colour can generate 50 per cent more readership than black and white.[4]

In part it may be a function of the position within the medium. An insertion facing the contents page at the front of a Sunday colour supplement will be more effective than one buried in the mass of advertisements; though those at the back may receive 65 per cent greater readership than those at the front.[5] A commercial run during a prestige programme will have more impact than one during an early evening soap.

As we have seen, the medium itself may contribute to the impact. This may relate to the specific product; a luxury food product may have more relevant impact in an up-market woman's magazine than in the national press. But the medium may also carry some inherent impact. Thus, it has long been a saying in agencies that 'we carefully evaluate the best, most cost effective, media plan and then choose television anyway!' For those campaigns which can afford it, television normally has the highest impact.

When it comes to the stage of deciding exactly what **message** this vehicle is to carry the picture is much less clear. This is where the creative departments of advertising agencies earn their keep – and it is almost impossible to suggest any generally meaningful guidelines in

---

4. Daniel Starch, *Measuring Advertising Readership and Results* (McGraw Hill, 1966).
5. *Ibid.*

this area. Perhaps the best advice of all is KISS (Keep It Simple Stupid). This another way of saying 'less is more', a philosophy I have already referred to a number of times. It is especially relevant, however, in the case of advertising (or any other form of promotion). The simpler the message the greater the impact it will make and the greater the attention it will receive.

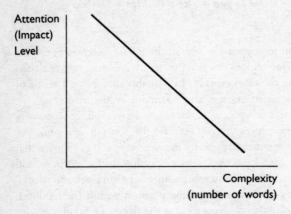

This is best tracked (by marketing research) in terms of 'spontaneous awareness' of the advertising. In practice the pattern is not the simple line shown above, but is the one indicated below:

○ Rule O53 – *True KISS*

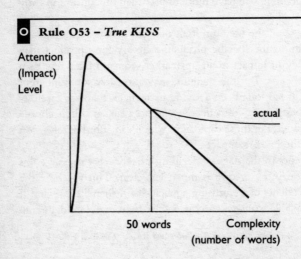

Where the line first rises from the origin it represents the impact of *very* few words. It simply indicates that when you remove almost any trace of message the advertisement will not even be read let alone convey any useful information – it becomes mere graffiti.

That departing from the straight line at 50 words is rather more significant. It reflects the observation[6] that up to 50 words or so impact progressively decreases at a quite rapid rate, but above this limit the fall-off becomes much slower.

The opposite is true of the information content of each message. This grows linearly with the number of words, not saturating (in the context of the promotional role) until 1,000 words or so. It should be noted, too, that there is an assumption that all the words used do in fact convey information. All too often communications are blurred by superfluous words, both detracting from the working limits and also confusing the genuine messages.

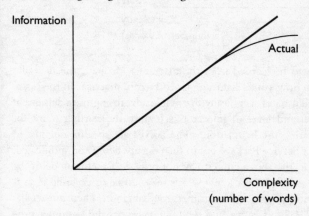

If we impose this actual curve on the earlier one and combine the two (by multiplication rather than addition) we get the picture below, showing the compound outcome, which we describe as 'appreciation'. In general, but with many exceptions, this may be highest at the extremes of short and long advertisements. This is a measure of what information has been transmitted to the average customer. It is best tracked by prompted recall.

6. David Ogilvy, *Confessions of an Advertising Man* (Atheneum, 1964).

⚪ Rule O54 – *Genuine Appreciation*

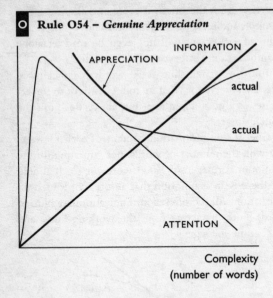

Complexity
(number of words)

The lesson to be learned from the diagram is, in part, the necessity for tracking how your advertising is working in practice. In the main, though, it illustrates graphically that while advertising must achieve at least a threshold level of impact this is only the starting point for communicating the brand story. The curves are specific not just to the Product:Service Package but to the concept being communicated. In particular, the above curves may not provide a useful model if the concept is so simple that a few words may suffice to describe it, as is the case with quite a few consumer goods brands. Then impact has to be all. The limit varies, and typically grows, as the customer progresses through the 'campaign' (essentially following the AIUAPR process).

⬤ Rule O55 – *Practical KISS*

Thus the headline, which is primarily intended to contribute to the impact, will usually be very short, and followed by more lengthy body copy which explains the product (and creates the attitude changes necessary for the first trial purchase). Then, depending upon the product, the label copy may be longer still and the instructions – if provided – even longer (though few suppliers realize the promotional potential of such instructions – especially when they may be used to turn the purchaser into a peer reference for other prospective purchasers).

Finally, it is worth noting that, as (direct) database marketing grows in importance, the message will be increasingly tailored (and be variable in content) to match the needs of the *individual* customer.

9 / *Conviction Marketing*

As we have seen earlier, the objective of your message determines not just its content but the medium which conveys it. Most important, of course, is the message itself – how well it relates to the existing positioning and how well it achieves the planned repositioning.

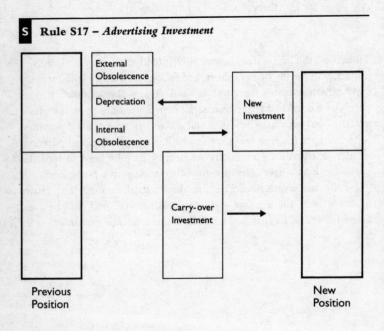

Investment in Advertising

Over time there is a general decline in the investment in brand position, as evidenced by the Long-term Competitive Saw, for instance, and as 'measured' by the current 'appreciation level'. In the chart above this stems from two main sources. 'Depreciation' simply represents the attrition which the brand suffers as customers' attention is distracted by all the other stimuli which inundate them. It also reflects the drift away from optimal positioning, as tastes change over time. The second, 'external obsolescence', reflects the attrition caused by the activities of competitors. Their promotions will reshape the market, so that your own brand's positioning again drifts away from the optimum.

The chart shows one further element, 'internal obsolescence'. This is a polite description for the self-inflicted wounds, often caused by overly anxious creative departments, where the brand positioning is actively moved away from the optimum position by new advertising! It reflects the work which, as we saw earlier, needs to be carried out before a combative advertising campaign can even start to work.

Opinion Leaders

So far we have looked at the message, and the campaign overall, in isolation, as if there were no influence on the customer beyond what he or she is exposed to in the media. But it is often argued that, especially in the case of a new product, the effects of promotion are seen in two stages. The promotion itself (usually advertising) persuades the more adventurous opinion leaders in the population to try the product or service. These opinion leaders then carry the message to those who are less exposed to it. This is not the same as the trickle-down theory, much favoured in certain parts of the social sciences, which assumes that patterns of consumption are led by the upper classes and then 'trickle down' to the lower classes. It is important to note that 'opinion leaders', on the contrary, influence members of their own class – horizontally in terms of class groupings.

As a result, it is clear that the impact of media advertising may be much more complex than many of its practitioners allow for. Thus, a more generalized aspect of communications within the community as a whole is word of mouth. Much of advertising theory concentrates upon the 'direct' receipt of these 'indirect' communications; it assumes that the consumer receives the message directly from the media, and only from the media. In practice, as we have seen, the message may well be received by word of mouth from a contact (who may have seen the advertising or may, in turn, have received it from someone else). Equally, even if the consumer had previously seen the advertising, word of mouth comments may reinforce (or undermine) what this has achieved directly.

Cognitive Dissonance

One unexpected but not wholly unrelated feature of 'audience behaviour' was that reported by Leon Festinger.[1]

⊙ Rule O56 – *Cognitive Dissonance*
Interest in all forms of promotion, particularly advertising, reaches its maximum after the consumer has made his or her purchase.

The usual explanation for this apparently illogical behaviour is that the consumer is then searching for the proof which will justify his or her recent decision. In looking at the competitive advertising, for example, the consumer is seeking out its flaws in comparison with the chosen product or service, in order to obtain reassurance that the decision was the correct one.

The importance from the advertiser's point of view is that advertising still has a job to do even after the sale has been made! In addition, the messages needed to address cognitive dissonance may be subtly different. Here they are needed to provide reassurance and should take account of the fact that these purchasers will also represent the main source of future sales, as well as serving as peer group references.

Indeed, there is in general one dimension of advertising which is often forgotten – that of:

---

1. L. A. Festinger, *A Theory of Cognitive Dissonance* (Row, Peterson & Co., 1957).

T **Rule T31 –** *Advertising Believability*

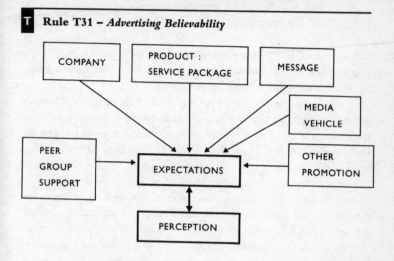

The inputs to the believability equation are many and, as can be seen from the diagram, often lie outside the advertising itself, so that the whole process becomes complex and difficult to manage. These outside factors often place quite constricting limitations on what may reasonably be said within the advertisement itself.

T **Rule T32 –** *Satisfaction Equals Perception Minus Expectation*
If you EXPECT a certain level of service and PERCEIVE the service received to be higher, you will be a satisfied customer. If you perceive this same level where you had expected a higher one, you will be disappointed and therefore a dissatisfied customer.[2]

The most important element here is how that pre-purchase belief (expectation) is in practice satisfied by the actual offering – a highly believable message may cause serious problems when the Product: Service Package fails to live up to it. The point is that both what is perceived and what is expected are psychological phenomena – not reality,[3] and it is the relative level which is important, not the absolute one.

2. David H. Maister, 'The Psychology of Waiting Lines' in *Managing Services: Marketing, Operations and Human Resources* (Prentice-Hall, 1988).
3. *Ibid.*

Push/Pull Promotion

Where a supplier uses any form of distribution chain, as most of those in the mass consumer markets do, he or she is faced with two extremes in terms of promotion: push or pull.

In the case of push the supplier directs the bulk of the promotional effort at selling the 'product' into the channel (into the various organizations which make up the chain of distribution) in order to persuade the members of that channel to 'push' the product forward until it reaches the final consumer. This aspect tends to revolve around sales promotion and is sometimes referred to as 'below the line' (derived from the days when advertising agencies managed all promotional activity, and the items on the accounts which did not relate to advertising were put below the line which divided off the agency's main activity on the expenditure reports). This is a technique particularly favoured by organizations without strong brands who are involved in price competition.

In the case of pull the supplier focuses the promotional effort (typically advertising) on the consumer, in the belief that he or she will be motivated to 'pull' the product through the channel (by demanding it, for example, from retailers). It is (due to its association with advertising) sometimes referred to as 'above the line'. This is the technique usually favoured by the owners of strong, differentiated brands.

T   **Rule T33 – *The Distribution Tube***

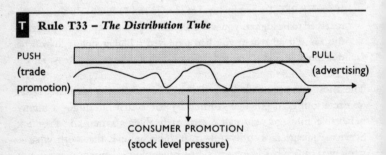

PUSH
(trade
promotion)

PULL
(advertising)

CONSUMER PROMOTION
(stock level pressure)

In practice, most suppliers choose a route somewhere between these two extremes, blending both elements to obtain the optimum (balanced) effect. In any case, brand share is often dependent upon the percentage distribution and, in turn, distribution just as often reflects brand share.

> **O** **Rule O57 –** *The Distribution Multiplier*
> If you can lever up either brand share or distribution then BOTH may rise.

Conviction Marketing

Conviction marketing, sometimes called 'commitment marketing', is in many respects alien to most of the traditional marketing concepts. It has a long and chequered history. The propaganda machine developed by the Nazis offered some of the most potent, and widely deplored, demonstrations of its power (and this represents one possible reason why discussion of this style of marketing is even now generally avoided). The religious 'marketing machines' had been even more effective in earlier generations (and can even now be very powerful, as evidenced by Islamic fundamentalism). In the commercial sector, though, its use has sometimes been just as powerful – and very productive! Indeed, the majority of the few truly global brands have embodied it to some degree: IBM, with its philosophy of 'customer service'; McDonalds, with Q. S. C. & V. (Quality, Service, Cleanliness & Value); Coca-Cola, with its embodiment of the American teenage dream; Marlboro, and the wide open spaces of the frontier!

It is different to 'selling', in that its focus is very firmly on the consumer, as all marketing is supposed to be, whereas the focus of 'selling' is internal (the customer is to be persuaded to take what the organization has to offer). On the other hand, conviction marketing's focus is still one-sided. There is little or no attempt to use market research to find out what the consumers need or want, though research is sometimes used to justify the organization's existing prejudices, and is frequently used, to great effect, to optimize the presentation of its chosen message.

The power-house of such conviction marketing is the powerful idea (the 'conviction' to which the organization has made its 'commitment'), to which the organization believes the consumers are also committed. Despite the focus on the consumer, and frequent reference to the importance of that consumer, the real organizational commitment is to the overarching idea (or set of ideas, often a 'lifestyle'). The essence and the strength of such 'conviction marketing' is the power it gives to the marketing organization. In this respect, religious as well as political parallels are often more relevant than those of conventional marketing theory.

S **Rule S18 – *Conviction Marketing***
The power of the campaign(s) is dependent upon the power of the idea(s) behind it.

In turn this power derives from a number of factors.

T **Rule T34 – *The Powers of Conviction***

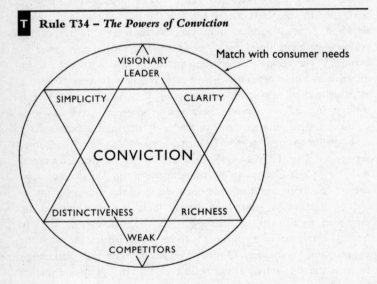

First, the concept being marketed must be distinctive. Successful conviction marketing is not the province of the marketer who is dedicated to pallid incrementalism. It has to be readily identifiable, as Coca-Cola was – in terms of the very powerful image created by the unique slope of the bottle. Beyond that, it has to be based on an identity, a brand personality. The beneficiaries of conviction marketing are typically not products where the technical features are predominant. Coca-

Cola and Marlboro are a matter of personal taste, but it is the images associated with them, their brand personae, which add the necessary richness to the relatively mundane. Even in the case of IBM it was the marketing and support (rather than the very complex technology) which were its outstanding feature.

As well as the richness of the concept it has to be instantly communicable, clear and simple. It has to be conveyed by simple messages, such as the shape of the bottle (or now the graphics on the can) of Coca-Cola, or the cowboy and Marlboro. If the product is complex, and none could be more complex than that of IBM, it has to be enshrined in an associated philosophy – 'Customer Service' (personified by the field personnel in the now rather outdated, but very necessary, dark suits and white shirts). It is frequently associated with a distinctive form of quality – McDonalds' 'Hamburger University', for example.

Conviction marketing is, above all, dependent upon the consumer's belief in what the communicators say. Even if unrelated to the basic needs, the 'vision' of the 'product' (of its identity) has to be conveyed to the target audience. They, in turn, have to enter into a 'belief' in the 'product' before they can fully appreciate it. This means that the message being communicated has to be believed; and that in turn means that the communicators themselves need to be believed. In some cases the 'communicators' can be those of conventional marketing: the Marlboro cowboy in the advertising, or the bright clean image of McDonalds' outlets. But behind them there is often a human face. In IBM it was the sales force, immensely capable and imbued with (many would argue indoctrinated in) the IBM culture. But, above all, it usually requires a strong (and almost obsessively dedicated) human personality at the centre to make the vision work: the Watsons at IBM and Ray Kroc at McDonalds developed very rich cultures which were aimed more at their own employees (the 'communicators' the public see) than at their markets.

There is one element of conviction marketing which is beyond the control of the organization itself, and that is what its competitors choose to do. Almost by definition, a 'conviction marketed' brand will develop a new segment of the market. Its unique identity will, at least for a time, give it a monopoly there. Eventually, though, competitors will recognize the success of the brand and will want some of the action.

> **◉ Rule O58 – *Separation by Conviction***
> Competitors can be mesmerized into accepting convincing brand dominance.

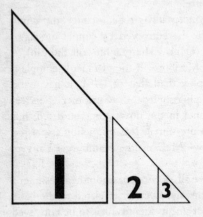

It is a peculiarity of conviction marketing that the almost hypnotic effect of the message also seems to infect competitors. They usually attempt, with only marginal success, to copy the original. Inevitably, the copies turn out to be pale imitations of the original: Burger King could not match the evangelical dedication to standards of McDonalds; Pepsi, for many decades, had to follow Coca-Cola. The competitors usually have to wait, therefore, for the leader to make a mistake, or for the market to change: Pepsi was eventually rewarded when the market did change, and Coca-Cola made a very public mistake with its change in recipe! Compaq similarly capitalized on both the changes in the PC market and IBM's uncharacteristically unsure handling of its own responses.

Although customer needs are at the heart of conventional marketing, they are only an enabling factor in the case of conviction marketing. If the 'vision' is too far removed from the consumer's view of reality, it will not be accepted. Even so, Clive Sinclair's C5 electric/pedal-power car (derisively called the 'electric clog') was initially accepted with praise by the media, based on his own charismatic image and obvious commitment to it. It took nearly three months for commentators to admit that the idea was in reality laughable.

This realization probably brought down the remainder of his business empire (which was unconnected to the C5, and more soundly based). There have been other spectacular mismatches to reality: IBM's PC Junior, Ford's Edsel. These are, however, the recorded exceptions, for most mismatches fail at the 'new product' stage and disappear with the 90 per cent of such new products which do not achieve acceptance.

Conviction marketed products can be broadly divided into two groups:
- product based
- value based.

The former are products, or services – frequently in the high technology field – whose creator has a blinding faith in what product or service features are needed. Steve Jobs at Apple believed in the special technology of his products (even after IBM set new standards and John Sculley had to be recruited from Pepsi to inject more conventional marketing expertise); Alan Sugar believed in his personal ability to put together low-priced electronics packages. The problem with conviction marketed products in this category is that they can be very rapidly overtaken by changes in the market. Typically, new technology supersedes them (as the Commodore Pet, one of the original PCs, was displaced from the business market by Apple, which in turn was superseded as brand leader by IBM), or tastes change (as Woolworth found out as its traditional place on the high street was undermined).

⊙ Rule O59 – *Conviction Value*

The strongest 'conviction marketed' brands are those in very general markets where the distinctiveness comes from the image; from the intangible VALUES associated with the brand.

These value-based brands are usually much more capable of change, since the identity is not usually locked into 'physical' features. The customers (and the organization's own employees) can easily accept the new features needed to accommodate developments in technology and taste. IBM's 'Customer Service' carried it through decades of revolutionary change. Disneyland is constantly absorbing new rides – but still keeping them immaculately clean! Even McDonalds, which should perhaps be one of the most product-based of retailers, is in reality based on conviction marketing of values: Q. S. C. & V. It has managed to change what it serves (adding a breakfast menu and lines based on chicken and fish, as well as pizza) and how it serves (increasing the size of its 'sit down' sections, so that it has become a restaurant rather than just a take-away outlet).

The challenge for less charismatic marketers, committed to the wisdom of the 'outside-in' viewpoint, is to understand to what extent the success of 'conviction marketing' undermines traditional marketing theory. This is a question mark which hung over much of marketing theory through the 1980s and, in particular, drove practitioners and academics alike to look for alternative approaches – such as competitive advantage. The reality is that most products and services (at least in terms of numbers of lines, if not of value of sales) are managed without reference to the principles of marketing, and have been throughout history. The difference is that 'conviction marketers' have very successfully extended this common 'inside-out' approach by adopting some of the tools of marketing. Indeed, the conviction marketers probably make greater use of marketing tools (albeit to somewhat perverted ends) than do many of those who would pay lip-service to traditional marketing. Philip Morris, which owns the Marlboro cigarette brand, also owns the Miller Brewing Company of Milwaukee. In applying the same sort of charismatic (and 'macho') image to 'Miller High Life' they used extensive market research to fine-tune the positioning. More important, the company continued to be aware of the demands of its market-place, and subsequently launched the highly successful Miller-Lite (low calorie beer) as a 'less filling' beer which fitted this image.

At the end of the day, the basic justification for conventional marketing, in the absence of the blinding (and hopefully viable) vision of the conviction marketer, is simply that it is generally the most successful approach to product or service management. Giving the customer what he or she wants rarely fails!

As already stated, what often makes the task easier for conviction marketers is that their competitors seem even more mesmerized than their customers. Many organizations are 'dedicated followers'; they always look to their competitors to take the lead. Their adherence to this creed goes beyond that required of 'followers', the subsidiary brands in a market which are simply not in any position to set the pace. It goes beyond the IBM approach of 'constructive following', where that organization (in its days of market dominance) deliberately let other smaller organizations explore (and take the risks inherent in) new developments, only to recapture the initiative (by deploying the vast resources at its command) when the markets proved viable. This strategy usually proves successful (at the risk of losing leadership, as IBM eventually found out). 'Dedicated followers' assume that the market leader always knows best. So that even IBM's mistakes were assumed to have some ultimate value and these too were copied! 'Dedicated followers' are organizations which, in effect, sub-contract their policy making to their competitors. As such, they deserve to, and usually do, pay the ultimate price for this!

The main problem facing conviction marketers is that the necessary strength of their commitment may blind them to the realities facing them and their customers. It is difficult enough for any marketer to adopt the unbiased perspective essential to understanding the customer's needs and wants. It may be impossible for a conviction marketer, whose vision may be so powerful that it precludes any doubts about the product. The Concorde airliner development team were convinced of the market for their 'baby', and their market research supported that view. It was only the market which disagreed. Even IBM fell foul of this problem, in the case of its personal computers, when its immensely strong corporate vision got in the way of any meaningful recognition of the scale of the problem posed by its wayward dealers.

Catastrophe theory is derived from science and technology but it may be very applicable to conviction marketing. In a very simplified form it states that some systems can be 'over-stressed', so that they will support loads beyond the point at which other systems would obviously start to deteriorate. When they pass the point of no return, however, their performance degrades (they fail) suddenly and catastrophically. This compares with most other systems, where the fail point may be reached much more quickly but the subsequent degradation in performance is much more gradual and, hence, predictable and controllable (even allowing for the possibility of recovery).

⬤ Rule O60 – *Conviction Catastrophe*

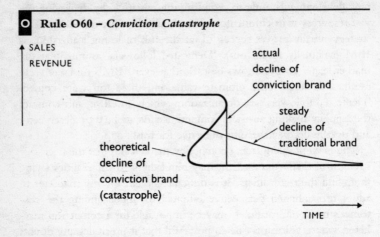

Above, the thinner line illustrates the decline of a traditional brand. Following (unspecified) changed circumstances, the position (relative to the brand share of the brand leader) declines gently until it reaches its new, lower equilibrium. This gentle change allows the brand owner to adjust the business to these new circumstances, and may even allow the brand to be restored to its original leadership position. On the other hand, the thicker line shows the path followed by the conviction marketed brand. This is maintained at the higher level far beyond the point where a traditional brand would have been well into decline, allowing a greater recovery of funds (and possibly even allowing it to override a short-lived challenge). When the line does begin to dip, it does so very steeply indeed. The problem this poses for the brand owner is the suddenness of the change. There is no time for adjustments to be made, and certainly none to allow any recovery plan to work – and the business as a whole may be destroyed by the shock.

This phenomenon is characteristic of conviction marketing. The conviction marketer often goes further than the steady state shown above, and persuades the customers (and the competitors) to defy the laws of 'marketing gravity' and slowly pushes them uphill! Often this is a process of incrementalism, making many gradual changes which are not noticed individually by the customers. As a result the marketers appear to achieve market positions, often of dominance, which are apparently unassailable. IBM achieved this feat in some respects before the introduction of the PC brought about the start of its own catastrophe phase. 'Salami Slicing' (gradual reduction) of quality is another way of producing high profits in the short (and even medium) term, but contains the seeds of its own catastrophic demise.

Coarse Marketing

A final comment before I finish this chapter. Marketing was not developed, nor dramatically advanced, in the laboratories of its academic theorists. It was the outcome of the practical explorations by practitioners, gradually probing the frontiers of what could be achieved by their activities. The academics usually came later and served a very valuable function by documenting, in a form which could be transferred to other managers, what had been learned by this practice. The marketer, in real life, does not face each decision with a copy of a text-book in his or her hand. The marketer starts with a quite specific environment with a limited range of options to be explored. The position will be further constrained by the resources available to deal with them. For instance, theory always says that the first step is marketing research, but if your competitor has just made a major change in strategy you may have just days to react – where research may take months.

S **Rule S19 –** *Coarse Marketing*

Real-life marketing revolves around the application of a great deal of common sense, to handle a limited number of factors based on imperfect information and limited resources (complicated by uncertainty and tight timescales).

Use of marketing techniques, in these circumstances, is inevitably partial and uneven.

Thus, for example, new products will emerge from irrational processes, and the rational development process may be used to screen out the worst non-runners. The design of the advertising, and the packaging, will be the output of the creative minds employed, which management will screen, often by 'gut-reaction', to ensure that it is reasonable.

O Rule O61 – *Gut Reaction*

The most successful marketer is often the one who trains his or her 'gut reaction' to simulate that of the average customer!

For most of the time, the marketing manager is likely to be using his or her considerable intelligence to analyse and handle the complex, and unique, situations being faced – without easy reference to theory. This will often be 'flying by the seat of the pants', or 'gut reaction', where the overall strategy, coupled with the knowledge of the customer which has been absorbed almost by a process of osmosis, will determine the quality of the marketing employed.

This almost instinctive management is what I would call 'coarse marketing' to distinguish it from the refined, aesthetically pleasing form favoured by the theorists. It is often relatively crude and would, if given in answer to a business school examination, be judged a failure of marketing. Nevertheless, this is the real-life world of most marketing!

10 / Public Relations

We will now move on to look at some of the other forms of promotion. Of these the first and often the most neglected is that of PR. This encompasses public relations, which may include a wide range of activities, and press relations, which concentrates on the more direct promotional aspects. It can be a very effective (and very inexpensive) part of the marketing mix, but it is one that many organizations neglect. Often the money spent on PR can be many times more productive than that spent on other types of promotion (including advertising). This is just as true of a small company (which may find such PR the most effective vehicle for promoting its products, where it simply cannot afford large budgets).

Press Relations

PR (in the narrower context of press relations) is a particularly valuable promotional device for services since the 'authority' of independent recommendations in the media can add vital credibility to an intangible service. It is also an easy device for non-profit-making organizations to use: the Open University, for example, has little need to advertise, for it is still a very legitimate topic for editorial comment.

There is a wide range of vehicles available for press relations, including:
- Media contact
- News stories
- Media events
- Press office.

One of the most important tasks of the PR professional is to maintain **contact with the key journalists** in the relevant media (usually national press, journals, radio and television). This is a two-way process, which should be the province of experts (often from an outside agency). The PR professional learns about, and can contribute to,

features which will be appearing in the media; on the other side of
the fence, the journalists become more receptive to news stories from
the PR professional. Again it is an 'investment' process. The relationship with the media (and especially with individual journalists) has to
be cultivated until a valuable mutual trust has been established.

T   Rule T35 – *The PR Ramp*

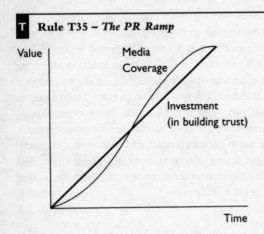

It is significant that a US survey (carried out by Sheila Tate, press
secretary to Mrs Nancy Reagan, as reported by Roger Haywood)
revealed that more than 90 per cent of journalists rated candour as
the key quality they required in an executive responsible for public
relations; and the same percentage said they were more likely to deal
with PR people they knew personally.

The backbone of PR is the **news item**, either genuine or 'manufac-
tured', which shows the client product or service in a good light (and,
most important, is interesting and entertaining enough to be run by
the news media). Such stories are best placed, as described above, by
personal contact.

O Rule O62
You get the PR coverage the story is worth.

Consequently you need the professional (journalistic) experience to recognize just what is a newsworthy story, and then to be able to present it in a way that interests a (very cynical) press corps. Public relations handbooks tend to stress that you must have good writing skills to deliver such stories but that is only the starting point. PR is like any other form of marketing. You must know the customers (in this case the journalists) and provide (sell) the right 'product' (the story they want). The personal touch helps. The same US survey quoted above showed that most press releases were read by journalists (who were even happy to be reminded, by telephone, of press events). Journalists need sources for their stories, just so long as they are worthwhile. This is tempered by a UK survey which showed that press releases achieved only a 22 per cent rating as a 'source of information most useful to your work as an editor' compared with 86 per cent for articles in other newspapers.

One device often used is a **media event**, such as the launch of a new product. Unfortunately, despite the journalists' reputation for being able to smell a free drink from more than a block away, this ploy rarely works unless the groundwork has already been done and the personal contacts with the media well and truly established. Once again the material will get the coverage that it deserves – if it has been presented and explained in a way that attracts the attention of journalists. The US survey showed, though, that two-thirds of journalists believed that news conferences were abused as a communications technique. It seems that discreet use of bona-fide executives from the organization may pay better dividends. The UK survey rated interviews with 'company officials' at 58 per cent compared with 19 per cent for 'company public and/or press relations officers' and a mere 14 per cent for 'public relations agencies' (and, surprisingly perhaps, only 22 per cent for trade or industry associations). The diagram below illustrates the importance of using (correctly trained and prepared) senior executives as the 'front-line' troops.

⭕ **Rule O63** – *Executive PR*

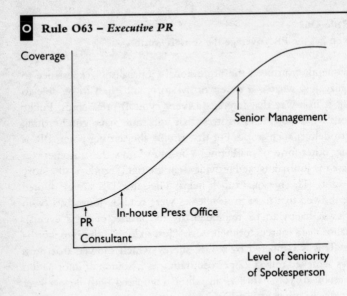

It is just as important that you are able to react to press enquiries. A continuously manned **press office**, which can handle any level of question from journalists, and is almost effusively enthusiastic to help, is essential if PR is to be taken seriously. Again, professionalism is essential: you must find answers quickly, to meet the deadlines by which almost all journalists are driven.

PR is very cost-effective and the amount which can be spent on it is relatively low in comparison with the other promotional spends (it is also self-limiting as there are only so many events you can arrange, and so many journalists you can entertain). Thus, there is a good argument for saying that, in setting budgets, PR should come at the head of the queue. Only when you have obtained the maximum you can achieve from PR should you allocate the remaining funds to other promotional activities. Since you get what you pay for, it is also better to pay more for high-calibre personnel than waste the rest of the PR budget.

Corporate Relations

PR is often used as a global term to cover a wider range of activities. Of these perhaps the most important may be that of acting as the corporate interface with the outside world, usually the province of corporate PR personnel.

The organization will often be exposed to the activities of external pressure groups and the corporate PR department, if one exists, will typically be the one that 'defends' the organization against these onslaughts, and handles relations with such groups – though an important first line of defence, one which is often ignored in the heat of the moment, is simply that of actually remedying what these groups are attempting to rectify themselves!

How the organization then responds to such pressure, and responds to the bodies which wield influence (most often, via the media and public opinion), is most clearly the responsibility of the corporate PR function. Only the larger organizations use PR to positively influence external activities, such as those in the political arena, to their advantage, mainly because considerable resources may be needed. It requires special personnel, with expert skills and knowledge, and will usually (even in the case of larger companies) require the employment of an outside agency, for example one that specializes in lobbying politicians.

In many of these fields it will be top management who have, and build upon, the most important contacts, but the corporate PR function should co-ordinate and support these. It should be assumed, incidentally, that lobbying is best handled in-house (or by agencies employed directly). Some trade associations (particularly those of the professions and farming) are powerful lobbyists, but rather more are not, and even those that do often represent key members within the association, so that individual members may find their interests not represented (even opposed).

The first task of corporate PR is to determine what issues, relevant to the future of the organization, are likely to emerge over the next few years. As with 'scanning' the environment this is not an easy task. It can either be more directly based upon opinion research – though this may be expensive, particularly where it has to be carried out world-wide. Alternatively, it can be obtained by buying syndicated reports from the specialist consultancies (such as the Henley Centre for Forecasting or Stanford Research Institute, SRI). Such research is important, in that the effectiveness of PR decreases rapidly over time as an issue builds up. It is much more effective to 'nip it in the bud' before it develops:

T **Rule T36 – *Rule of 10s***

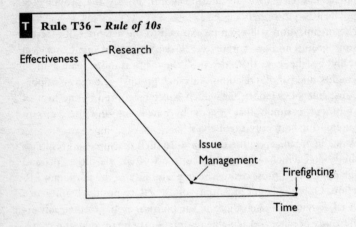

This is described as the **Rule of 10s**, since the amount of effort needed to rectify the situation increases by a factor of 10 at each stage. It is recommended that no more than 10–20 issues are 'managed' at any one time; more than this will simply cause confusion and spread effort too thinly. You can use rigorous methods to force these issues to emerge but the general view is that they emerge by 'osmosis' – based on discussions, over time, by the experts involved. Once identified, it is important to try and understand the issues and, in particular, to obtain political input on their perceived importance. It is also important to start lobbying (possibly on an international scale) as soon as possible.

Sales Promotion

Sales promotion is normally an adjunct to personal selling or advertising, usually of products, but some techniques can also be applied to services. It is very different to the promotional techniques which have been described so far, since it is generally a short-term activity which can justifiably be considered an operating cost rather than an investment. It is typically directed towards the sales force, distribution channels, or consumers, or some combination of these groups, in order to stimulate specific action in the short term.

In essence it should have a very short-term influence on sales, and may thus be used as a powerful tool added to the competitive balance to sway current sales in the supplier's favour as well as bringing forward sales, or even generating extra sales. Sales promotions can also be targeted to achieve specific objectives, for example, to increase repeat purchases or to recruit specific competitors' customers.

In most cases the effect is immediate; there is rarely any lasting increase in sales and many of the costs are not accounted for in the reported direct costs. At worst, one-off sales promotions can conflict with the main brand messages and present a confusing image to the customer. It is believed, for instance, that Burger King's promotional activities, in its war with McDonalds at the end of the 1970s, may have had an unfavourable influence on consumers' brand perceptions.

Perhaps the most obvious disadvantage, and this applies to many types of promotion, is that they offer a price-cut, in effect, and this persuades users to expect a lower price in future. At the same time, they may damage any element of 'quality' in the image.

Their greatest disadvantage, though, may be their lack of effectiveness. Abraham and Lodish[1] report that '. . . only 16% of the trade promotion events we studied were profitable, based on incremental sales of brands distributed through retailer warehouses. For many promotions the cost of selling an incremental dollar of sales was greater than one dollar.' They go on to record that, despite this, '. . . promotions have become so popular that they now account for more than 65% of typical marketing budgets'.

1. M. M. Abraham and L. M. Lodish, 'Getting the Most out of Advertising and Promotion', *Harvard Business Review*, May–June 1990.

T **Rule T37 – *Sales Promotions***

The regular use of sales promotions on a large scale must be questioned. As a general device for promoting brands they are expensive, ineffective and often damaging. The short-term sales increases are usually bought at the expense of the long-term investment in the brand and may eventually lead to its demise.

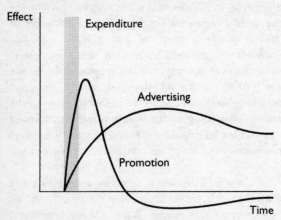

Accepting their essentially short-term nature, however, promotions may be used very effectively to achieve certain limited objectives, for example, some promotions are expressly planned to induce trial purchases; the classic example being 'money-off coupons' distributed house to house (or in the press), or even samples of the product, at the time of the launch (again delivered door to door or 'banded' as a free gift on a related product).

O **Rule O64 – *Sampling*** is generally thought to be the most powerful form of promotion for 'new products'.

The free sample is normally used as one of the very early elements in a new product launch, though Schultz and Robinson[2] say 'Sampling seems to work best for new products when it is preceded by four to six weeks of advertising. That generates interest which the sample then converts into trial.' It is a very expensive promotional device, but it is the most effective, direct and immediate way of obtaining consumer trial. Retailers also recognize its power to pull in customers, and accordingly it may also help to achieve distribution. It is often combined with a money-off voucher to ensure that a successful trial is rapidly followed by a purchase.

Other promotions are designed to stimulate the user's decision at point of sale: on-pack price-cuts are the obvious example. A cheaper alternative may be to offer more of the product ('free 20 per cent extra') for the same price. Yet others are meant to build repeat business, for example, 'money off next purchase' coupons. Most recently, retailers have used loyalty cards to very effectively stimulate repeat visits. Perhaps the greatest number, though, are intended only to have an indirect effect, to provide additional interest (to differentiate the product) for an advertising campaign (for example, free gifts such as drinking glasses with petrol), or to obtain better display at point of sale (for example, a competition, with the prize of a 'holiday in Hawaii', jointly run with a retailer), where it is the extra shelf space that sells the product, rather than the promotion itself.

It should be added that sales promotion and advertising (or, indeed, any of the other forms of promotion) are not mutually exclusive. In practice they are complementary, and the most effective, well-balanced campaign will often include a mix of several types of promotion (advertising and sales promotion tend to go hand in hand).

As sales promotions are almost always set up for their direct and immediate effect, it is possible and desirable to set specific performance objectives. Performance should be monitored to ensure that these objectives are attained, and as a basis for judging the usefulness of such promotions in the future.

2. D. E. Schultz and W. A. Robinson, *Sales Promotion Essentials* (Crain Books, 1982).

11 / Selling

Deploying your sales force is quite different to all other aspects of marketing. It is much more dependent upon relationships between individuals: between sales personnel and customers, and between sales management and their sales personnel, and it is the management of these relationships which should take priority.

Territory Management

To begin with you must decide how responsibilities are to be allocated within the sales team. The traditional breakdown is now by territory. Most territories are based on a geographical area, ranging from a whole country down to a single postal district. One advantage of such an approach is that the boundaries of such territories are relatively easy to define, and so not contentious.

 Rule O65
    Selling time costs far more than sales management think.

Sales activities are very expensive!

Most managers who have little practical experience of selling are surprised by how short a time is actually spent with the customer. The table below, which is derived from figures detailed in Malcolm McDonald's book,[1] shows a breakdown of a salesman's daily workload in one consumer goods company. It indicates that less than a third of his time was spent on the customer's premises and almost a quarter of this time was spent waiting for the customer to see him! McDonald's understandable conclusion is that it is important for salespeople to plan their time effectively.

1. Malcolm H. B. McDonald, *Marketing Plans*, 2nd edn. (Heinemann, 1989).

Breakdown of a salesman's daily workload

	Time spent %
Travel	43
General call-time	26
Actual selling	6
Administration	25

The traditional view of selling has been that it is a 'professional' role rather than a management one. In practice, though, a large part of the sales professional's role is actually concerned with management.

○ Rule O66 – *The Sales Professional's Management Responsibilities*

The sales professional is usually solely responsible for everything that happens on his or her territory, for all activities, with a range of responsibilities (albeit on a smaller scale) comparable with those of a brand manager, or even of the chief executive of a subsidiary. In addition, every sales professional will have, to a greater or lesser extent, some organizational resources at his or her command, including service support, marketing support and possibly even budgeted amounts of territory-based promotional funding. All of these resources will have to be managed in the same way that the rest of the organization's resources are managed by its team of managers.

It is conventionally assumed that sales professionals do not manage people and very few actually have formal responsibility for subordinates. Yet, many indirectly control the activities of support personnel, often under difficult circumstances, on customer premises, without any formal authority.

T **Rule T38 – *Customer Interface Management***

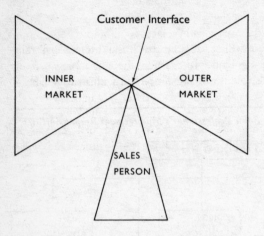

Above all, the sales professional manages that most important asset of any organization, the relationship with the customer. As we will see, this demands a great deal of skill, and it is a role which contains many of the key elements of management.

Customers and Prospects

The most important split between different sales activities is usually that between supporting – and developing – existing customers and recruiting new prospects.

S **Rule S20**
CUSTOMERS are almost universally more productive than **prospects**. All marginal prospects have to be treated as outcasts.

Existing customers are generally more productive than many sales professionals (or their management) allow for. What is more, assuming that an organization has previously offered good customer service, they are already tied to it and competitors will have to justify breaking these links before they can even begin their selling process.

Yet many, if not most, sales professionals devote disproportionately less time to existing customers. The model, discussed later in this chapter, persuades them to spend their time unproductively, touting for new business when they should be spending at least adequate time defending and growing their existing customer base.

So the first priority of any sales professional must be to allocate resources to the customer set, as well as differentiating between customers according to what they are worth. Some will be 'bankers' and will bring in a large part of the easy 80 per cent of business – and these investments must be cosseted. Some, on the other hand, will be totally unproductive, demanding resources for little return.

The sales team should know their customers well enough to be able to predict the sales performance of each. But the real skill comes in being able to separate out the sheep from the goats amongst the prospects. They need to decide which are the 10 per cent or so of prospects who will bring in 50+ per cent of the new business. This is partly a function of their size (in terms of potential business) and partly of their probability of closing. These are the prospects that should take first cut of the resources left after the planned support of customers.

No matter how much marginal prospects plead, the efficient sales force will have to be ruthless and refuse to fritter away resources in unproductive areas. The main danger is that they allocate some of their precious resources, only to find the prospects are happy for the sales professional to spend considerable time talking to them, indeed demanding this, but never really likely to buy (despite their loud promises). So the true sales professional must insist they prove their good intentions.

 Rule T39 – *Good Salesmanship* is as much about managing scarce resources – and walking away from losers – as it is about winning friends and influencing people.

T **Rule T40 –** *The Numbers Mountain*

The more contacts that are made the greater will be the business booked.

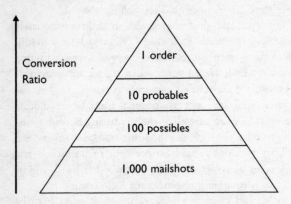

The basic building block of any sales campaign has to be its calls. Generally speaking, a number of calls are needed to get the business; this is often described in sales circles as the 'numbers game'. I prefer to call it the 'numbers mountain', for each level must rest firmly on the one below if you are to be able to climb to the peak. Thus, for every 1,000 mailshots there will be a certain percentage of returns which justify a sales professional calling personally. Telesales and cold calling will also generate proportional results. From these subsequent calls a proportion will turn into serious prospects (some of whom will progress to demonstrations and proposals). And out of these serious prospects a proportion will place orders, and a proportion (hopefully a good proportion) will place those orders with the organization undertaking these activities rather than with its competitors.

At each stage, therefore, there is a conversion ratio. It is clearly the sales professional's personal skills (backed by sound account management) that ensure that this conversion ratio is as high as it can be. Converting a good prospect into a customer requires all the skills a sales professional possesses, but it is a basic fact that providing the prospects in the first place is just sheer hard work. The more mailshots sent out, the more teleselling done and the more cold calls made, the greater the raw material for the conversion process. The eventual outcome is almost directly proportional to the numbers that are fed in.

Complex Sales

The professional salesperson is more likely to come into contact with the 'complex sale', where a number of individuals are involved in the buying decision, and the sales campaign extends over a number of calls. Miller, Heiman and Tuleja[2] have this to say:

> In a complex sale, you have short-term and long-term objectives. In the short term, you must close as many individual deals as you possibly can, and as quickly as possible. In the long term, you want to maintain healthy relations with the customers signing the deals, so they'll be willing to make further purchases in the months and years to come. It would be great if these two objectives always coincided, but you know that they don't.

In many ways this environment is very different to that of the single-call sale, which is the staple diet of many (if not most) sales trainers. The complex sale differs most markedly in the complexity introduced by the multiplicity of buyers involved. It is no longer sufficient to persuade just one buyer; the sales professionals have to convince a whole range of individuals, all with different (often contradictory) requirements! The first problem this poses is quite simply that of identifying the various buyers. The buyers involved in the complex sale can range from the chief executive down to members of the typing pool. The convention is to split these buyers into 'Decision-Makers' and 'Influencers', with the clear implication that the small group of 'Decision-Makers' should be the prime target, though 'Influencers' should not be neglected. This is a useful distinction in that it correctly focuses the sales professional's attention on the key decision-makers, and forces him or her to contact these; too many sales personnel never progress beyond the 'Influencers'.

Selling has traditionally been seen as a confrontational activity, with the salesperson hierarchically subservient to the buyer, trying to persuade the latter to buy something not wanted or needed. It is seen as a 'zero-sum game', where each of the participants can gain only at the expense of the other. This is at odds with the trust which is so

2. Robert B. Miller and Stephen E. Heiman *Strategic Selling* (Kogan Page, 1989).

important in building relationships with customers of all types. In recent years, it has been argued that the most productive relationship in such sales deals is based on the 'win–win' approach so that both sides start out with the intention of producing a mutually beneficial arrangement.[3] This concept is, as we saw earlier, encapsulated in my Win–Win Triangle – where both sides must win if the balance is to be maintained:

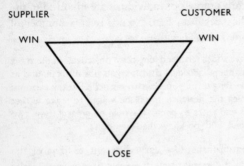

An increasing number of organizations have, indeed, come to see the relationship as one of interdependence; where the two sides adopt a 'peer to peer' relationship. The sales role here is sometimes described as 'relationship management'. As this type of relationship requires a higher level of personal support, from a more skilled sales professional (a 'relationship manager'), it will typically be limited to the five or ten most important customers.

Theodore Levitt comments:

> The relationship between a seller and a buyer seldom ends when the sale is made. In a great and increasing proportion of transactions, the relationship actually intensifies subsequent to the sale. This becomes the critical factor in the buyer's choice of the seller the next time around ... The sale merely consummates the courtship. Then the marriage begins. How good the marriage is depends on how well the relationship is managed by the seller.[4]

3. *Ibid*.
4. Theodore Levitt, 'After the Sale is Over', *Harvard Business Review* (1983) September/October.

Thus, regular contact is essential to maintain rapport and to maintain the partnership. It is also very productive in terms of growing the account. Once more, the investment in a satisfied customer may not show on the balance sheet, but it contributes handsomely to the bottom-line profit!

Probably the most important activity in developing these key relationship accounts is the development of an account plan. Unlike the overall sales plan, which will deal with groups of customers, each account plan (or 'key account plan') deals quite specifically with a single customer. This plan should match (at least in its scope) the overall marketing plan. It should detail the specific objectives, which will be individually related to the customer's needs and wants. It should detail the activities which are planned to meet these objectives, and to build the relationship. If such a plan is produced within the selling organization it will be a productive exercise. However, if it is produced in co-operation with the customer, it may make a major contribution to the development of the business relationship.

T | **Rule T41 – *Account Management***

In its most general sense, covering prospects as well as customers, this is the essence of professional salesmanship. Customer account management, in particular, is the epitome of this.

Account management is probably the most important single skill (apart from selling itself) required of a sales professional, and yet it is almost entirely neglected by sales trainers.

It is worth, here, making reference to the traditional stereotype of the salesman. For the rest of society the salesman is often to be despised, or to be feared, or even to be pitied. What is more harmful is that many members of the sales profession themselves hold very similar views! The buyer–seller relationship as seen by them is aggressively competitive; a 'zero-sum game' where the sales professional can only win by the customer losing. This then becomes an environment in which the sales professional's effectiveness is seen simply in terms of his or her use of techniques of deception. It is therefore vital, if the relationship with the customer is to be saved, that the sales force is persuaded (by training or leadership) to switch from being cowboys to being relationship managers.

Distribution Channels

There is one special category of customers, those who control the distribution channels for the product or service. In many respects they need to be cosseted in exactly the same way as any other customer. Suffice it to say that their main 'product' requirements are likely to be quite simple (albeit very different to those of other customers): the maximization of profit and the minimization of risk, from the business arising from your own organization. Your own sales will directly depend upon how efficiently they conduct their sales operations in general, and upon how well motivated they are to direct customers to your product or service in particular.

Managing distribution channels is a very sophisticated process. It requires all the techniques needed to run your own sales force, but at a distance! Two contrasting philosophies can help this process:

Rule O67 – *Integrated Partnership*
Ideally you should take customer partnership to its logical conclusion, by integrating your operations – especially sales and promotion – with those of your distributors.

If you reward them with the status and rights of your own staff there is a chance that the distributors' staff will also take on at least some of the accompanying responsibilities.

Rule O68 – *Private Disbelief*
Your (senior) management must recognize exactly where the real organizational boundaries lie. In particular, they must always understand what motivates distributors and their staff. They should not be seduced by proximity into assuming that the distributor *really* is an extension of your own operations.

Rule O69 – *The Proximity Trap*
You must not be fooled into forgetting that your real customers are
those beyond the distributors.

It is too easy to react to the very close relationship with the distributor's
staff, and direct your business to meet their needs, rather than match
the indirectly registered needs of the customers of the distributors,
who are the real buyers of the service or product.

 Rule O70 – *Customer Service Levels*
The product should be available when and where the customer wants
it. If it is not available, an immediate sale may well be lost. More
important, long-term sales may also have been lost if the customer
is forced to change to another brand, and then decides to stay with
that brand.

The percentage availability is described as the service level in the
diagram below. It might seem that the simple answer would be to
achieve 100 per cent availability. The problem is that the cost of
achieving these service levels rises very steeply as it approaches 100
per cent.

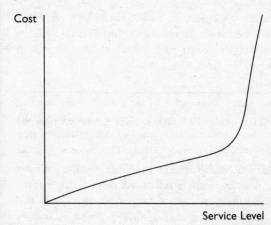

Cost

Service Level
(% in stock)

There is a very clear trade-off here between customer service (level) and cost. Fortunately, the indications are that, in terms of demand generated, customers are not significantly affected by minor variations if there are generally high levels of availability.

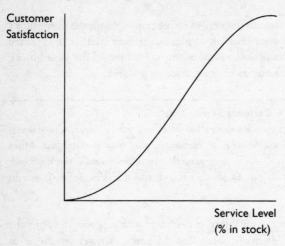

Lead Time

There are, however, other elements of customer service level. Some of these relate to the time it takes to meet an order. This is called the 'lead time' (or sometimes the 'order cycle time'); clearly, the shorter the lead time the better the service.

Ⓞ Rule O71
The RELIABILITY of the lead time is more important than the time itself.

However, a customer who has to arrange a number of other activities to mesh in with the delivery of the product will often prefer that the delivery date is certain, albeit at a later date. A secondary but related factor is how long it takes a customer to find out what is actually happening to the order (the response time).

○ Rule O72 – *Queuing*

In the specific context of queues associated with provision of a service, David Maister[5] lists a number of principles which have wider applicability:

- Unoccupied time feels longer than occupied time . . .
- Pre-process waits feel longer than in-process waits . . .
- Anxiety makes waits seem longer . . .
- Uncertain waits are longer than known, finite waits . . .
- Unexplained waits are longer than explained waits . . .
- Unfair waits are longer than equitable waits . . .
- The more valuable the service the longer the customer will wait . . .
- Solo waits feel longer than group waits . . .

These are all reasonably well-known, indeed almost obvious, principles, yet they are often ignored by management.

Laws of Service

David Maister[6] also formulates two 'Laws of Service'. The first of these is expressed by the formula we looked at earlier: 'Satisfaction equals perception minus expectation. If you expect a certain level of service and perceive the service received to be higher, you will be a satisfied customer. If you perceive this same level where you had expected a higher one, you will be disappointed and therefore a dissatisfied customer.'

5. David H. Maister, 'The Psychology of Waiting Lines', in *Managing Services: Marketing, Operations and Human Resources* (Prentice-Hall, 1988).
6. *Ibid.*

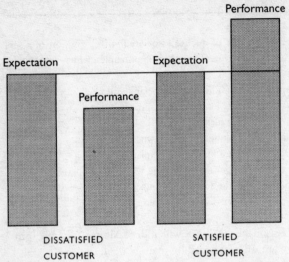

As explained earlier, both what is perceived and what is expected are psychological phenomena not reality (and it is the *relative* level of service, related to expectations, which is important, not the absolute one).

David Maister went further, to posit:

> ○ **Rule O73 –** *The Second Law of Service*
> It is hard to play 'catch-up ball'. There is a halo effect created by early stages of any service encounter . . . the largest pay-off may well occur in the earliest stages of the service encounter (a problem early in the provision of the service sours the whole process).

Customer Complaints

Complaints are often treated as a nuisance by many organizations, and yet they have considerable value for a number of reasons:

• Although there will always be a small proportion of frivolous complaints, the genuine ones usually highlight something which has gone wrong with a part of the overall marketing operation. This could be that a sufficiently high level of quality, which should be fundamental, has not been achieved. Whatever the reason, the sensible marketer will want to know exactly what has gone wrong so that remedial action may be taken.

• The way a complaint is handled is often seen by customers, and their many contacts, as an acid-test of the true quality of support. What is more, it is also a powerful reminder to the organization's own staff of the importance of quality.

• Finally, customers who complain are usually loyal customers (those who are not loyal tend just to switch to another supplier), and will continue to be loyal (and valuable) just so long as their complaint is handled well.

> ○ **Rule O74 –** *Encourage Complaints*
> The first requirement is that complaints should be positively encouraged.
>
> The second requirement is that all complaints should be carefully handled by painstakingly controlled and monitored procedures.
>
> The third, and most important, requirement is that the complaint should then be fully investigated, and the cause remedied.

The first requirement is that complaints should be positively encouraged. This is not the same as saying that the reasons for complaint should be encouraged. But, assuming that the problem has occurred despite your best efforts, you should put nothing in the way of any customer who wants to complain and, indeed, should positively encourage such complaints. The main problem lies with the many more customers who do not complain and instead change to another supplier rather than the few who abuse the system.

The second requirement is that all complaints should be carefully handled by painstakingly controlled and monitored procedures. Complaints must be handled well, and must be seen to be well handled, by the complainant and by the organization's own staff.

The third, and most important requirement, is that the complaint should then be fully investigated, and the cause remedied. Complaints are only symptoms. The disease needs to be cured! There may be an understandable temptation to overlook complaints until they reach a significant level. Holding off will usually mean that the problem has already damaged the organization's image. It is far better to assume that 'one complaint is too many'!

COMPLAINTS

ENCOURAGE → HANDLE → INVESTIGATE

The reality in most organizations is very different. The number of complaints are minimized, not by remedying the reasons for them but by evading the complainants! An assumption is usually made, wrongly, that complainants are trouble-makers, and have to be handled in a confrontational manner. In fact, most dissatisfied customers do not complain (a US survey[7] showed that 97 per cent didn't), but they do tell their friends (the same survey showed that 13 per cent complained to more than 20 other people).

7. K. Albrecht and R. Zemke, *Service America* (Dow-Jones Irwin, 1985).

○ Rule O75 – *Satisfaction Surveys*

It is essential that an organization monitors the satisfaction level of its customers. This may be, all else failing, at the global level, as measured by market research. Preferably, though, it should be at the level of the individual or group.

IBM, at the peak of its success, conducted a survey every year of all its direct customers. The results were analysed to produce overall satisfaction indices, and made available to field management so that they could rectify any individual problem situations, for example, where the customer was dissatisfied with some aspect of the IBM service and the sales representative was unaware of it.

There are a number of advantages to conducting satisfaction surveys (particularly where any individual problems highlighted can be subsequently dealt with):

• Like complaints, they indicate where problems lie;
• If they cover all customers, they allow the 97 per cent of non-complainers to communicate their feelings and vent their anger;
• They positively show, even the satisfied customers, that the supplier is interested in the customers and their complaints – which is at least halfway to satisfying those complainants;
• They help persuade the supplier's staff to take customer service more seriously.

The importance of very high standards of customer service is supported by two examples. The marketing philosophy of McDonalds, the world's largest food service organization, is encapsulated in its motto 'Q. S. C. & V.' (Quality, Service, Cleanliness & Value). The standards, enforced somewhat quixotically (but memorably) on its franchisees and managers at the 'Hamburger University' in Elk Grove Village (Illinois), require that the customer receive a 'good-tasting' hamburger in no more than five minutes, from a friendly host or hostess, in a spotlessly clean restaurant. The second example, Disneyland, also insists on spotless cleanliness, and on the customer being 'The Guest'. It is salutary to observe how few of the competitors in either of these fields manage the simple task of keeping their premises clean, let alone being able to think of their customers as 'guests'. Interestingly, the terms used in the fairground trade (with which

Disney competes, albeit at a very different level) usually see the customer as some form of victim ('pigeon', 'mark', 'punter' etc).

Inner Marketing

Marketing is, by definition, primarily concerned with the world outside the organization. However, if it is to optimize its use of the resources, it also has to be concerned with what lies inside the organizational perimeter. This is referred to as inner (or internal) marketing.

Increasingly, the most valuable resource of any organization (and particularly those in the service sector) is its people and the skills they possess. In tapping this internal resource, many of the traditional tools of marketing can be used to great effect in areas of internal communication and motivation, to harness and focus the 'people' resource to meet the objectives of the marketing plan. In the recent past, such campaigns have tended to focus on Total Quality Management (TQM) on the basis that the overall quality that the customer perceives comes from every part of the organization, from support and administrative staff just as much as from the workers (or the robots) on the production lines. Inner marketing is in many ways the ultimate extension of TQM in that it fixes 'quality' exclusively in terms of the marketing context for every employee.

In a similar vein, many organizations in the service sector, and not a few in the manufacturing sector, have customer service programmes. These use many of the promotional devices of marketing – advertising, incentives, seminars etc. – to persuade employees (particularly those in contact with customers) to adopt the correct attitude to those customers. Such campaigns have received a mixed response. The problem has often been that the management implementing them are themselves unconvinced of the message and cannot, therefore, expect a positive response from the employees. Probably the most frequent shortcoming is that such campaigns are run as short-term programmes – the flavour of the month, which everyone knows they can ignore, since the next month is likely to bring a newer flavour still!

S **Rule S21 –** *Inner Marketing* is a powerful concept. It says quite simply that EMPLOYEES should be 'marketed' to in exactly the same way as CUSTOMERS.

O **Rule O76 –** *Stages of Inner Marketing*
For memorability I think of these as the four Cs:

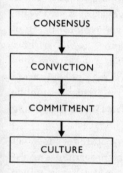

The first requirement, and the one which distinguishes it from almost all other customer service programmes, is some form of marketing research to be conducted on the organization's own employees. This should be used to determine their perception of the customer (is the customer seen as friend or foe?), and of the customer service programmes which are likely to be the main focus of the research (does anyone do anything more than pay lip-service to them? why?). It should also attempt to explore employees' attitudes and motivations. (Do they really want to offer a good service? If not, why not? How can they be persuaded to change their views?) The objective of the research should be to reach some positive conclusions, especially in terms of values, to which all the participants (in this context members of staff at all levels, as well as the managers and customers themselves) will be able to commit themselves, i.e. to achieve a consensus.

O **Rule O77 – *Internal Opinion Surveys***

Internal research may have great benefits. Such opinion surveys are extremely effective devices for obtaining information on the inner market. If applied regularly to all staff, they are also remarkably good motivators and contributors to a positive culture.

One of IBM's most powerful tools, in developing its justly famed relationship with its staff, was the 'Opinion Survey'. Every two years, all employees of the company took part in an anonymous survey of how they felt about IBM, and what it was doing, as well as how they felt about their immediate management. The results were then published, making it difficult to ignore them, and very publicly acted upon. This benefited the 'inner market' because the employees (unlike those in most other organizations) recognized that IBM was listening to them.

Only with this basic information on employee attitudes (however derived) can the 'inner marketer' start to devise the programmes necessary to create new attitudes, and faith in the company goals, which will eventually deliver the requisite service to the external customers. It also needs to be recognized that it may take far longer to achieve these desired results than in a traditional consumer marketing campaign – often fundamental shifts in attitude are required.

At the most basic level, the staff will need to understand what is expected of them by their own management and, in particular, by their customers. It is remarkable how many 'improvements' in customer service are advertised to the customers but never explained to, let alone agreed with, the employees who are to deliver them. Beyond this, the essence of any marketing campaign, as with any military one, is that all the actions happen at the right time, and in the manner planned. The inner marketing campaign is thus essential (whether it is formally or informally implemented).

Most difficult of all, however, is the process of changing attitudes, of developing the necessary conviction. Staff who have been bound by the rigid rules of a bureaucracy, for example, will not suddenly become receptive to the concept that 'the customer is always right' just because a memo from head office states that this is so. The most important input from management at this stage is leadership. If senior management are believed to be highly committed (and very publicly so) to goals, and especially to values, which take account of the consensus views then the majority of staff are likely to be convinced by the validity of those goals. Thus, the first stage must be to match the organization's external goals to a realistic appreciation of what the inner market can (and is willing to) deliver. This role of management is illustrated below:

⊙ Rule O78 – *The Management Balance*

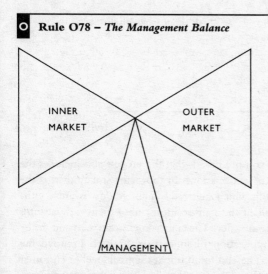

INNER

MARKET

OUTER

MARKET

MANAGEMENT

But the process does not stop there, for the most important, but least well appreciated, aspect of inner marketing is that it is a process of managing change, and the marketing department must be seen as an agent of change. The end result should be an alignment of customer and staff expectations and a positive commitment by staff to the jointly agreed goals.

O   Rule O79 – *The Inner Marketing Bonus*

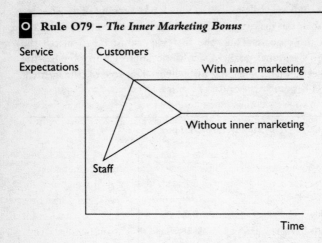

Service Expectations

Customers

With inner marketing

Without inner marketing

Staff

Time

An important fact to note here is that the process also includes the lowering of customers' expectations. In too many situations it is the customers' expectations which are steadily adjusted downwards (without any improvement of the staff positions) until their view accords with the lower levels on offer. The upper line shows what might be achieved with the application of inner marketing to improve the response rate of staff. The end result is that the final level of customer perception is significantly higher, potentially offering a major competitive advantage.

The techniques here may often be closer to those of education and may revolve around significant amounts of retraining. Indeed, the service offered to customers, for instance, is in many cases only as good as the skills available to provide it, and those skills may, and usually do, need developing. The route to this must be the investment, once again, in raising the level of these skills by a comprehensive programme of high-quality training for all staff.

Culture

In pursuing the concept of inner marketing further, Peters and Waterman[8] stress that the resulting culture of an organization (generally speaking, the common values that its employees share) can be a very important contributor to its success. It can be even more important in determining what customer service is provided. They conceptualize this cultural element as 'shared values' but they do not spell out the very lengthy steps needed to achieve it.

The culture of the company is often what conditions customer service. IBM maintained a philosophy of 'Customer Service' throughout the whole company (applying to all employees) as its only marketing objective for more than half a century, with spectacularly successful results (and an equally spectacular disaster when it abandoned it). Both McDonalds and Disney have similarly strong cultures, and it shows in their bottom-line profits.

To be realistic, changing the 'cultural dimension' of any organization takes time, often years. If existing cultures are strong, and the changes are major, the process may take decades. Both IBM and the Japanese corporations, who probably have the strongest cultures of all, needed as much as fifteen years to fully develop all the detailed aspects of the new, rich cultures they were introducing. Such an undertaking is not, therefore, to be taken lightly. More minor changes (particularly those which complement the existing culture) may be accepted more rapidly, but even then, not in days!

Based on my experiences with IBM, which at its peak had the most successful culture of all, I postulated a number of management philosophies. Although they are mainly concerned with organizational development (OD), I will briefly mention them here (now grouped under six main headings) since, in their impact upon organizational culture, they have significant implications for marketing.

They fall into two categories. The first represents the legacy of paternalistic management practices, derived from IBM's earlier days. These were later copied by the Japanese, so they also lie at the heart of their management culture:

8. T. J. Peters and R. H. Waterman, *In Search of Excellence* (Harper & Row, 1982).

G Rule G6 – *Philosophies I*

Driven by conviction
- Strong beliefs
- Guided by philosophies not objectives
- Shared ethical values
- Development of a strong culture
- Holistic approach to employees

Employee oriented
- Full employment policies
- Job enrichment
- Personal incentives
- Non-specialized career development
- Personal involvement in decisions
- Implicit (value) control

Within this category, the most important points are those related to the culture itself – and these reflect many of the values of conviction marketing described earlier. The second group relates much more to inner marketing, reflecting the degree to which organizations recognize their intimate relationship with all their employees. To a degree all of these concepts are recognized by management thinkers (though less often put into practice by managers).

The second category, however, is not likely to be recognized by anyone outside IBM, yet it contains the most important points of all.

G Rule G7 – *Philosophies II*

Empowerment of the individual
- Strong (published) beliefs in individualism
- Personnel processes to guarantee these
- Single status across the organization

Manager as team leader
- Maximal delegation to the lowest levels
- Emphasis on team leadership by planned constraints on management
- Encouragement of dissent

Creation of the best human resource
- Recruitment of the highest calibre personnel
- Extended training

Structures for change
- Development of horizontal communications
- Institutionalization of change

Of the four groups above, the first is probably the most powerful and the most neglected. It is paradoxical that the recognition of the power of the individual, which fuelled many of the political developments of the 1980s, was accompanied by many organizations taking draconian steps to reduce the rights of their staff.

The middle two groups should be obvious developments of our times, and are at the heart of the very fashionable human resource strategies, but again the lessons seem not to have been genuinely accepted by many Western organizations. The final group reflects the obvious and much reported fact that the endemic change which is sweeping through organizations (including now, paradoxically, IBM itself) needs to be dealt with at a structural level, not just at the tactical one.

Since the time when these two stages of philosophy held sway, IBM has experienced the catastrophic downside of the cultural approach, and has abandoned many of these philosophies in the process. This has led me to add a new series – Philosophies III – which indicates the pitfalls awaiting the exponents of strong culture/conviction marketing:

G Rule G8 – *Philosophies III*

Culture undermined collapses
- Culture needs success to breed on
- Failure of confidence leads to catastrophe

Core competences cannot be sub-contracted
- Customers cannot be ignored
- Experts are no substitute for expertise

Paradigm dissonance confuses
- False data reinforces groupthink

A successful culture can be immensely strong, but one that becomes unsuccessful (relative to its own standards) and loses confidence (and, as a result, many of the resources needed to maintain standards) can rapidly fail. When the paradigm (described in the next chapter) changes, which is usually the trigger for the loss of confidence, all the cultural landmarks disappear, and the organization's leaders lose their sense of direction. False data can then be disastrous, if the leaders seize upon it and use it to reinforce their prevailing groupthink (also described in the next chapter). The organization may then even forget its core competences (as IBM did) and ignore its customers (as IBM also did), even though these were central to the dying culture.

12 / New Products

Before coming to grips with new products strategy you must first put it in perspective. In particular, you must put behind you some of the myths which stand in for theory in this field. Just as the stereotype of the salesman would lead us to believe that success comes from a concentration on new prospects rather than by supporting existing customers, so a number of these marketing myths would have us believe that the future lies only in developing new products and not through investment in existing ones.

Product Life Cycle

The concept of the 'life cycle', which was discussed in chapter 3, has become a very important element of marketing theory. As a result, it is incorporated as a basic assumption in many other theories, including those relating to new product introduction. It is now accepted as a basic fact of life by many managers, and fuels the drive for change (especially in terms of new product launches) in many markets. In my view, its supposed universal applicability is largely a myth – but it does have relevance in terms of new products.

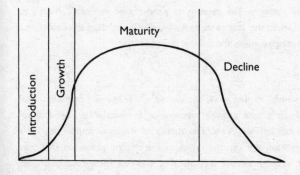

Introductory stage

At this first stage of a product's life, the supplier can choose from a number of strategies, ranging from 'penetration', where the supplier invests (typically in terms of promotion, but possibly by a low price) to gain the maximum share of a new market, through to 'skimming', where the maximum short-term profit is derived (typically by a high price) from the 'innovation' factor.

Growth stage

By this stage customers are becoming aware of the product or service and its benefits. Accordingly, usage is growing, often rapidly. More people want it, and want to use more of it. During this stage, the suppliers often have to increase the capacity of their plant and run promotional campaigns to consolidate and extend their share of the new market. In the process they frequently make substantial investments, which usually absorb the profit that is made. It is accepted that this part of the life cycle will not be a profit generator, and may even demand further net investment.

In recent years, another feature of this phase has been the battle for distribution, especially in the retail market where distribution is concentrated in the hands of a few major operators. It is vital to the success of a brand to obtain the widest possible distribution, so there will probably be much energy expended on negotiations with these key operators.

Maturity

No market can grow forever and eventually all the significant potential uses will have been exploited. The sales curve will flatten, and the market or product will have reached maturity. The majority of products or services currently in the market-place are at this stage and, as we have seen, much of the theory and practice of marketing revolves around this 'steady state'.

Decline stage

Eventually the whole market may decline or other newer products may be introduced, leading to a terminal decline for the established product or service – which can last for years. The theory of the PLC implies that you should constantly look out for the onset of the decline phase, so that you can change your strategy to take account of it. The rule for successful brands is longevity rather than imminent decline. However, the effect of the PLC may be to persuade the manager to see a short-term dip as a long-term decline, resulting in the onset of an inappropriate milking strategy and premature withdrawal.

The problem, unfortunately, is that the model does not reflect reality. The main reason for describing it, therefore, is to warn you *not* to use it, despite the fact that it is probably the most widely known theory in marketing, and the most seductive one. Nevertheless, many leading marketers now recognize that it can easily give the wrong signals.

To a certain extent, the first two stages do reflect reality, and are especially relevant to new product development, although research on the practice of new product development shows that, in the United Kingdom at least, almost two-thirds of organizations put less than 10 per cent of their total new product development effort into 'new products in new markets'. The bread and butter of new product development is, much more prosaically, 'existing products development', on which two-thirds of organizations reported that they spent more than 20 per cent of their development effort (the greatest share recorded by any category we looked at).

This emphasis on the further development of existing products is fully justified when you look at the results of our research into the long-term record of brand leaders in the UK consumer goods markets.[1] The top three brands on (unweighted) average took 82 per cent of the 'most used' penetration in 1969 and 72 per cent in 1989. The first-position brands by themselves took 46 per cent in 1969 and 39 per cent in 1989. A reflection perhaps of the value of the brand name, and/or of the (resulting) domination by the well-resourced large corporations, is the fact that no less than ninety-nine of the brands appeared in two or more markets/segments, between them providing almost half of the total number of products in the leading (first to third) positions.

Perhaps the most significant finding, however, was the length of brand life. The majority (53 per cent) of the 150 brand leaders in 1969 remained the brand leaders in their respective markets/segments in 1989. Indeed, of the 451 brands holding the first three positions in 1969 (and accounting for 82 per cent of 'most used' penetration)

---

1. D. S. Mercer, 'A Two Decade Test of Product Life Cycle Theory', *British Journal of Management*, Vol. 4 (1993) pp. 269–74.

91 per cent were still alive two decades later, and 68 per cent remained in fourth place or better.

There were just nineteen totally new brands which (from this list of 150 markets) rose to brand-leader position in the twenty years to 1989 – a period when there was intense new product activity in these consumer goods markets – and almost all of them appeared to incorporate a significant degree of new technology; for example, Duracell offered longer-life batteries; Gillette Aerosol Shaving Foam replaced cream products. Some new formulations were also developed to match changing consumer tastes (Heinz slimming soups replacing biscuit product; the more exotic L'Oreal replacing the relatively mundane Amami as a hair-setting product). But the power of existing brand names was still reflected in the fact that existing 'extended' brands took first place in 60 per cent of the new markets/segments added between 1969 and 1989.

The first requirement in deciding your new product strategy is, therefore, that you decide just what category of 'new product development' you are to undertake. It should be clear by now that in almost all cases the priority should be given to development of *existing* products.

Development of Existing Products

In most markets customer requirements change over time, as a result of social factors or changes in fashion or – perhaps more likely – technological changes in the market. These changes may be relatively slow for long-established brands or very rapid for some fashion products. It is imperative, therefore, that you develop your existing products in line with these changing requirements. This is just as true for long-established brands as for new ones. If you do not develop existing brands in a regular and rigorous manner you may find yourself the victim of 'position drift'.

Position drift

You will remember the positioning map which was the key element behind our approach to product:service strategies.

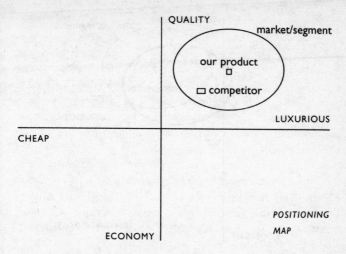

You will also remember that you should use this map to position your brand as close to the ideal as is possible for the segment(s) you wish to address, and hopefully dominate. The problem is that this shows only a static picture. Over time 'position drift' can significantly change the picture for one of three main reasons:

• *Consumer drift* – as consumer tastes change, the segment (cluster) which contains them will shift its position. Its centre of gravity will move, and its size may change as consumers switch to other, perhaps newer, segments.

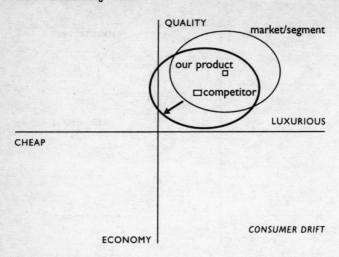

The position of your brand relative to the ideal position within this cluster will reflect this drift.

• *Competitor drift* – alternatively, your competitors may shift their positions, with the effect that your own relative position, your competitive advantage, may become less than optimal.

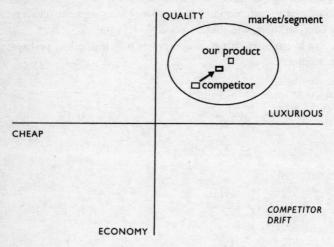

This may pose a particular problem if you are trying to target several segments with just one brand, since any move to respond to a competitive threat in one segment may leave the rest of the segments exposed.

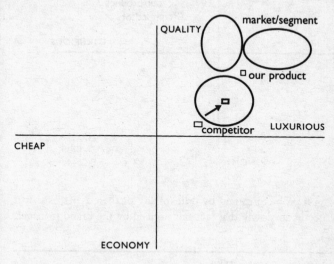

- *Ego drift* – perhaps the most prevalent drift of all occurs where brand managers (or their advertising agencies) gratuitously reposition their own brand in a less optimal location. This is usually justified on the basis that consumers are bored with the existing messages, and an exciting new approach is needed. The real reason is that members of the management team, frequently persuaded by an agency's creative team itching to make their own distinctive mark, are themselves bored.

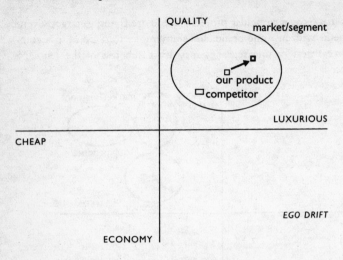

The biggest problem caused by drift, of any of these types, is that it usually occurs so slowly that it is not noticed by the brand manager.

T Rule T42 – *Position Drift*
Brand positioning maps must be updated regularly, and the changes plotted as accurately as possible – so that the trajectory of any drift may be determined, and corrected.

If drift does occur most Product:Service Packages will need to be redeveloped to compensate. In the rational approach to strategy this repositioning takes place as part of the planning process, usually on an annual basis. A good summary of this approach was outlined by Argenti.[2]

1. *Target Setting*
- Clarify corporate objectives
- Set target levels of objectives

2. *Gap Analysis*
- Forecast future performance on current strategies
- Identify gaps between forecasts and targets

2. J. Argenti, *Practical Corporate Planning* (Allen & Unwin, 1980).

3. *Strategic Appraisal*
- External (environmental) and internal appraisal
- Identify corporate advantage
- Redefine targets in light of stage 3 information

4. *Strategy Formulation*
- Generate strategic options
- Evaluate strategic options (against targets and internal/external appraisals)
- Take strategic decision

5. *Strategy Implementation*
- Draw up action plans and budgets
- Monitor and control

Rational planning and repositioning once a year are, however, the exception rather than the rule. The reality is that much of strategy is set by small decisions taken, as the need arises, throughout the year. These small decisions then accumulate to dictate the overall strategy, when this comes to be formalized, in written form, at the end of the year. The result is the 'logical incrementalism' described by Quinn.[3]

T **Rule T43 – *Logical Incrementalism***

The manager must be prepared in practice to follow a number of stages which are quite different from those traditionally described for (annual) planning:

1. *Scanning* – a rigorous approach to environmental analysis is needed.
2. *Information Networks* – the widest possible networks to obtain the input which will tell managers what is happening in their environment.
3. *Generation of Alternatives* – before committing to any one approach.
4. *Building Credibility* – preparing the ground for the necessary changes.
5. *Tactical Moves* – experimental tactics rather than strategy.
6. *Political Support* – building of political coalitions.
7. *Creating Commitment* – throughout the organization.

I'll now examine these stages in more detail:

1. *Scanning* – since the trigger for the incremental change in strategy

---

3. J. B. Quinn, *Strategies for Change: Logical Incrementalism* (Dow-Jones Irwin, 1980).

is a change in the environment, this approach is very dependent upon perception of the signals which indicate such changes in the environment. Hence the rigorous approach to environmental analysis needed.

2. *Information networks* – a consequent requirement is that managers develop the widest possible networks (of human contacts not just computers) to find out what is happening in their environment and, more important, to help them sense when change is likely to be needed. The human neural network is a very good analogy for this.

3. *Generation of alternatives* – it might seem that incrementalism would imply instant decisions, yet a key requirement, observed by successful managers, is that they develop a range of alternative solutions which they then think through with their colleagues before committing themselves to any one approach.

4. *Building credibility* – having taken the personal decision, this may be started – by CEOs for instance – by making symbolic moves (by, say, a very public commitment to a new philosophy). It is often accompanied by moves to legitimize new viewpoints, for example, by setting up workshops (or retreats) to talk through the issues, preferably off-site so that they are not interrupted.

5. *Tactical moves* – even then, the changes may first be introduced as (experimental) tactics rather than strategy. Here incrementalism can be used to bypass opposition which might otherwise emerge against a formal announcement of the change in strategy.

6. *Political support* – these new moves will still require the building of political coalitions if they are to be sustained; committees and task forces are favourite devices for developing such support. At the same time opposition will need to be neutralized.

7. *Creating commitment* – when the strategy is finally in place then it is necessary to actively build commitment to it throughout the organization.

This concept of logical incrementalism is important in two contexts. The first is that managers moving into the rational phase of the annual planning process need to be aware of the limitations imposed by the legacy of incremental decisions which have built up since the last annual exercise. The second is that an understanding of this process helps you put such incremental decision-making in perspective. Most important of all, it alerts you to the fact that it is happening all the time.

If brand managers understand the implications of logical incrementalism they will inject some of the rational thinking which is supposed to lie at the heart of the annual planning process – it is, after all, a logical process. A recognition that an immediate response may be necessary if a position drift is detected is not the same as the random decision-making which infects many organizations. Because it recognizes that decisions are driven by real events rather than a theoretical planning process, it may indeed be rather more effective.

One of the implications of the above processes is that the making of strategy is a much more diffuse process than most managers think. Decisions can take place almost randomly throughout the year rather than tidily during the annual planning process.

A less obvious implication is that the process of logical incrementalism is not limited to senior management alone, as traditional theory would suggest. In practice, the process works through several layers of management, with different degrees of involvement depending on what particular incremental aspect of strategy is under review. This has major implications for managers throughout the organization, who may not have realized just how important their contribution could be.

T | Rule T44 – *Ringi*

The Japanese *ringi* system requires that any significant decision is formally agreed upon by ALL those involved.

This takes the form of signing a *ringi* – a document detailing the decision. All those affected by the decision have to agree to support it by adding their signature to the *ringi*, before the decision can receive final approval.

A somewhat similar process may be seen in some Western organizations where the approval of ('signing off' by) key departments must be obtained before certain decisions can be implemented. The important differences in Japan are that *all* significant decisions are handled in this way, and that *all* the managers affected have to sign the *ringi*. Where in the West the signing-off process might involve five or six signatures at most, in Japan it will typically require fifty or more.

Although this becomes a lengthy process in Japan the gains are considerable: it forces them to gain active commitment from all involved, where the Western equivalent may just demand grudging commitment. Subsequently, the Japanese implementation phase is usually much shorter than in the West and, as the implementation phase is normally far longer than the decision-making one, overall they make significant savings in time.

At the other end of the scale individual commitment is often what is needed to ensure success.

◉ Rule O80 – *The Product Champion*
Often, the most important ingredient of all for ultimate success is a 'champion', a manager who is so committed to the strategy that he or she will fight for it – often beyond any reasonable call of duty.

The 'product champion' is the manager who pushes for his or her pet product. This has its negative aspects, since it may lead to non-viable products being launched (the Concorde airliner was a classic example of this), but effective management control by senior management, especially if there is a *ringi* system in place, should be able to resist obvious no-hopers. The positive aspect is that many, if not most, of the great product breakthroughs, and strategic breakthroughs, can be traced back to one individual champion.

First, of course, you need to find such a product champion. Fortunately, it is usually possible to find someone in the organization who has a strong interest (for reasons of self-advancement if no other) and who can be persuaded to take on at least part of the role. A more important corollary is that you should never neglect an existing product champion unless he or she poses impossible problems. Such enthusiasm is rare, and is a valuable commodity which no organization can afford to throw away.

To sum up this section, then, even though logical incrementalism is quite different to the traditionally described theory it is still a very rational approach to management, and one where the manager is still very much in control. However, it neglects one very important aspect, which is that a considerable amount of strategy emerges as a result of unpredictable changes in the environment rather than from rational control by management. This emergent strategy means that managers are forced to follow courses of action which they had not planned.

Emergent Strategy

The diagram below shows very clearly how the intended strategy, decided upon traditionally or incrementally, can be overtaken by events in two main ways. The first is **unrealized strategy**, where it proves impossible to implement the chosen strategy in practice. Less obvious is the **emergent strategy** which is decided by events in the external environment, and so forced upon the organization. As markets become more complex such emergent strategies are becoming more common.

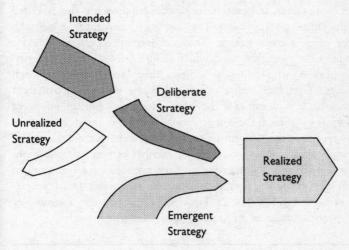

Many organizations see both these processes as a sign of failure; they have been forced, usually by unpredictable events, to abandon their own strategy. Accordingly, they may try to ignore the events until they simply cannot be avoided. This is a major error. Such deviations must be recognized (probably through one or other form of environmental analysis coupled with networking) as soon as possible so that the organization can react in good time.

A much more positive approach is to be proactive; to seize upon these deviations as the basis for future developments.

G **Rule G9 –** *Emergent Strategies* are the most powerful strategies of all. They must, by definition, be directly derived from the needs of the market.

Emergent strategies are, thus, likely to be vigorous ones. There are two main approaches to capitalizing on such emergent strategies. The first of these, favoured in the West, is the **umbrella strategy**. The overall strategies – the umbrella – are very general in nature and allow the lower-level managers, who are closest to the external environment, the freedom to react to these changes.

A more direct, and even more powerful approach is that favoured by the Japanese corporations. They integrate emergent strategies with those of their own making. They deliberately go out to look for symptoms of emergent trends which can be detected in the performance of their own products. In addition, they often deliberately launch a range of products rather than a single one to see which is most successful. It is almost as if they deliberately seek out the emergent strategies by offering the best environment for them to develop – the very reverse of the Western approach which seeks to avoid them! The Japanese then build on these with a number of very effective tools, above all recognizing that time is of the essence. Time management techniques (including parallel development along with flexible manufacturing and JIT – Just in Time) offer the Japanese a significant competitive advantage in handling such emergent strategies.

T **Rule T45 –** *Paradigm Shift* is the ultimate emergent strategy. In this case the emergent effects are so powerful that they force a complete shift in perspective by the organization.

The phenomenon of 'paradigm shift' forces an organization to rethink completely its strategic position. It is most obvious in the field of science (and indeed the term 'paradigm shift' was coined by the historian of science, Thomas Kuhn, to describe the dramatic changes which take place in science when a new set of theories, the new paradigm, supersedes the old set). The important implication of this theory is that a paradigm shift is a discontinuous process (rather like catastrophe theory). There is no gentle move from one viewpoint to the other taking place over a long period. Instead, there is an instantaneous, almost violent, shift from one to the other. The reason for this is the investment (in terms of management commitment) in the previous paradigm.

○ Rule O81 – *Paradigm Blinkers*
Because it is too painful to abandon their cherished viewpoint, managers may adopt a number of devices to deny or minimize the existence of the changes, including blindness, misinterpretation, opposition.

- *Blindness* – most basic of all, they simply will not see them, or will persuade themselves that they do not apply to their own position (thus the British motorcycle industry convinced itself that the Japanese were only making small bikes, which was a different market and no threat to themselves!).
- *Misinterpretation* – or the signals may be forced to fit the existing paradigm.
- *Opposition* – if the signals are too obvious to ignore, then the management may fight change by a number of means. These may include referring to the basic philosophies of the organization (the new paradigm is a 'heresy'), developing highly political defences within the organization, and/or partially assimilating those elements which can be accepted by the existing paradigm.

The above may be taken as stages which have to be gone through before the new paradigm overpowers the old. Assuming its overthrow is inevitable, these delays in recognition may be very damaging, and are often fatal. Even if the new paradigm is eventually accepted, there is likely to be, as shown in the diagram below, a period of 'paradigm dissonance' when the organization is demoralized and its confidence sapped.

⊙ Rule O82 – Paradigm Dissonance

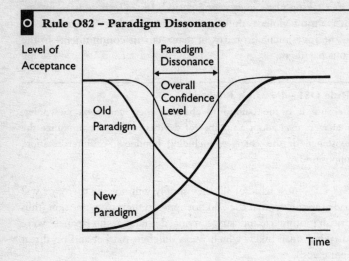

The paradigm freezes everyone in the organization and it will probably require a very strong lead from the CEO, even the appointment of an outsider (and a charismatic one), to lead them out of the trap. Groupthink is a related process which only applies to a group of managers. Based on his research into the 'Bay of Pigs' adventure by President Kennedy, Irving Janis[4] derived a number of symptoms which may be detected when groupthink is taking place.

⊙ O83 – *Groupthink Symptoms*
1. Invulnerability
2. Blindness
3. Moral superiority
4. Stereotyped enemies
5. Pressure
6. Self-censorship
7. Unanimity
8. Mindguards.

4. I. L. Janis, *Victims of Groupthink* (Houghton Mifflin, 1972).

The first group of these relates to ways of perceiving the outside world, and may be similar to those involved in a paradigm shift:

1. *Invulnerability* – excessive optimism about their (illusory) position
2. *Blindness* – collective avoidance (rationalization) of unwanted warnings
3. *Moral superiority* – unquestioned (but unwarranted) belief in their ethical position
4. *Stereotyped enemies* – black and white, good versus evil.

The remainder, however, relate to how the group (and individuals within the group) organizes itself to combat these 'enemies':

5. *Pressure* – on any group member who dissents
6. *Self-censorship* – of anything which deviates from the group consensus
7. *Unanimity* – an illusion that there is no possible dissent within the group
8. *Mindguards* – some members of the group may set themselves up to police the rest.

The impact of groupthink is felt in the extent it divorces the group from reality. Once you have seen it in action, which fortunately is rare, you will probably never forget this almost manic abandonment of reality (and the accompanying damage to the organization). Lesser manifestations can be seen in more humdrum management situations (the well-known 'yes-men' syndrome can have similar effects).

To put all of the above theories into a more practical, simpler light: marketing simply requires you to adopt the most realistic view of the world around you – keeping your eyes open to all the changes that are happening. These changes may relate to your customers, or your competitors, or to the wider external environment, but you need to create, incrementally, commonsense strategies which take account of them in order to ensure that the investment in your Product:Service Package(s) is protected and developed.

In general, the thrust of the development for existing products should be clear – especially if you are fortunate enough to own one of the market leaders. If, however, you are dissatisfied with your position, and are willing to consider the investment needed to improve your position, then you may wish to employ gap analysis as a tool.

Gap Analysis

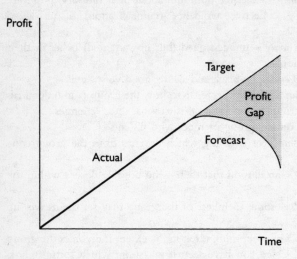

This diagram represents a very crude approach to gap analysis – but one which has a degree of immediacy for many companies. The bottom line shows what the profits are forecast to be for the organization as a whole. The upper line shows where the organization, and in particular its shareholders, want to be. The shaded area between these lines represents the 'planning gap'; what is needed of new activities in general and of 'new products' in particular.

In gap analysis this 'gap' derives from four main causes:

- Usage gap
- Distribution gap
- 'Product' gap
- Competitive gap.

The relationship between these is best illustrated by the following bar chart.

O Rule O84 – *Potential Gaps*

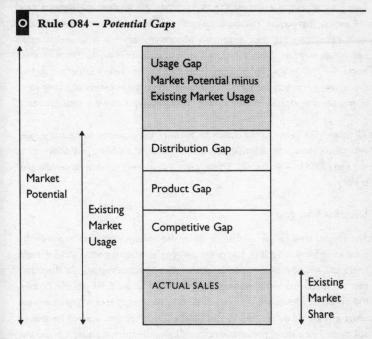

Usage gap

This is the gap between the total potential for the market and the actual current usage by all the consumers in that market:

• *Market Potential* – the most difficult estimate is probably that of the potential of the whole market, including all segments covered by all competitive brands. It is often achieved by determining the maximum potential individual usage, and multiplying this by the maximum number of potential consumers.

• *Existing (Market) Usage* – the existing usage by consumers makes up the total current market, from which market shares are, for example, calculated. It is usually derived from market research, or panel research, but also from ad-hoc work. Sometimes it may be available from figures collected by government departments or industry bodies.

The usage gap is thus:

USAGE GAP = MARKET POTENTIAL – EXISTING MARKET USAGE

This is an important calculation to make. Many, if not most, marketers accept the existing market size, suitably projected over the timescales of their forecasts, as the boundary for their expansion plans. Although this is often the most realistic assumption, it may sometimes impose an unnecessary limitation on their horizons. This 'usage gap' is most important for the brand leaders. If any of these have a significant share of the whole market, say in excess of 30 per cent, it may become worthwhile for them to invest in expanding the total market.

All other 'gaps' relate to the difference between the organization's existing sales (its market share) and the total sales of the market as a whole. This difference is the share held by competitors. These 'gaps' will, therefore, relate to competitive activity.

Distribution gap

The second level of 'gap' is that posed by the limits on the distribution of the product or service. If it is limited to certain geographical regions, as some draught beers still are, it cannot expect to make sales in other regions. At the other end of the spectrum, the multinationals will sell their products globally. Equally, if the product is limited to certain outlets, as some categories of widely advertised drugs are limited by law to pharmacies, then other outlets will not be able to sell them. More likely, perhaps, is that not being the market leader a brand will find its overall percentage of distribution limited. Unfortunately, it is not so easy to maximize distribution unless you are one of the obvious market leaders.

Product (or service) gap

This could also be described as the segment or positioning gap. It represents that part of the market from which the individual organization is excluded because of particular product or service characteristics. This may have come about because the market has been segmented, and the organization does not have offerings in some segments, or it may be because the positioning of its product excludes it from certain groups of potential consumers. Segmentation may well be the result of deliberate policy. As we have already seen, segmentation and positioning are very powerful marketing techniques, but the trade-off is that some parts of the market may effectively be put beyond reach. Or it may simply happen by default; the organization has not thought about its positioning, and has simply let its offerings 'drift' to where they now are.

It is in the 'product gap' that the organization can have the most productive input; hence the importance of correct positioning.

Competitive gap

What is left is the gap resulting from your competitive performance. This is the share of business achieved amongst the similar products, sold in the same market segment, and with similar distribution patterns. It represents the effects of factors such as price and promotion, in terms of both the absolute level and the effectiveness of the messages. It is what marketing is popularly supposed to be about. But, as we have already seen, the product or service itself will still be the prime focus of marketing activity.

Gap analysis should be used as a tool to help you examine as thoroughly and objectively as possible your current marketing position and the strategies which you could follow to improve on it. It offers a starting point for developing fresh product:service strategies and alerts you to the need for developing new and improved products.

In the type of analysis described above, gaps in the product range are looked for. Another perspective (essentially taking the 'product gap' to its logical conclusion) is to look for gaps in the market, regardless of where the company's current products stand. This is called **Market Gap Analysis**.

Many marketers would, however, question the practical worth of (theoretical) gap analysis. As with most management techniques it has too often been oversold by its supporters. Instead, these practising managers would adopt a more pragmatic approach to development.

 Rule O85 – *The Customer Bonus*
The best R & D of all is to let the CUSTOMER or consumer tell you how the product or service should be developed.

This approach is most obvious in those industrial markets where some customers naturally undertake a substantial share of application development, that is, the work on the uses to which the product or service is put. Sound development strategy in these cases may simply be observing what the customers are doing, selecting the best solution and then translating it to the wider customer set. In the process the required changes to the product or service itself may also emerge.

The same principle can as successfully be applied to consumer products. The Japanese, for example, take enormous pains to find out what changes their customers want to their products, and are helped by having a Japanese public educated to try the many new products brought to market.

 Rule O86 – *Creative Imitation*
The greatest innovation threat usually comes from known competitors. It is important, therefore, to monitor their developments very closely, and to respond in kind immediately.

Any major new change introduced by competitors must be taken seriously and immediately evaluated to see if it is a genuine threat to (the position of) the brand. At the same time, where time is of the essence in such competition, contingency plans must be prepared (and development work on a response begun). The main point to remember is that a brand/market leader with a strong position rarely loses that position even to a serious threat – just so long as it delivers an effective counter (usually by imitation) fast enough. Creative imitation can offer wider benefits. Many ideas can be productively transferred from other fields of human activity.

 Rule O87 – *Creative Scanning*
The major technique for finding major new product developments is scanning the horizon – preferably a decade or more ahead (since such major developments take time as well as money).

It is true to say that the seeds of major innovations can usually be seen a number of years (or even decades) ahead. The scientific breakthroughs which lead to new technologies normally follow this rule, but so also do the changes in lifestyles which lead to new consumer demands.

Rule O88 – *Leapfrog*
A more sophisticated version of creative imitation is not just to launch an imitation (though that may also be done to protect the immediate market position) but to put a very high level of resources into developing the next 'generation' of product based on the imitation – and launching this BEFORE the competitor.

The Japanese have managed to turn this almost into an art-form by their mastery of time management in the field of product development. In part, this comes from the practices which they have built up in their manufacturing systems, which stress time (JIT, for example) as much as flexibility. What is not appreciated, however, is that these are not production techniques in the Western sense, but are the outcome of training their workforce to apply such approaches over many years. Despite those 'experts' who would promise to provide you with these secrets instantaneously, you would be wise to assume that they take decades (as they did at Toyota), rather than a matter of days, to become fully effective.

Better communications can be facilitated by siting the developers in the plant. This may reduce the productivity of the developers slightly, at the early stages, but it vastly improves the implementation stage – where (as we have seen earlier) the Japanese gain nearly all their advantage.

In the area of product development, the Japanese use another technique – parallel development. Western organizations complete one stage of development before they start the next because they believe, quite correctly, that otherwise development effort may be wasted (as each stage sets unexpected requirements for the next). The Japanese recognize this inefficiency, but believe that the benefit gained from a much faster overall development process, with overlapping of stages, far outweighs the extra cost of having to redo some work – since it gives them market leadership. It should be noted, though, that more recently some Japanese corporations (Toyota among them) have been reducing the amount of parallel work because it had become *too* expensive.

Existing market leaders may take this process a stage further, by having two development teams working in parallel. While one is implementing the last stages of the next generation the other is working on the earlier stages of the next generation but one.

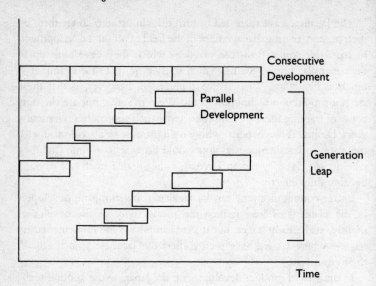

Product Strategies

There are said to be four basic product strategies for growth in volume and profit (which is what shareholders conventionally demand), as described by Igor Ansoff,[5] and subsequently developed as the well-known 'Ansoff Matrix':

5. I. Ansoff, 'Strategies for Diversification', *Harvard Business Review* (1957) September–October.

⭕ Rule O89 – *Ansoff Matrix*

PRODUCT

	Present	New
Present	Market Penetration	Product Development
New	Market Development	Diversification

MISSION (MARKET)

Market penetration

The most frequently used strategy is, as we have already seen, to take the existing product (or service) in the existing market and try to obtain improved 'penetration' (or more accurately an increased share) of that market. This can be achieved either by increasing sales to existing customers or by finding new customers in the same market. In general, the former means persuading users to use more. This may be achieved by motivating them to use the product on more occasions: perhaps by replacing an indirect competitor (for example, a household might eat beans on toast an extra time each week, instead of fish fingers). It may, on the other hand, simply be to use the product more often without any need to take business from competitors, as Unilever used Timotei to promote the more regular shampooing of hair. Possibly it may be to use more each time: promotions offering '30% more free' may have, as one objective, the intention of persuading customers to get into the habit of using more (two spoonfuls of baked beans on their slice of toast rather than one).

The second category relates to taking business directly from competitors, increasing both penetration and market share.

As such penetration is the main objective of much of marketing, almost any of the relevant techniques can be brought into play. Product performance may be improved, price may be reduced, distribution may be extended, promotion may be increased or the marketing mix as a whole may be restructured. All of these, singly or in combination, could be used to improve penetration.

Product (or service) development

This approach, which most closely matches what is thought of as new product development, involves a relatively major modification of the product or service in terms of quality, style, performance, variety and so on. To be most effective, such developments should extend the 'product' into a new segment, or to a new competitive position in relation to the clusters of consumers.

Market (extension) development

This involves finding new uses for the existing product or service, thereby taking it into entirely new markets, as Apple did in persuading customers to use its PCs for desk-top publishing. Alternatively it may be achieved by moving into other countries; most export operations can be viewed as 'market extensions' in this context.

Diversification

This involves a quantum leap – to a new product and a new market. Consequently it involves more risk, and is more normally undertaken by organizations which find themselves in markets with limited, often declining, potential. One obvious example was the tobacco companies, which extended, at considerable cost, into areas as diverse as cosmetics and engineering, because they could clearly see the limitations of their existing markets. Diversification can be a positive move to extend the application of existing expertise, as Amstrad did, moving from consumer electronics to home computing and thence to business computing. Heinz, as another example, has steadily (and successfully) extended beyond its '57 varieties' core business (which revolved around baked beans and soups). Its 'Weight Watchers' brand is now worth more than $300m in the US. But it should be noted that, in common with many other similarly successful diversifications, this was built on a logical extension of the company's existing strengths.

In his original work, which did not use the matrix form, Igor Ansoff stressed 'the diversification strategy stands apart from the other three. While the latter are usually followed with the same technical, financial, and merchandising resources as are used for the original product line, diversification usually requires new skills, new techniques, and new facilities. As a result it almost invariably leads to physical and organizational changes in the structure of the business, which represent a distinct break with past business experience.'

For this reason, amongst others, most marketing activity revolves around penetration; and the Ansoff Matrix, despite its fame, is usually of limited value. It does, however, always offer a useful reminder of the options which are open. Its most important lesson is quite simply that **risk** increases dramatically the further you move away from your home base in the top left-hand corner of the matrix.

 Rule O90 – *Market Penetration* really is a very much safer activity than diversification!

Acquisition strategies (or those for joint ventures) are rarely discussed in the context of new product development, yet there is normally a lower risk attached to buying a going concern (or developing another form of binding commercial relationship with it) than to developing your own offering. Whatever route you choose you should be aware of, and be prepared to meet, the levels of investment and extended timescales involved. Both of these are significantly higher than most product developers are willing to admit to, even to themselves. Thus, a survey by Ralph Biggadike[6] of new corporate ventures by 200 members of the Fortune 500 showed that on average they suffered severe losses through their first four years of operation and needed eight years before they reached profitability (and it was twelve years before they generated cash-flow ratios comparable with the existing businesses)!

More importantly, if despite all the odds against it you are determined to go ahead, Biggadike offers the most important other recommendation to emerge from his research:

 Rule O91
The way to improve the odds and to build a portfolio is to commit substantial resources to each venture and to defer immediate financial performance in favour of market position.

6. Ralph Biggadike, 'The Risky Business of Diversification', *Harvard Business Review*, May/June 1979.

Genuinely new product development is a very expensive process indeed, and it takes a very long time to pay off – though the results then may be spectacular.

One further piece of advice emerges from our own research.

Rule O92 – *Quantum Leap*

Totally new development **must** represent a quantum leap in 'product characteristics' if it is to succeed.

Our results,[7] for consumer goods brands, show that almost all genuinely new brand leaders have depended upon such dramatic changes. These are most obvious in terms of physical (technological) changes, but they can just as easily be based on dramatic changes in taste or image.

Rule O93 – *Brand Extension*

Investments in existing brands can be transferred (extended) to emerging markets – just so long as they are clearly complementary to the existing brand's positioning.

Almost half the new consumer goods brand leaders which emerged during the 1970s and 1980s fell into this category,[8] demonstrating, yet again, the power of the brand investment.

7. D. S. Mercer, 'A Two Decade Test of Product Life Cycle Theory', *British Journal of Management*, Vol. 4 (1993) pp. 269–74.
8. *Ibid.*

Logistic Curve

The logistic curve offers the best solution to predicting and then tracking the post-launch development of new products:

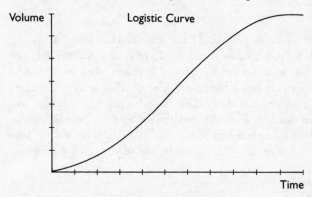

The great advantage of this curve, as compared with the purely descriptive product life cycle (which aims to illustrate the same exponential growth for new products), is that it can be described by a simple equation:

Rate of Growth (at time 't') = $R \times N_t \times (1 - N_t/N_{max})$

where R is the constant which determines the overall rate and N_t is the number (of users, say) at time 't', compared with N_{max}, which is the maximum number available in the market. This equation only contains three values which need to be inserted and then multiplied or divided to give a useful result. There are few other equations in management theory which give such practical results for so little effort.

The key fact is that the consumer sales curve is likely to start to grow very slowly, until it eventually accelerates rapidly over the central part of the growth period, before once more slowing down as saturation approaches. This, unfortunately, means that during the initial stages of the launch – when many of the critical decisions need to be taken – the sales levels are likely to be so low that it is difficult to measure them without error.

13 / Pricing

Finally, we come to pricing. Its late appearance is quite deliberate, since it has let you become accustomed to the idea that it is only one of the elements of the Product:Service Package, albeit an important one. This short chapter is, therefore, primarily designed as an antidote to the hype which has traditionally surrounded pricing. Its exaggerated importance descends from the tradition set by the economic disciplines. Central to the writings of neo-classical economists are the 'laws of supply and demand', which describe one theory of how prices are set.

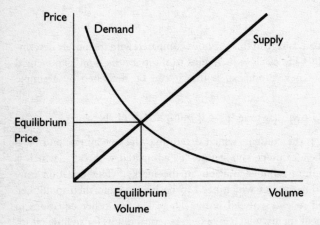

The (equilibrium) price is reached when demand matches supply. For most markets that now exist, however, more practical demand curves might look rather different from this classical model:

◉ Rule O94 – *Real Demand*

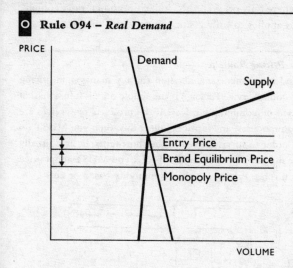

The typical demand curve of most products or services is much steeper than traditionally assumed and the demand is relatively inelastic (with respect to price). In other words, increasing the price makes little difference to sales levels. At the same time the supply curve is very elastic above the entry price (the price at which the market becomes attractive to new entrants); below this point, however, it is inelastic. In other words, new entrants require a given price level before they will make the investment necessary to enter. Above it they will produce in ever larger quantities, but below it they will not even consider production.

In recognition of this entry-level price, the existing tenants will maintain the actual brand equilibrium price in the market somewhat below the theoretical equilibrium level. This discount can be described as the 'competitive insurance', since it represents their uncertainty as to what is the exact level. Contrary to much of economic theory, the evidence suggests that (except for those protected by patents) the monopoly price will often be lower still, representing the 'monopoly insurance', which the monopoly-holder is willing to pay in order to avoid the monopoly being taken away (directly by competitive activity or indirectly by government regulation).

The problem is that these models describe price activity in only one context – where only price counts, and 'commodity' prices obtain. Fortunately, this applies to only a small minority of markets.

S ### Rule S22 – *Pricing Roulette*

The first, and most important, decision for any manager in pricing his or her Product:Service Package is the simple one: is it in a market which is based on commodity prices? If the products or services are treated as commodities, and if prices reflect this, then you MUST do the same in order to survive, even in the short term. If, as is usually the case, the market is not commodity based, you MUST adopt price maximization rules. Pricing is either commodity based or not!

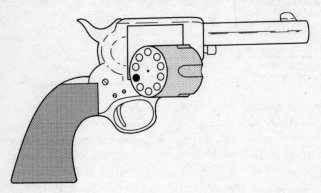

Much the same as you play Russian roulette with a revolver, suppliers often play pricing roulette with the market. The odds are a little bit better – our research indicates that only a tenth of markets indulge in commodity-pricing. The end effect may be much the same, however, if your spin of the chamber lands you on a commodity-based market – it is often tantamount to commercial suicide!

If the products or services are treated as commodities, and if prices reflect this, then you must do the same in order to survive, even in the short term. You have no pricing choice. You must hope that the situation changes in the future, so that you can make a reasonable profit, but in the short term you can only reduce costs to staunch the bleeding. Fortunately, 90 per cent of the markets are not commodity based.

So if, as is usually the case, the market is not commodity based, you should adopt the price maximization rules described below. This is one of the very few situations in marketing where there are no grey areas, no spectrum of options. Beware though! One of the great temptations in marketing, to which many succumb, is to think that a significantly lower price will improve your position. The odds show that this is likely to be a mistake, and may switch the whole market to commodity-pricing (so that everyone loses, especially the initiator). This is not to say that a drive for reduced costs, which is typically initiated by commodity-pricing, should be abandoned. Commodity-pricing may one day emerge in your market, and your organization must (while making its investments in the future) develop a cost structure which will enable it to survive this eventuality, and in the meantime it will reap even higher levels of profit.

Price Maximization

For the great majority of markets suppliers can, happily for them, count on achieving more than the base commodity price. The difference is known as the 'price premium'.

Rule O95 – *Price Premium* simply states that you can achieve a premium price, above the commodity price level.

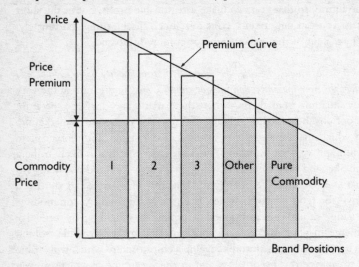

This is a simple concept, but a useful one – not least because it acts as a restraint on the very strong temptation to indulge in price-cutting. The diagram also indicates that, in general, the brand leaders are progressively better placed to achieve such premiums (though they may choose to trade this off against higher volumes of sales).

The premium may be justified by a variety of factors, including those of image, quality, differentiation, positioning etc. The precise reason for the premium is not important, it will vary from situation to situation. What is crucial is that you recognize it as a possibility, and work to maximize it.

If you avoid the pitfall of commodity-pricing, along with those of the many 'guaranteed' techniques offered by academics and consultants, then most pricing turns out to be relatively simple. This is because most products are either existing products with a known track record, or are new products entering markets where there are already similar products with known track records. The two main alternative methods I would suggest, both of which tend to be scorned by academics, are, in my opinion, eminently sensible.

1. *Historical pricing* – this is probably the most prevalent form of pricing.

> **⊙ Rule O96 – *Historical Pricing***
> For good reasons, what the price has been in the past is, for most products or services, the best starting point for what it should be in the future.

The first caveat is that you must be aware of how the price needs to change to reflect the consumer's changing needs and different competitive conditions.

The second caveat is that it assumes the historical price was correct, and exactly matched the value as perceived by the consumer (what he or she is willing to pay for it). This is just what the positioning process, which is at the heart of the marketing processes described in this book, sets out to achieve. Pricing is just one of the variables involved in the positioning, but the process should be no less powerful for that.

2. *Competitive pricing* – the one additional aspect which may modify historical pricing, and may sometimes replace it (and always will in the case of new products), is what the competitors are doing. The positioning exercise takes full account of the position relative to competitors. Once again, this should be a natural part of the pricing process.

Cost-plus pricing

Another approach used by many organizations, adding a fixed percentage (to show a 'profit') to costs, should *not* usually be considered. Costs should be minimized, but prices should be maximized, based upon what the customer is willing to pay. The one exception, where cost-plus pricing may be justified, is where a large number of items have to be priced and the logistics of making a large number of individual decisions become a significant hindrance. Here a guide price may be determined, on the basis of historical/competitive/perceived value pricing, for a group of products, and then extended to the individual products as a percentage uplift on their cost. A cost-plus approach may also be required for new products entering new markets, where no track record of any kind is available.

⊙ Rule O97 – *New Products Pricing*

The decisions here are encapsulated in the strategic decision between 'skimming' and 'penetration'.

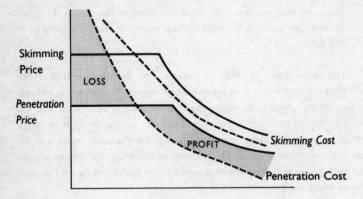

To sum up, then, the most productive approach to pricing is not to view it as a separate technique, but to see it as the natural outcome of the positioning process.

14 / Marketing Planning

Traditionally the production of the marketing plan, which will determine activities for the next year, is seen as an important milestone in marketing activities. In practice, few managers base their day-to-day decisions on the contents of a marketing plan, even though many of them have gone through the motions of producing a plan.

The reasons for this are eminently practical: their actions are dictated by the reality revealed by subsequent events rather than the historical theory contained in the plan. But there is also a psychological aspect. As Bernard Taylor[1] says: 'Planning is an unnatural process. It is much more fun to do something.' John Preston of Boston College (quoted by Bernard Taylor) went further: 'The nicest thing about not planning is that failure comes as a complete surprise, and is not preceded by a period of worry and depression.'

Despite these shortcomings in practice, we should not dismiss the production of a marketing plan as a total irrelevance. It may not be as central to marketing actions as theorists would like, but it still has some important benefits:

• *Review* – the process forces a full review of *all* the marketing factors, not just those which are currently the focus of attention.

• *Agreement* – it acts as a positive stimulus to the involvement of a wide range of personnel in the strategic decision-making, and then as a framework for generating formal agreement amongst them.

• *Communication* – the output, the marketing plan itself, can be an especially useful vehicle for communicating the organization's marketing intentions more widely amongst its staff.

The traditional framework of marketing planning is best explained by Malcolm McDonald in his book.[2] The main steps in the process he describes are:

1. B. Taylor, 'Corporate Planning for the 1990s: the New Frontiers', *Long Range Planning*, Vol. 19, No. 6 (1986).

2. Malcolm H. B. McDonald, *Marketing Plans*, 2nd edn. (Heinemann, 1989).

1. Corporate Objectives
2. Marketing Audit
3. SWOT Analysis (Strengths, Weaknesses, Opportunities, Threats)
4. Assumptions
5. Marketing Objectives and Strategies
6. Estimate Expected Results
7. Identify Alternative Plans and Mixes
8. Programmes
9. Measurement and Review.

The essence of the process is that it moves from the general to the specific; from the overall objectives of the organization down to the individual action plan for a part of one marketing programme. It is also an iterative process, so that the draft output of each stage is checked to see what impact it has had on the earlier stages, and is amended accordingly.

He suggests a specific layout for the plan itself:

1. Mission Statement
2. Summary of Performance – to date, including reasons for good or bad performance
3. Summary of Financial Projections – for three years
4. Market Overview
5. SWOT Analyses for Major Projects/Markets
6. Portfolio Summary (a summary of SWOTs)
7. Assumptions
8. Setting Objectives
9. Financial Projections for Three Years – in detail.

More important, he deliberately separates this three-year strategic marketing plan (sometimes just called the 'strategy') from the one-year operating plan (often what is called the 'marketing plan' itself), which is derived from the overall strategic plan.

His suggested format for this one-year plan includes:

1. Summary of Strategic Plan
   Overall Objectives – in numeric terms
   Overall Strategies
2. Resulting Annual 'Strategies'
   Sub-Objectives – relating to specific products/markets/segments/customers
   Strategies – the means by which these will be achieved
   Actions/Tactics

3. Summary of Marketing Activities and Costs
4. Contingency Plans
5. Operating Results and Financial Ratios
6. Key Activity Planner.

It can be seen from this list that the short-term (one-year) plan should concentrate on very specific and quantifiable actions. Indeed, he provides a very useful set of 'forms' which can be filled in to create most of this plan.

My approach is simpler, since it assumes that most of the work has already been undertaken, and consists of a genuine review of what has been happening and what needs to be changed to improve performance in the future.

There are just five simple steps, which follow closely the conventional process (the comparable stages of which are shown in the brackets below):

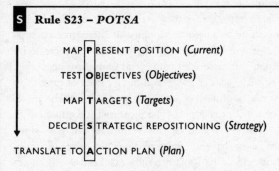

S **Rule S23 – *POTSA***

MAP **P** RESENT POSITION (*Current*)

TEST **O** BJECTIVES (*Objectives*)

MAP **T** ARGETS (*Targets*)

DECIDE **S** TRATEGIC REPOSITIONING (*Strategy*)

TRANSLATE TO **A** CTION PLAN (*Plan*)

If you need a mnemonic to help you remember these stages, then the underlined letters above spell out POTSA (of profit?).

Map Present Position (*Current*)

The starting point must be a definitive statement, ideally a formal 'map' of some kind, positioning your Product:Service Package(s) in the market(s). This is arguably the most important step of all, and the one where most organizations fail. If you cannot recognize where you currently are then you will not be able to plot how you will reach your objectives. You need to produce just a one-page summary (of no more than 500 words and preferably shown in terms of diagrams/maps or, at least, in measured numeric terms). If you feel that there must be some explanatory expansion, put this into an appendix – but be ruthless in limiting yourself to one page here. This not only makes the document dramatically shorter than most such exercises, and correspondingly easier for the recipients to read, but it forces you to decide on the key parameters.

An especially important outcome of the analysis of the current position, is the key **assumptions** about the future. It is essential to spell these out. Most companies, however, do not even realize that they make such assumptions. IBM's key product marketing document is entitled 'Forecast Assumptions', and the agreement on what are the assumptions is often the key to understanding the marketing plan. You should, however, make as few assumptions as possible and explain those you do make very carefully.

When, in the later steps, you estimate the results expected from your strategies, you should also explore a range of alternative assumptions. For example, if you have assumed the market will increase by x per cent, you might estimate sales from your chosen strategy at y. You should also estimate sales at lower and higher rates of growth in the market, say: At rate of growth of $x - 2$ per cent, sales will be $y - 3$. At a growth rate of $x + 2$ per cent . . . The most useful component of this part of the exercise may well be this 'sensitivity analysis', since this indicates which factors have the most influence over the outcomes, and so which factors should be most carefully managed.

Test Objectives (*Objectives*)

The organization will have existing marketing objectives, by design or by default, stating where the organization intends to be in the future and when it intends to be there. Indeed, these marketing objectives may be the most important elements of the overall corporate objectives – especially where the organization primarily justifies its existence in terms of what it offers its customers or clients. They must, in any case, complement these corporate objectives. They typically relate to *what* products will be *where* in what markets (and must be realistically based on customer behaviour in those markets). They are essentially about the match between the products and the markets. Objectives for pricing, distribution, advertising and so on are at a lower level and should not be confused with marketing objectives: they are part of the marketing strategy needed to achieve marketing objectives.

These objectives must emerge naturally from the core competences enjoyed by the organization, mediated by the values enshrined in its culture. To be most effective, objectives should be capable of measurement and therefore quantifiable. This measurement may be in terms of sales volume, money value, market share, percentage penetration of distribution outlets and so on. An example of such a measurable marketing objective might be 'to enter market A with product Y and capture 10 per cent of that market by value within one year'.

I should add one caveat: formal corporate objectives tend to be documented in terms of profit projections – our managerial culture demands as much – but the unpublished, informal objectives which really drive the actions of most organizations range much wider. It is these wider objectives which need to be taken into account here.

One technique which might be usefully considered at this stage is that of 'objective trees':

O   **Rule O98 – *Objective Trees***
Objectives are usually described consecutively, without any clear relationship between them. A useful technique is to write them in the form of a hierarchy – a tree structure where sub–objectives are clearly related to overarching ones:

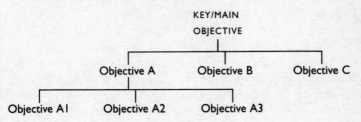

In practice it may prove difficult to assign objectives to such a hierarchy, but it should not be impossible, and it often provides a very illuminating insight into the relationship between them, and any underlying conflicts.

Map Targets (*Targets*)

General long-term objectives need to be quantified as a progressive series of targets and given timescales as well as numeric projections. Even intangible objectives, such as those relating to image, should be quantified in terms of measurable marketing research results.

Forecasting

This is the point at which you are likely to enter into the complicated world of forecasting. In the next few pages, however, I will attempt to guide you through a few of the most useful, and most practical, techniques.

Forecasting can be roughly divided into two parts:

Short-term forecasting

This is the type of forecasting you will recognize. It is normally based upon a projection of historical trends, usually focused on sales volumes. There are many sophisticated techniques, increasingly using large amounts of computing power, but all of them cover the four main components:

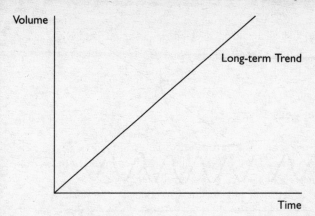

Long-term trends probably represent the most important information you are trying to extract from the mass of data before you.

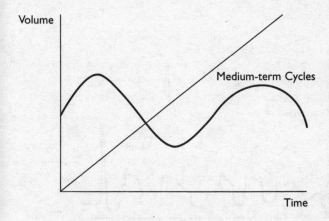

Medium-term cycles are supposed to result from regular economic ups and downs (from boom to bust), but this, which used to be encapsulated in a five-year 'business cycle', unfortunately became unpredictable in the 1980s. The much-quoted 'Kondratieff Cycles' are much longer, if they exist at all, being of the order of twenty-five to fifty years; and hence do not normally enter into shorter term forecasts.

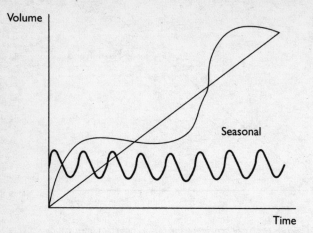

Seasonal is the pattern within a single year, a pattern which most suppliers who are affected by it know well.

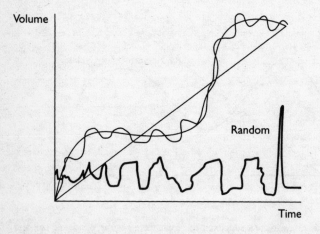

Random fluctuations, which do not fit regular patterns, afflict all products and services, and make computer analysis a very difficult proposition.

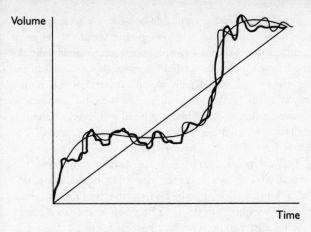

Volume

Time

Having described some of the approaches on offer, by far the best advice is still to keep it as simple as possible. The human eye is much better at resolving the complications shown above than the most powerful computer. Unnecessary complexity hinders your understanding of what is going on under the covers of the computer (and hides the fact that most forecasts are really based on human judgement). In any case, even if historical trends are accurately analysed, there is no guarantee that the future will be the same as the past. It is much better to consider all the assumptions, and make your own judgement in full knowledge of what is involved.

T **Rule T46**
The best approach to forecasting (and certainly the best check on any more sophisticated technique) is 'eyeballing' the sales charts! With some practice you should be able to sort out the main features of what is happening – and that is better than most computer models achieve.

I will now recommend two very simple techniques to use (if nothing else but as a check on the forecasts others are trying to sell to you):
• *Eyeballing* – the technique I mentioned above is the first, and best, method. It merely requires you to plot historical results graphically, and then look for the patterns. Trust your own judgement – until you are proved wrong.
• *Exponential smoothing* – this is the mathematical technique which

reportedly gives the best results, probably because it is so simple, and consequently easily understood. It allows greater weight to be given to recent trends. Instead of, for example, the average trend over the whole of the last year being calculated, the sales data for each of the months is given a weighting, depending on how recent that month was. It simply takes the previous forecast, and adds on the latest 'actual' sales figure, except that it does this in a fixed proportion, which is chosen to reflect the weighting to be given to the latest period. The general form is $F_{t+1} = F_t + aE_t$ where F_{t+1} is the new forecast you are calculating, F_t is the previous one, E_t is the deviation (or 'error') of the latest actual performance recorded against that previous period forecast, and 'a' is the weighting to be given to the most recent events. For example, if a weighting of 0.1 is to be given to the latest figure, then the new forecast will be (Previous Forecast) + (0.1 × Deviation of Last Actual from the Forecast).

Exponential smoothing will not, in this simple form, allow for seasonality; though more sophisticated (but less easily understood) versions can do this.

Long-term forecasting

This tends to be qualitative (as compared with the quantitative, numeric focus of short-term forecasts). It is even more dependent on judgement; and most of the more complicated approaches to it (such as Delphi or Jury methods) aim to reduce the risks implicit in the judgement by involving panels of experts. It does not, in the final analysis, absolve the manager from backing his or her own judgement (which is probably better informed, in terms of the specific situation, than that of the 'experts').

Of all the techniques the most useful involves developing alternative scenarios, which allow for the uncertainties involved and broaden the views of all the managers involved in the process. Unfortunately, it can also be the most complex and sophisticated of these techniques – and in this form perhaps only the very large corporate planning team at Shell have used it really effectively. A more simplified approach, based on the version which Shell recommend for their line managers who are not part of their corporate planning group, is more practical for most organizations:

T **Rule T47 – *Simple Scenarios***

As described by Shell[3] the four steps to this process are:

1. Identify the important variables
2. Brainstorm to find the possible outcomes
3. Link these together in a series of alternative scenarios
4. Refine these scenarios.

I'll now examine each of these steps in more detail.

1. *Identify the important variables* – what (taking into account the whole of the external environment) are the most important factors which will determine the future of the organization. This is usually the climax of the environmental analysis (scanning) work described in an earlier chapter, and is undertaken over the few weeks or months before the main planning phase begins. Indeed, the raw material for this planning phase will mainly have been generated while conducting that analysis. It is not, however, the analysis itself which is most important for the input to the scenarios, but the emerging ideas about the future trends/ events. This is usually a process of informal debate, often with colleagues, with insights emerging at various times as you make sense of the information you are gathering. It is often the most stimulating and enjoyable part of the whole planning cycle and, because of its very informal nature, is often not recognized as part of planning and is accordingly neglected in theory. Yet it is probably the part of the process which contributes most to successful scenario planning.

The first formal stage of scenario planning is to collect these ideas together and rate them in terms of importance. The topics to be discussed in the scenario planning debates must be those of most importance to the future of the organization. The 80:20 Rule is applicable here. Managers will need to have their attention focused on the fewest possible key issues: experience has proved that offering a wide range of topics merely allows them to select those which interest them and not necessarily those which are most important to the organization.

The second requirement, as described by Shell, is that the topics covered by scenarios must be 'variable', that is, there must be a number

---

3. Contribution by Graeme Galer to an Open University computer conference in 1992.

of possible outcomes. If there is certainty (or a reasonable degree of confidence about the likely outcome) then these topics, too, must be taken out of the process.

2. *Brainstorm to find the possible outcomes* – work through the outcomes which different alternatives for these variables may lead to. This is the most important part of the formal scenario planning process and the stage where all the participants come together for the debates which lead to the agreed scenarios. It is essentially a group process, since it depends upon the interaction of the individuals to generate a diversity of views which is the strength of the whole scenario planning process.

The initial input to this stage will be the topics generated in stage 1. These are then modified in four main ways:

• New topics – the juxtaposition of the various topics usually results in more topics being suggested. This is a genuine strength of the process in terms of creative decision-making, since it 'forces' the emergence of such new ideas.

• Re-description – whilst the various topics may be agreed in a general sense, it is often the case that the way they are described (by the group rather than by the individual who introduced them) is different and the detailed sense may be changed.

• Importance – the topics, which up to this point have largely represented the views of individuals, are then further edited to make sure that those remaining are genuinely important.

• Outcomes – the true 'brainstorming' commences at this stage, when the links between the various elements are explored and the possible outcomes are debated.

It is possible that this stage will be accomplished in one meeting but it is more likely that it will be spread over several meetings held at intervals. This way individuals have the opportunity to assimilate and expand the ideas generated previously.

3. *Link these together in a series of alternative scenarios* – start to build six to eight scenarios ('stories' about the future of the organization, or more importantly its market) which are able to contain these different alternatives. This stage follows much the same process of informal debate as the previous one. It is important that the six to eight people who (ideally) are involved at this stage should not be constrained by any hierarchical pressures – all must be able to contribute equally (there should be no chairperson in the conventional sense). Now the emphasis is on finding patterns. The topics are gradually aggregated

together into clumps of topics, or 'mini-scenarios', which seem to make sense. This sounds difficult, but in practice you quickly discover that there are roughly six to eight of these groupings into which most of the topics naturally fall.

4. *Refine these scenarios* – work on the scenarios until they are condensed to two or three meaningful alternative (but complementary) descriptions of the future. This is the most unnatural, and usually the most difficult stage. You have to reduce the six to eight 'mini-scenarios' to just two or three. There is no theoretical justification for this, just a very practical one. In one form or another, these scenarios will be delivered to other managers (line managers usually) to be used as a basis for planning. It is our experience (and that of Shell) that these managers cannot usefully deal with more than two or three scenarios. The challenge, therefore, is to find, say, just two scenarios, and the process often produces fundamental insights into what are the really important drivers for change affecting the organization. The final two scenarios are used in a number of ways:

• Containers for the topics (groups) – they are a logical device for presenting the individual topics (or coherent groups of these). In this context, which scenario contains which topic, or issue about the future, is irrelevant.

• Tests for consistency – even at this stage it is necessary to iterate, to check that the contents are viable and make any necessary changes to ensure that they are; the main test is to see if the scenarios are internally consistent. If they are not then you must loop back to earlier stages to correct the problem.

• Positive perspectives – the main benefit deriving from scenarios comes from the alternative glimpses of the future their different perspectives offer. It is a common experience, when the final scenarios emerge, for the participants to be startled by the insight they offer. At this stage it is no longer a theoretical exercise but a genuine framework (or rather set of alternative frameworks) for dealing with the future.

○ **Rule O99 –** *Wall Post-it* is one very simple technique which is especially useful for handling scenario planning debates, but may be used to support any form of planning process.

It only requires a conference room with a bare wall and copious supplies of Post-it Notes!

The six to eight people taking part in the debates should be in a conference room environment which is isolated from outside interruptions. The only special requirement is that the conference room has at least one clear wall on which Post-it Notes will stick (and most walls, in my experience, pass this test – I have used it just as effectively in hotel lounges in small towns in the Third World as in the headquarters of multinationals).

At the start of the meeting itself the topics, which were identified in the first stage of the scenario planning process, are written (preferably with a thick magic marker, so they can be read from a distance) on separate Post-it Notes, in black. These Post-it Notes are then, at least in theory, *randomly* put on the wall. In practice, even at this early stage the participants will want to cluster them in groups which seem to make sense. Later they can be taken off and moved to a new cluster, and the old description quite simply crossed out and the new one written above it.

The most important stage comes next, when the participants try to group them to make the six to eight 'mini-scenarios'. This is where the Post-it Notes are almost essential – they will continue to stick no matter how many times they are moved around (and they may be moved dozens of times over the length – perhaps several hours or more – of each meeting). While this process is taking place the participants will probably want to add new topics – so more Post-it Notes are added to the wall. At the same time the unimportant ones are removed and, more important, the 'certain' topics are also removed from the main area of debate, to be grouped in a clearly labelled area of the main wall. It is important that all the participants feel they 'own' the wall, and are encouraged to move the notes around themselves. The result is a very powerful form of creative decision-making for groups, which can be applied to a wide range of situations.

The great benefit of Post-it Notes is that there is no bar to changing your mind. If you want to rearrange the groups, or simply to go back to an earlier stage, then you strip them off and put them in their new position. A Polaroid camera is also a help here; every so often take a picture of the wall to record where you are, and do so especially before you make any major changes.

O **Rule O100 –** *Role Playing*
When you have your final two or three scenarios, act through (role play) what they mean to each of the key 'actors' involved (the parts of your own organization, competitors, government, say).

It helps to produce a table with the scenarios listed across the top and the key actors down the side so that you can record what each of these groups feels about each scenario (and what the reaction of each is to the outcomes). It also helps if a number of planners/managers repeat the process (and then debate their views to achieve a consensus). Governments often use role-playing by itself, without scenarios, to see how the various actors may react to political/diplomatic develop-ments (and in this case it becomes an expensive process since those role-playing the key actors, often at great length, have to be experts). Combining it with scenarios is still more powerful.

To return from forecasting to the overall planning documents which are the main subject of this chapter, the setting of measurable targets, so that progress may be monitored and changes made to plans to allow for any divergence, justifies a separate main section in the marketing plan – though once again it should only be one page in length. A further page should be dedicated to four (two-dimensional) maps of the eight most important parameters, with each one showing the current position (along with that of the customers' ideal and that of key competitors), the targeted future positions and the planned path to both of these. This should primarily be used to summarize the whole plan, but should in the process be used as a further check on the validity of the proposed moves. Full-sized maps (along with further dimensions if needed) should be relegated to an appendix.

Decide Strategic Repositioning (*Strategy*)

This step, contained yet again on just one page, should simply explain what marketing strategy is to be adopted to move the organization, over the longer term, from its present position to its targeted future positions. These strategies describe, in principle, how the objectives will be achieved. James Quinn[4] gives a succinct general definition: 'A strategy is a pattern or plan that integrates an organization's major goals, policies and action sequences into a cohesive whole.' The strategy statement can be a purely verbal description of the strategic options which have been chosen, or, perhaps most positively, it might include a structured list of the major options chosen.

One aspect of strategy which is often overlooked is that of timing. Deciding exactly the best time for each element of the strategy to be implemented is often critical. Taking the right action at the wrong time can be almost as bad as taking the wrong action at the right time. Timing is, therefore, an essential part of any plan, and should normally appear as a schedule of planned activities in the last section of the document as well as being allowed for in the strategies themselves.

Having completed this crucial stage of the planning process, you will need to recheck the feasibility of your objectives and strategies in terms of the market share, sales, costs, profits etc. and look at your conclusions from all possible angles.

Translate to Action Plan (*Plan*)

Finally, the shorter-term (more certain) elements of the strategies need to be translated into action. This could be in the form of a table which describes the key activities in terms of the most relevant parameters. Their prioritization levels and resource requirements should be listed along with their quantified targets and times.

4. J. B. Quinn, *Strategies for Change: Logical Incrementalism* (Dow-Jones Irwin, 1980).

Rule O101
The action plan should confine itself to tabulating the prioritized key activities (together with their quantified targets and deadlines) and should allow space for subsequent entry of actual results.

Allowing for updating, in this way, emphasizes the true role of the plan and its relationship to the subsequent monitoring.

Rule O102
The whole marketing plan – POTSA – should be contained in no more than six pages. It should also be, as far as possible, free-form.

Other Specific Planning Techniques

The content of each section of the plan should be dictated solely by what is important to the organization – the philosophy we have been following throughout the book. The more traditional approach uses techniques at each stage that have been pre-specified by the 'experts' who have devised the planning process. Of these techniques the most prevalent is probably that of SWOT (Strengths, Weaknesses, Opportunities, Threats):

SWOT Analysis

This groups some of the key pieces of information into two main categories (internal factors and external factors) and then by their dual positive and negative aspects (Strengths and Opportunities, as the former aspects, with Weaknesses and Threats representing the latter):

Internal factors: Strengths and Weaknesses

The factors internal to the organization – but relating to its strategies and position in relation to its competitors, may be viewed as strengths or weaknesses depending upon their impact on the organization's positions (for they may represent a strength for one organization but a weakness, in relative terms, for another). They may include all of the four Ps, as well as personnel, finance etc.

External factors: Opportunities and Threats

The external factors, presented by the external environment and the competition, again may be threats to one organization while offering opportunities to another. They may include such matters as technological change, legislation, sociocultural changes, as well as changes in the market-place or competitive position.

The technique is often presented as a form of matrix:

Internal

STRENGTHS	WEAKNESSES
OPPORTUNITIES	THREATS

External

SWOT is just one aid to categorization, and in my opinion its weaknesses often outweigh any benefits it offers! In particular, it tends to persuade companies to compile lists rather than think about what is really important to their business. It also presents the resulting lists uncritically, without clear prioritization, so that, for example, weak opportunities may appear to balance strong threats.

O **Rule O103**
Do **not** use SWOT unless you really understand it!

As you might expect, I favour the freedom offered by the 'Analytical 4-Step'. This does not impose alien structures on your planning, but lets you develop your ideas to match exactly what the organization needs.

In general, the most useful strategic planning techniques (such as logical incrementalism and the Competitive Saw) have already been covered in the earlier chapters, but there remains one other group of techniques which tend to be associated very closely with planning – those relating to balancing 'product portfolios'. This means planning the overall collection of Product:Service Packages so that the result is a balanced performance for the organization:

GE (General Electric) Matrix

This is a little-taught matrix, but one which is probably used more than others by practising corporate strategists. Once again, though, it can only be used at the business unit level and above, since it is a device for managing portfolios rather than individual products or services.

The factors it plots are more 'intuitive' than those used by some other approaches. Thus, the vertical axis simply plots the 'product/market attractiveness', in other words, how worthwhile is the business. The horizontal axis covers 'business strength/competitive position': the organization's competitive advantage in each. It is also a 3×3 matrix where most others in management theory make do with 2×2 matrices. In practice, this adds little to the complexity – and much to the flexibility – as you will see below from the outcomes for the various boxes:

Business strength/competitive position

	Strong		Weak
High	invest	invest	evaluate
Product/ market attractiveness	invest	evaluate	disinvest
Low	evaluate	disinvest	disinvest

The addition of the 'evaluate' boxes diagonally across the middle softens the harsh yes/no outcomes which are characteristic of 2 × 2 matrices. The whole approach can, however, be considerably simplified without losing its inherent value:

T **Rule T48 –** *The Three Choice Box*

The simpler version of the GE Matrix is just:

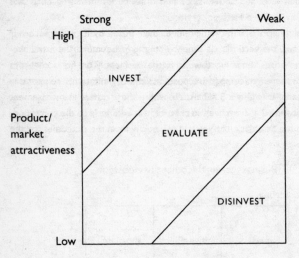

Business strength/competitive position

For most relatively unsophisticated users this simpler version (which we dub the 'Three Choice Box') offers a more immediate picture. It retains the flexibility and intuitive practicality of the original and its great virtue is that it surfaces the very many subjective decisions which are hidden beneath the surface of the original approach. Both the attractiveness of the product/market and the strength of the business involved are clearly subjective (if informed) values. It also highlights the fact that there is a range of outcomes.

To help provide more information immediately to hand, it is conventional to show the chosen position as a circle (whose area is proportional to the size of the market) with a solid (pie) sector within this, whose size represents your share of that market.

Boston Matrix

The most often taught matrix, again for use with portfolio strategy, is the Boston Matrix. Like the Boston Advantage Matrix, described in an earlier chapter, it was developed by the Boston Consulting Group for use in a narrow range of portfolio situations. It works well in such situations where you are balancing cash-flow across a range of market leaders in quite distinct markets (and in high-tech markets which are growing rapidly). The axes (which are relative market share and market growth rate) indicate the special nature of this matrix and tend to be counter-intuitive, so that managers find them difficult to understand.

It is mentioned here to warn you of the dangers posed by its incorrect use! It is one of the two or three most frequently taught management 'theories', but it is probably the least used in practice. It is almost invariably taught incorrectly (except in the best business schools, and even in these its limitations are perhaps stressed less than they might be). The main problem is that, like many management theories, it has been corrupted by later additions, aimed at making it easier for the less sophisticated manager to use. The version which is usually taught uses very memorable descriptions for the quadrants:

stars	problem children
cash cows	dogs

The main danger of this gross oversimplification is that it is very seductive, and in the seduction almost all the value of the original is lost. Managers tend to categorize the positions of their own 'product' offerings by gut-feeling and as a result the positioning within the matrix reflects personal prejudices rather than (as in the original) objective facts. Worse still, the meaning of these positions is then distorted by the emotive labels given to the boxes. In particular, the 'Cash Cow' has to be milked. It has no future, even though, as we saw earlier with the Rule of 1:2:3, such offerings represent the future of the organization as well as its past. Stars demand our attention, which may result in too much emphasis on new products at the expense of the main strength of the business.

 Rule O104

All in all, therefore, IGNORE the Boston Matrix (in any form) unless you need its specific insights, and even then only if you really know what you are doing!

Perhaps the most crucial shortcoming of these techniques, especially of the Boston Matrix, is that they emphasize the short term (and operating costs). We believe that marketing should be seen as a long-term investment, and should be viewed as such on the balance sheet rather than as a cost on the operating statement.

The next theory, the 'Investment Multiplier', is best looked at in comparison with the Boston Matrix.

The Investment Multiplier

In earlier chapters we saw that the most successful brands have very long lives, and the Rule of 1:2:3 celebrates this fact since it is the normal state in stable markets (that is, markets where brand leadership positions do not change, even over the longer term). Thus a new Product:Service Package entering the market (which we would call a 'Starter' in a more positive vein than the equivalent 'Problem Child' of the Boston Matrix) can be plotted on two dimensions – that of the cumulative investment level itself, and that of time.

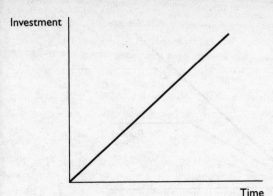

If the product:service is (like the great majority) unsuccessful (called in our terminology a 'Loser' rather than a Dog), the investment is eventually cut off and 'death' occurs. If it is not clear whether it will be a long-term success, the investment will continue until it reaches a plateau. When it is realized that it does not after all have major potential (in view of its equivocal position, we would describe this as a 'Runner' rather than a Star) further investment is usually limited.

Relatively few products or services will reach long-term positions as brand leaders, but these will be the major cash generators which drive successful organizations (and are called by us 'Winners', not the rather derogatory Cash Cows). Eventually the investment levels – for a successful brand – are likely to reflect its profit performance. High investment will return high profits (once again, assuming success) and lower investment lower profits. Hence, the investment graph also is a good indicator of performance.

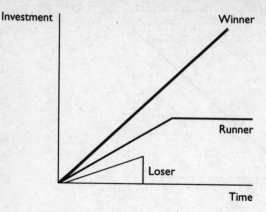

The difference in philosophy is most evident in the terminology: Runners versus Stars and Winners versus Cash Cows. We believe that Winners are to be cared for (and are not Cash Cows to be milked), and that Runners have to be carefully assessed (and not automatically presumed to be future Stars).

If you plot the historical performance of your current brands (allowing them to plateau as investment is eventually matched by depreciation) it is likely that you will get a pattern like this:

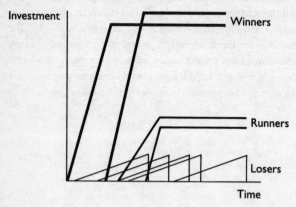

This can be simplified if we ignore the cumulative figures building during the launch, and extend the plateau back to the launch time:

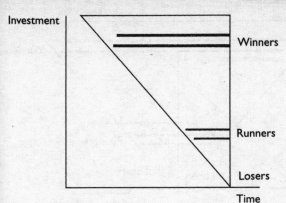

It should be obvious from this that the normal pattern is that of an inverted pyramid. The higher performance brands are also the longer lived ones.

A more general approximation, or rule of thumb, can also be derived. This is:

G **Rule G10 –** *The 'Rule of History'*
The past performance of a brand is the best indicator of its future. If it has been a high performer, it will continue to be so. If it has been long-lived, it most probably will have a long life in the future too.

The 'Investment Multiplier' incorporates this 'Rule of History' by simply mirroring in the future what has happened in the past:

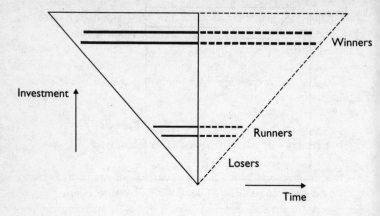

The 'multiplier' in this case is the life of the brand. A successful high-investment brand multiplies its return by having a longer life – over which the annual returns accumulate.

S **Rule S24 – *The Investment Multiplier***

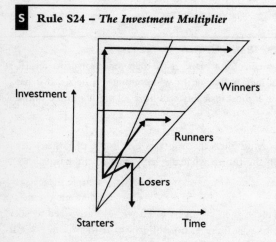

This diagram still contains the important lesson of the Boston Matrix, that of impending mortality. Complacency, even when you have the brand leader, is ultimately rewarded by death (a message even more strongly conveyed by the Competitive Saw). More than this, though, it graphically illustrates the odds against long-term success, and the significant leverage to be gained if success can be achieved. It highlights the importance of maintaining those few winners, whereas the Boston Matrix, and much of marketing mythology, takes exactly the reverse view (and demands that you milk them to death).

The Positive Philosophy of 'Do Nothing'

Even with all this marketing theory available to them, many organizations by default 'do nothing'. They simply do not recognize the need for change, or they are afraid of what it involves. Such organizations have, justifiably, been criticized and not a few of them have later paid a high price for their neglect.

There is, therefore, a commendable incentive for management to 'do something'. This approach, though, becomes a problem in its own right when no obvious solution is immediately to hand. The pressure to 'do something' quickly turns into pressure to 'do anything'. Managements, accordingly, tend to grasp at very short-term fixes, while they try to find the right long-term one.

T **Rule T49 –** *Positively Do Nothing*
Under some circumstances, if you are brave enough, the best solution is literally to 'do nothing'.

If you do not know what to do, then doing nothing will force those closer to the problem (the staff on the ground) to take the necessary actions instead. They are, in any case, the people most likely to develop the best short-term fixes – and to implement them. A long-term solution can then be investigated without any need to take account of these fixes – there is no obligation to incorporate them incrementally in any final solution.

This is a very brave philosophy, which demands a management confident of its own position, but it can remove many of the short-term pressures which lead to panic – and thence to disaster.

The Planning Process

Returning to marketing planning in general, the most important aspect is normally not the output (the plan) but the process leading up to it. Very real benefits can be derived at each of the stages:

Input

At this stage there may be, if the process is well managed, considerable benefit to be gained from the active involvement of a wide range of staff, including all the managers who will be asked to implement the plan. Involvement in the planning of their own future is highly motivational for all levels of staff and management; exclusion from the process will lead to frustration and fear.

Corporate mission

In recent years the term 'corporate mission' has become very fashionable. Most organizations now routinely include such a statement as part of their annual report. This 'corporate mission' can be thought of as a definition of what the organization is and what it does. To be really effective it should not just be a routine gesture, but must have the power to determine the future of the organization. Perhaps a more important factor in successful marketing is a genuine 'corporate vision' rather than a bland 'mission'. This was the main theme of a book by Peters and Waterman,[5] under the heading 'Superordinate Goals'. As Theodore Levitt[6] says, 'Nothing drives progress like the imagination. The idea precedes the deed.'

If the organization in general, and its chief executive in particular, has a strong vision of where its future lies then there is a good chance that the organization will achieve a strong position in its markets (and attain that future). This will be not least because its strategies will be consistent; and will be supported by its staff at all levels. Robert Townsend[7] echoes the statement: 'Things get done in our society because of a man or woman with conviction.' Such visions tend to be associated with strong, charismatic leaders.

5. T. J. Peters and R. H. Waterman, *In Search of Excellence* (Harper & Row, 1982).
6. T. Levitt, *The Marketing Imagination* (Free Press, 1986).
7. R. Townsend, *Up the Organisation* (Coronet Books, 1971).

Debate

The review process should, again if properly managed, lead to a stimulating challenge to the embedded wisdom. In reality, 'logical incrementalism' is more often replaced by 'illogical incrementalism'; a decision is taken on the spur of the moment and subsequently becomes institutionalized as a strategy which is never challenged (regardless of whether it is right or wrong).

Marketing myopia

Theodore Levitt,[8] in his very influential article, stated that: 'The viewpoint that an industry is a customer-satisfying process, not a goods-producing process, is vital for all businessmen to understand. An industry begins with the customer and his needs, not with a patent, a raw material, or a selling skill. Given the customer's needs the industry develops backwards, first concerning itself with the physical delivery of customer satisfactions. Then it moves back further to creating the things by which these satisfactions are in part achieved. How these materials are created is a matter of indifference to the customer, hence the particular form of manufacturing, processing, or what-have-you cannot be considered as a vital aspect of the marketing.'

His reason for this emphasis, supported by considerable anecdotal evidence in the rest of the article, was that most organizations defined their business perspectives (now more often referred to as the 'corporate missions' described earlier) too narrowly. His view, which was enthusiastically seized upon by the more adventurous organizations, was that the link with the consumer, the 'customer franchise', was the most important element.

The corporate vision must, therefore, be defined in terms of the customer's needs and wants. Adopting a wider perspective has helped many organizations to better appreciate how they could develop. Some organizations, though, took the process very literally. Holiday Inns, for example, decided it was not in the 'hotel business' but in the 'travel industry' and acquired a number of businesses, including a bus company. It soon discovered that its management skills were not in those areas and divested itself of them, retrenching to the business it knew best. Levitt recognized the danger of the possible over-reactions in his later book, where he added the comment: 'Marketing Myopia was not intended as analysis or even prescription; it was intended as a manifesto. It did not pretend to take a balanced position . . . My scheme, however, tied marketing more closely

---

8. T. Levitt, 'Marketing Myopia', *Harvard Business Review* (1987) July–August.

to the inner orbit of business policy.' The last sentence seems to me to be the best comment on the true importance of his contribution.

This debate should be as wide-ranging as possible. Nothing should be exempt from scrutiny, and no idea should be dismissed until fully considered. The range of creativity tools, such as brainstorming, should also be brought into play. It is the one chance, during the year, to think the unthinkable.

Agreement and understanding

Probably the most productive part of the whole process is the opportunity to gain a shared understanding of what the marketing plan means. This internal communication process is best accomplished in an extended meeting away from the pressure of day-to-day business; a two to three-day meeting in a suitable hotel is normally the way this is achieved. The fact that this is an extended meeting, in a neutral environment, is critical – the discussion in the bar at the end of the day is probably just as important as that in the formal meeting, and the forced concentration over a lengthy period on the issues brings any misunderstandings over their interpretation to the surface. The meeting will inevitably cover far more than is eventually enshrined in the plan itself, and in the process will bring home to the participants (who must include all the key managers responsible for implementation, not just the favoured few) the 'flavour' of (and philosophy behind) what is intended. It is this shared 'flavour' which will inform their actions over the succeeding year – and is the most potent outcome of this part of the process.

This part of the process should go even further, to obtain agreement and wholehearted commitment from all those involved. The Japanese corporations' decision-making process typically requires that all managers involved in the implementation formally sign an agreement to this effect, called the *ringi*, as described in chapter 12.

Rule O105 – *Ringi*
Time invested in obtaining commitment to the agreement usually
pays handsome dividends in terms of reduced implementation time.

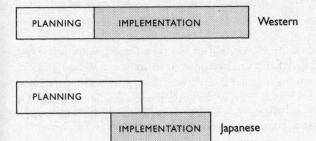

Expert Gobbledygook

One final caveat about communicating the plan to your staff, and
indeed about communicating with them in general.

 Rule O106
The words and concepts used in communicating strategy must be
easily and immediately understood by everyone involved.

This is not to say that you should talk down to them, but to warn
you quite specifically against the use of specialized words which are
only meaningful to experts. So you will need to fillet out all superfluous
jargon. Keep it simple is the best approach.

This has a further benefit. In trying to reduce your ideas to something others can understand, you will really have to understand what
they mean.

Rule O107
If it can't be explained simply (albeit with a great deal of effort on
your part) it probably isn't going to work in practice.

15 / *Strategies for Success*

At the end of this exploration of the rules for successful marketing practice, it is difficult to summarize so many ideas. What I will do, therefore, is bring together the relatively few *general* and *strategic* rules.

The *General Rules* provide the main framework for the book. Of these, the most basic is that which explains why 'rules' offer such a powerful approach.

G   **Rule G1 –** *Rules of Thumb* are valuable because they offer practical help which is immediately of use in building upon managers' existing skills and knowledge to develop specific solutions to unique problems whilst clearly highlighting the limitations of the 'theory' involved.

The main context for the book, however, is set by the Triple 'I' Triangle, which builds upon the individual manager's strengths in each specific situation:

G   **Rule G2 –** *Three 'I's of Marketing Success*

INSIGHT

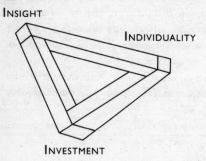

INDIVIDUALITY

INVESTMENT

• *Insight* – the skills required of a manager to conduct effective management in general, and marketing in particular, are those of simple common sense, coupled with a carefully cultivated insight into what is really important for the organization in general, and for the customers or clients in particular.

• *Individuality* – but those skills need to be applied to the specific problems which confront that organization; problems which are unique to each individual organization, and are usually obvious when dealt with individually – but cannot be effectively answered by general theories.

• *Investment* – the one guiding principle to be kept in mind should be the long-term nature of most strategy – with the related decisions best considered as resulting in investments rather than day-to-day costs.

G **Rule G3 – *The Critic's Charter***

The practical steps in evaluating a marketing theory for use in a given situation are:

1. Is it directly relevant to the specific needs of the situation? (*if not, discard it*)

2. What other theories attempt to explain the same phenomena? (*check for alternatives*)

3. Does it offer the (most) productive framework for meeting your specific needs? (*discard any explanations which are clearly less effective*)

4. How does it complement the theories you are using to examine other phenomena? (*if it clashes with the main techniques to such an extent that it could cause confusion then discard it, after checking to see that it is not the only one 'in step'*)

5. What reliance can be put upon it and what evidence is there of its effectiveness? (*discard all techniques which have no substantial, proven backing*)

6. Is it 'original' or has it been distorted by later interpretation? (*discard all theories which have been stripped of their meaning by popularization, or go back to the original*)

7. Does it match with your own experience, and does it make sense? (*discard anything which does not make sense, but only after you are sure you understand what it is trying to say*)

8. Then, and only then, use it – but only as a starting point (and as a framework) for further investigations to find the solution which best matches the unique needs of the specific situation. Unless persuaded

otherwise by the facts, assume your own judgement is better than that of any experts (who cannot understand the specific situation as well as you can)!

In line with the approach which encourages individual initiatives, a main feature is also a requirement to appraise critically every theory and technique before attempting to use it, and, indeed, to start the whole process devoid of any commitment to a specific theory.

G Rule G4 – *The Analytical 4-Step*

Step 0: START with nothing more than a blank sheet of paper.

Step 1: SEARCH without any preconceptions as to the outcome and, based upon your own knowledge and experience, write down what you think are the key factors involved.

Step 2: SELECT, then progressively discard the least essential until you have reduced the number to six.

Step 3: PRIORITIZE these six factors.

Step 4: SYNTHESIZE the relationships and patterns that exist, if necessary returning to Step 1 in order to reduce the six factors to no more than two 'prime directives' which encapsulate these.

The overall process is inevitably one of selection, and focus – concentrate on the few issues which are most important.

G Rule G5 – *The 80:20 Rule*

The most general and powerful rule of all is this one. It simply states that, across a wide range of situations, 20% of the contributors (customers, say) will account for 80% of the performance (sales volumes, for instance).

G Rule G6 – *Philosophies I*

Driven by conviction

- Strong beliefs
- Guided by philosophies not objectives
- Shared ethical values
- Development of a strong culture
- Holistic approach to employees

Employee oriented
- Full employment policies
- Job enrichment
- Personal incentives
- Non-specialized career development
- Personal involvement in decisions
- Implicit (value) control

G Rule G7 – *Philosophies II*

Empowerment of the individual
- Strong (published) beliefs in individualism
- Personnel processes to guarantee these
- Single status across the organization

Manager as team leader
- Maximal delegation to the lowest levels
- Emphasis on team leadership by planned constraints on management
- Encouragement of dissent

Creation of the best human resource
- Recruitment of the highest calibre personnel
- Extended training

Structures for change
- Development of horizontal communications
- Institutionalization of change

G Rule G8 – *Philosophies III*

Culture undermined collapses
- Culture needs success to breed on
- Failure of confidence leads to catastrophe

Core competences cannot be sub-contracted
- Customers cannot be ignored
- Experts are no substitute for expertise

Paradigm dissonance confuses
- False data reinforces groupthink

Awareness of change is also essential and, in particular, change driven by customers provides the basis for the most powerful strategies of all:

G | **Rule G9 – *Emergent Strategies*** are the most powerful strategies of all. They must, by definition, be directly derived from the needs of the market.

Even so, the overall process is one which recognizes the importance of the past investment in organizational activities in general, and especially those in the marketing relationship with the customer.

G | **Rule G10 – *The 'Rule of History'***
The past performance of a brand is the best indicator of its future. If it has been a high performer, it will continue to be so. If it has been long-lived, it most probably will have a long life in the future too.

The *Strategy Rules*, which are specific to marketing, start with a recognition of the wider marketing environment (including the internal environment as well as the external one).

S | **Rule S1 – *The Marketing Triad***

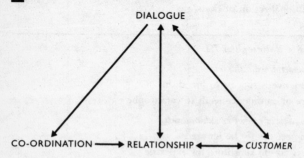

- *Dialogue* – to establish customer needs and to negotiate suitable solutions to these.
- *Relationship* – investment in the effective external exchanges neces-

sary to optimize these solutions, in practice, to the benefit of both sides.

• *Co-ordination* – management of internal operational resources across the whole organization in order to deliver these solutions.

A key aspect of this is the long-term relationship, which is justified in terms of the fact that:

S **Rule S20**
CUSTOMERS are almost universally more productive than PROSPECTS.
All marginal prospects have to be treated as outcasts.

In practice the relationship may be very complex, even in consumer markets. Marketing cannot be confined to the direct, short-term impacts which are addressed by conventional theory. Indirect influences may be even more important, and the key effects are certainly more long term.

S **Rule S12** – *The Three Pillars of the Purchasing Process*

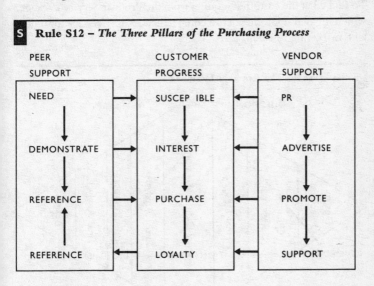

To service these customers the organization must first determine what are its core competences.

S Rule S3 – *The Core Competences Pie*

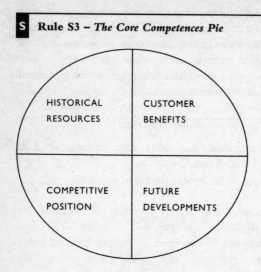

To find what the customer requires from the Product:Service Package, which is based upon these core competences, it is necessary to undertake marketing research.

S Rule S13 – *The Research Diamond*

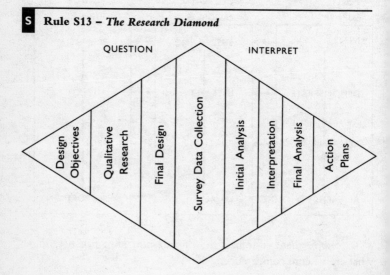

The most important parts of marketing research are, as indicated above, the parts which are usually unseen and unconsidered. Thus, at one extreme, the objectives of any research must be correct or all else fails. At the other, there must be some positive action to which the research leads. At the same time, the research must be put in the context of a process of exploration which starts wide, with scanning of the environment in general, and then gradually funnels down to the narrow focus which is where most marketers start!

S | **Rule S14 – *The Viewing Funnel***

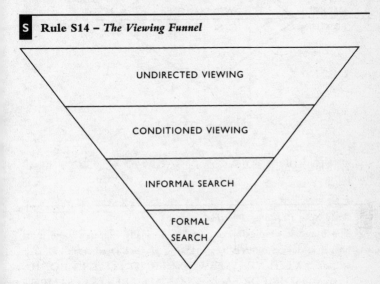

UNDIRECTED VIEWING

CONDITIONED VIEWING

INFORMAL SEARCH

FORMAL
SEARCH

The most positive outcome of such research is likely to be a definition of the Product:Service Package. This will, though, also need to take into account competitive strengths:

S Rule S2 – *The Power Diamond*

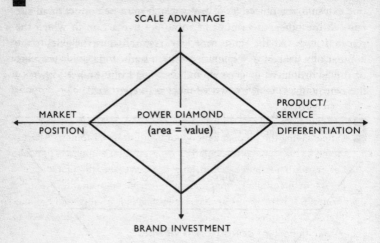

This already hints at the most positive device of 'differentiation': branding.

S Rule S6 – *Branding Practice*

The brand is simple in concept but normally represents the most powerful device offered by marketing practice *to all organizations in all fields*. WITH VERY FEW EXCEPTIONS, IT EMBODIES THE MOST IMPORTANT AND VALUABLE INVESTMENT THAT ANY ORGANIZATION CAN HOLD. It must be developed over the longer term – not milked for short-term results – and above all it must be safeguarded. IT ENCAPSULATES THE WHOLE PRODUCT:SERVICE PACKAGE and is the means by which the richness of this is conveyed to your customers in a personified form. It offers the best way of integrating (and protecting) all the intangible elements which contribute to the power of the Product:Service Package. IT MUST BE POSITIVELY TREATED AS THE MOST IMPORTANT INVESTMENT THE ORGAN-IZATION HAS.

This is reflected, externally, in:

S Rule S7 – *The Customer Franchise*

This is the prime asset of the organization. It is the external *alter ego* of the brand.

It may come from the individual relationships developed face to face by the sales professionals. It may also be the cumulative image held by the consumer, resulting from long exposure to all aspects of the product or service over a number of advertising and promotional campaigns.

The customer franchise may be so strong as to be exclusive, in effect giving the supplier a monopoly with those customers. Alternatively it may have a particularly strong position amongst a portfolio of brands being purchased making it, on average, the first choice.

As an investment, therefore, it must be seen in the long-term context. It has to be protected and husbanded. It must not be squandered by short-term approaches such as inappropriate advertising or promotional tactics.

The power of this is best seen in the almost impregnable positions attained by brand leaders.

S Rule S8 – *The Rule of 1:2:3*

The most competitive markets are typically dominated by 2–3 brands. Between them they account for around 70% of total sales.

For maximum stability the ratio of share should typically be that the BRAND LEADER SHOULD HOLD TWICE THE SHARE OF THE SECOND AND THREE TIMES THAT OF THE THIRD.

The brand leader usually has around 40% of the overall market; and is correspondingly profitable – justifying the investment needed to reach this position.

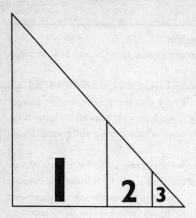

The basic strategic decisions, from which all subsequent decisions flow, are those of segmentation and positioning. Despite the inherent simplicity of the concepts behind them, these are the most powerful techniques in the whole of marketing.

S **Rule S9 – *Segmentation***

The value of discovering separate segments, each with rather different characteristics, is that they allow producers to offer products which target the needs of just one segment, and hence are not in direct competition with the overall market leaders.

This process represents, therefore, the most important practical application of marketing for most organizations.

S **Rule S10 – *Segmentation and Positioning*** are probably the most important decisions any marketer has to make. From them most other decisions will emerge naturally.

S **Rule S11 – *Product (or Service) 'Positioning'*** is, following segmentation, the most important activity in the whole of marketing. Carried out effectively by design, or poorly by default, it determines every other element of marketing.

Most marketing, however, revolves around maintenance of existing brands and of existing brand positions. The best illustration of this requirement is embodied in the Competitive Saw.

S Rule S4 – *The Competitive Saw*

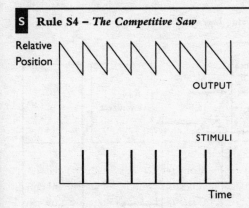

The extension of this, which emphasizes the investment aspect of the maintenance of the brand in the form of 'marketing depreciation', is an even more powerful concept. It lies at the heart of the book's view of the long-term role of marketing.

S Rule S5 – *The Long-term Competitive Saw*

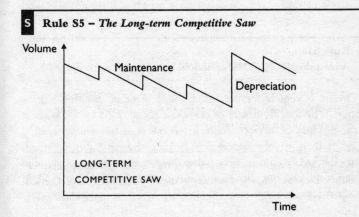

In practice, this concept of 'depreciation' is more clearly seen in the investment which has to be made in advertising just to maintain the brand's existing position.

S **Rule S17 – *Advertising Investment***

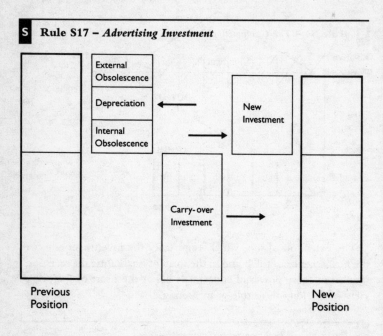

S **Rule S16**
Advertising INVESTMENT should be treated as a fixed ASSET.

The main vehicle for the maintenance of brand position is promotion. The specific nature of this is usually decided by the context of the product or service. Consumer goods tend to need advertising to reach their widely dispersed audience, whereas industrial goods justify the higher costs of direct sales. Long-term strategic moves tend to start with PR, but sales promotions are only justifiable, if at all, in the short term.

S Rule S15 – *The Promotional Lozenge*

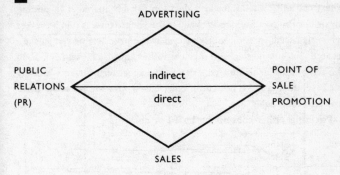

The message contained in such promotion will come directly from the prior positioning exercises. How this is conveyed most forcefully is the province of the best creative departments your money can buy! On the other hand, many of the most powerful campaigns have flown in the face of all marketing wisdom.

S Rule S18 – *Conviction Marketing*

The power of the campaign(s) is dependent upon the power of the idea(s) behind it.

The one marketing decision which is often considered to be separate from the Product:Service Package – though it too must emerge from the positioning exercises – is that of price. It is a key decision, though one which is often much simpler in practice than the economists (who tend to dominate theory in this area) would allow for.

274 / New Marketing Practice

S Rule S22 – *Pricing Roulette*

The first, and most important, decision for any manager in pricing his or her Product:Service Package is the simple one: is it in a market which is based on commodity prices? If the products or services are treated as commodities, and if prices reflect this, then you MUST do the same in order to survive, even in the short term. If, as is usually the case, the market is not commodity based, you MUST adopt price maximization rules.

Pricing is either commodity based or not!

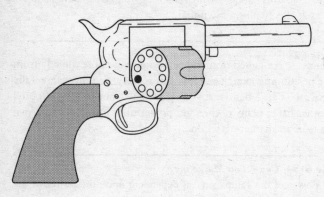

All of these factors are brought together in the annual marketing plan, though this typically formalizes the incremental decisions taken throughout the year.

S Rule S23 – *POTSA*

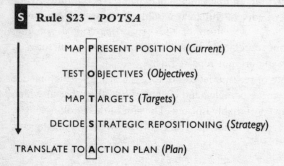

MAP **P**RESENT POSITION (*Current*)

TEST **O**BJECTIVES (*Objectives*)

MAP **T**ARGETS (*Targets*)

DECIDE **S**TRATEGIC REPOSITIONING (*Strategy*)

TRANSLATE TO **A**CTION PLAN (*Plan*)

The power of marketing is also increasingly dependent upon the people involved:

S   **Rule S21 –** *Inner Marketing* is a powerful concept. It says quite simply that EMPLOYEES should be 'marketed' to in exactly the same way as CUSTOMERS.

In the annual marketing plan the investment aspect must, yet again, be kept in mind. This is especially true in balancing the portfolio of products. It is all too easy to become enamoured of new products, and to milk the established winners.

S   **Rule S24 –** *The Investment Multiplier*

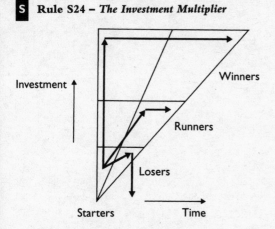

The real success of marketing, however, comes from the correct, common-sense implementation of the many operational activities which result from strategic decisions. These operational rules are far more numerous and are not repeated here.

On a final note of realism, let us not forget that marketing practice exists in a much more complex and chaotic world than that in which we academics are comfortably isolated. The aim of this book has been, therefore, to prepare you for the reality of that world – and to give you the confidence in your own common-sense judgement to succeed in its less than perfect markets.

S Rule S19 – *Coarse Marketing*

Real-life marketing revolves around the application of a great deal of common sense, to handle a limited number of factors based on imperfect information and limited resources (complicated by uncertainty and tight timescales).

Use of marketing techniques, in these circumstances, is inevitably partial and uneven.

Index

READ MORE IN PENGUIN

In every corner of the world, on every subject under the sun, Penguin represents quality and variety – the very best in publishing today.

For complete information about books available from Penguin – including Puffins, Penguin Classics and Arkana – and how to order them, write to us at the appropriate address below. Please note that for copyright reasons the selection of books varies from country to country.

In the United Kingdom: Please write to *Dept. EP, Penguin Books Ltd, Bath Road, Harmondsworth, West Drayton, Middlesex UB7 ODA*

In the United States: Please write to *Consumer Sales, Penguin USA, P.O. Box 999, Dept. 17109, Bergenfield, New Jersey 07621-0120.* VISA and MasterCard holders call 1-800-253-6476 to order Penguin titles

In Canada: Please write to *Penguin Books Canada Ltd, 10 Alcorn Avenue, Suite 300, Toronto, Ontario M4V 3B2*

In Australia: Please write to *Penguin Books Australia Ltd, P.O. Box 257, Ringwood, Victoria 3134*

In New Zealand: Please write to *Penguin Books (NZ) Ltd, Private Bag 102902, North Shore Mail Centre, Auckland 10*

In India: Please write to *Penguin Books India Pvt Ltd, 706 Eros Apartments, 56 Nehru Place, New Delhi 110 019*

In the Netherlands: Please write to *Penguin Books Netherlands bv, Postbus 3507, NL-1001 AH Amsterdam*

In Germany: Please write to *Penguin Books Deutschland GmbH, Metzlerstrasse 26, 60594 Frankfurt am Main*

In Spain: Please write to *Penguin Books S. A., Bravo Murillo 19, 1° B, 28015 Madrid*

In Italy: Please write to *Penguin Italia s.r.l., Via Felice Casati 20, I–20124 Milano*

In France: Please write to *Penguin France S. A., 17 rue Lejeune, F–31000 Toulouse*

In Japan: Please write to *Penguin Books Japan, Ishikiribashi Building, 2–5–4, Suido, Bunkyo-ku, Tokyo 112*

In South Africa: Please write to *Longman Penguin Southern Africa (Pty) Ltd, Private Bag X08, Bertsham 2013*

READ MORE IN PENGUIN

BUSINESS AND ECONOMICS

Trust Francis Fukuyama

'The man who made his name proclaiming the end of history when communism collapsed has now re-entered the lists, arguing that free markets, competition and hard work are *not* the sole precursors for prosperity. There is another key ingredient – trust . . . This is the heart of Fukuyama's theory . . . it is both important and full of insight' – *Guardian*

I am Right – You are Wrong Edward de Bono

Edward de Bono expects his ideas to outrage conventional thinkers, yet time has been on his side, and the ideas that he first put forward twenty years ago are now accepted mainstream thinking. Here, in this brilliantly argued assault on outmoded thought patterns, he calls for nothing less than a New Renaissance.

Lloyds Bank Small Business Guide Sara Williams

This long-running guide to making a success of your small business deals with real issues in a practical way. 'As comprehensive an introduction to setting up a business as anyone could need' – *Daily Telegraph*

The Road Ahead Bill Gates

Bill Gates – the man who built Microsoft – takes us back to when he dropped out of Harvard to start his own software company and discusses how we stand on the brink of a new technology revolution that will for ever change and enhance the way we buy, work, learn and communicate with each other.

Exploring Management Across the World David J. Hickson

This companion volume to *Management Worldwide* contains selections from seminal writings on centralization, individualism, work relationships, power and risk among managers and countries and cultures all over the globe.

Understanding Organizations Charles B. Handy

Of practical as well as theoretical interest, this book shows how general concepts can help solve specific organizational problems.